TWO CHEERS FOR DEMOCRACY

HOW EMOTIONS DRIVE LEADERSHIP STYLE

DAN HILL

Sensory Logic Books
www.SensoryLogic.com
1509 Marshall St., N.E., Suite 400
Minneapolis, MN 55413 USA

Publisher's Cataloging-In-Publication Data
(Prepared by The Donohue Group, Inc.)

Names: Hill, Dan, 1959- author.
Title: Two cheers for democracy : how emotions drive leadership style / Dan Hill.
Description: Minneapolis, MN : Sensory Logic Books, [2019] | Includes bibliographical
references and index.
Identifiers: ISBN 9780999741627
Subjects: LCSH: Heads of state--Psychology. | Leadership--Psychological aspects.
| Campaign debates--United States--Psychological aspects. | Facial expression. |
Emotions. | Personality.
Classification: LCC JF251 .H55 2019 | DDC 352.23--dc23

Printed in the United States of America

Book cover by theBookDesigners
Book's interior design by James Monroe

ADVANCE PRAISE FOR *TWO CHEERS FOR DEMOCRACY*

"Breathtaking in scope, Two Cheers for Democracy uses the science of facial emotions to assess which candidates win, which presidents succeed, and which world leaders champion democracy over dictatorships. It is packed with eye-opening insights that often turn conventional wisdom on its head."

—Ted Brader, author of *Campaigning for Hearts and Minds: How Emotional Appeals in Political Ads Work* and Professor, Political Science, The University of Michigan

"This book takes us one important step forward linking the social science of the study of cognition, personality traits, and emotion to where we need to be, that is, how they come together to influence political decision making and leadership. The main responsibility of political psychology is problem driven social science, and this book takes us farther along that path in an enjoyable narrative."

—Martha Cottam, co-author of *Introduction to Political Psychology* and Professor in the School of Politics, Philosophy, and Public Affairs at Washington State University

"What's in a face? Quite a lot, as Dan Hill's facial coding analysis of U.S. and world leaders reveals in this book. His analysis teems with surprises and insights into the past, present and future of political leadership. It's great reading about the qualities of those who have led us and may lead us in the future."

—Steven E. Schier, co-author of *The Trump Presidency: Outsider in the Oval Office* and Carleton College Congdon Professor of Political Science Emeritus

"Two Cheers for Democracy offers an original and insightful analysis of the emotional requirements of political leadership, particularly at the presidential level. Tapping into his deep knowledge of American history and world affairs, author Dan Hill examines the role personality plays in political performance, and how personal traits and feelings connect to a politician's ultimate success or failure. This accessible, well-written book gives readers a fresh way to think about familiar characters and familiar historical developments, from the Kennedy-Nixon debates to the rise of authoritarianism around the world. Two Cheers for Democracy is an engaging and informative read."

—Alan Schroeder, author of *Presidential Debates: Risky Business on the Campaign Trail* and Professor Emeritus, Northeastern University School of Journalism

"Two cheers for democracy."

—E. M. FORSTER

*"In politics, when reason and emotion collide,
emotion invariably wins. Although the marketplace
of ideas is a great place to shop for policies,
the marketplace that matters most in American politics
is the marketplace of emotions."*

—DREW WESTON

*"Don't trust anyone without a sense of humor.
I never met a KGB agent who had one."*

—MILAN KUNDERA

CONTENTS

PREFACE

Scary Times for Democracy

BACKGROUND & CONTEXT

I wrote this book because of Donald Trump. The Israeli writer Amos Oz often noted the bitter irony of the Jewish people being forever doomed to discuss Adolf Hitler. And now here in America and across the world, I fear we might be facing a similar—although admittedly much less horrific—fate. Trump has always sought fame, and now he has it . . . forever.

Maybe I'm wrong. Maybe 170 members of the American Political Science Association got it wrong, too, when they ranked Trump as the worst president the United States has ever had.[1] Maybe 50 leading economists surveyed by the University of Chicago got it wrong when they almost unanimously concluded that Trump's policies were "destructive".[2] Maybe U.S. allies gathered at the recent Munich Security Conference got it wrong when they offered only silence (no applause) after Vice President Mike Pence told the audience: "I bring greetings from . . . Donald Trump."[3] Maybe I'm wrong but I doubt it, given how even among our closest allies the percentage of people with a favorable view of America has declined by 30% in the United

Kingdom, for instance, and up to 80% in Canada, France, Germany, and Mexico since Trump took office.[4]

Yes, Trump is the "inspiration" for *Two Cheers for Democracy*. But he is by no means its exclusive focus. Not only in America, but around the globe democracy is under siege. Thomas Friedman opened a column in *The New York Times* last year by noting: "it's springtime for strongmen—and nobody has to worry what America thinks about that."[5] Emperor, Czar, Caliph, King, and Pharaoh: these are the titles to which current leaders aspire, from China to Russia, to Turkey, Hungary, and Egypt. And President Trump seems to be just fine with that.

The big debate underlying this book is over what form of government is best. Back in 1947, Winston Churchill wryly observed: "No one pretends that democracy is perfect or all-wise. Indeed, it has been said that democracy is the worst form of government except all those other forms that have been tried from time to time." An aspect of the debate over democracy's merits is whether individual leaders' personalities or the times in which they live play the most important role in bringing about historical greatness (or failure).

In 1947, the Great Man Theory—which posits that leaders are born, not made—was encountering stiff headwinds.[6] In the aftermath of Hitler's terrible greatness, faith in the beneficial potential of all-powerful leaders, a notion born during the heyday of the Industrial Revolution, was shattered. It did not help that no scholar back then—or now—has been able to pinpoint the key qualities necessary to make a great leader.

In recent years, technological advances in brain science have obliterated the notion that anyone—including political leaders—is capable of objective decision-making free of emotions and bias.[7] Personality rather than objective rationality is at the core of politicians' behavior as much as anyone else's. In an era of "strongmen" looking to dominate the world, with potentially catastrophic consequences, understanding the personalities of political leaders is of crucial importance.

Such a role has been commonly apportioned to psychologists, who seek to understand political leaders with the help of the usual array of rational, cognitive tools of analysis. The problem with this approach is that it seeks access to internal processes through the use of external techniques. It's not hard, but instead utterly impossible to directly access the *minds* of leaders.

Far easier in this media age is to access the *faces* of leaders and explore the emotions shown therein. People's facial expressions can be analyzed using a methodology known informally as facial coding and formally as the Facial Action Coding System (FACS).[8] Those familiar with Malcolm Gladwell's bestseller *Blink: The Power of Thinking Without Thinking*, Fox's #1 prime-time television hit series *Lie to Me*, or Pixar's phenomenally successful film *Inside Out*, will already have some understanding of how facial coding works. I propose that this tool can be effectively used to help understand the personalities and the behaviors of political leaders, past, present, and future alike. (More information about facial coding appears as an appendix item at the end of this book.)

For twenty-plus years, I have used FACS to identify and quantify human emotions. That work has ranged from learning people's responses to advertising and packaging for global blue-chip companies, to studying CEOs, celebrities, and professional and NCAA Division 1 athletes. For the winning PRI party in Mexico in 2012, I also predicted the outcome of that election within 1% after studying the reactions of 100 Mexican citizens watching the race's one and only campaign debate on television.

Intent & Structure

As the subtitle to my book indicates, the goal here is to investigate whether leaders have emotive tendencies that might indicate everything from whether they are likely to be effective in office (Part 1), able to connect well with voters during televised debates (Part 2), or have pro-democracy

as opposed to authoritarian instincts (Part 3). Wouldn't it be a relief, after all, for us to have leaders who prove to be competent, compelling, and compassionate in executing their official duties?

The specter of partisanship naturally looms large in a project like this. Because of that, I have taken every reasonable precaution I can to avoid personal bias, including the use of three benchmarks. In Part 1, I have relied on the rankings of greatness provided by the American Political Science Association as I analyzed all 44 U.S. presidents to date. In Part 2, which deals with every U.S. presidential debate from 1960 onward, I compared the candidates' emotional displays to the Gallup polling results released in the immediate timeframe after each debate. Finally, in Part 3, where the focus is on foreign leaders, I turned to Freedom House's annual survey of democracy's status, measured country by country, in considering the behavior of the 79 foreign leaders included in this study.

EMOTIONS WHEEL

The emotions in **bold** can all be identified (and quantified) using facial coding. At times, their opposite is noted (in italics). Happiness is classified using four, descending levels of happiness from joy and pleasure (most intense) to satisfaction and, finally, (mere) acceptance. For the presidential debates, acceptance isn't coded and instead is replaced by skepticism (an ironic smile usually accompanied by sarcastic comments); otherwise, skepticism isn't a category used for the U.S. presidents or foreign leaders (as I am working in those cases from photographs, rather than video).[9]

Speaking of Freedom House, I'm still smarting from the news that its latest annual report reveals America's lowest score since the survey began in 1972. It also mentions that nearly twenty countries have taken Trump's cue by pushing laws that censor the internet as a way to supposedly fight "fake news."[11] This illustrates just how much is interconnected or influenced by previous actions. While Trump apparently lifted "Make America Great Again" from Ronald Reagan, his promise to "drain the swamp" bears an unmistakable similarity to Benito Mussolini's own promise ("*drenare la palude*").[12]

To be fair, Trump is not the first president to betray America's highest ideals, as shown here. The litany of the 43 presidents who preceded him occupies the book's opening section. Lately, just to get to the White House requires, if not "winning", at least decently surviving the series of presidential debates that serve as the hallmark of each election campaign's home stretch. Therefore, coverage of those debates serves as the second part of *Two Cheers for Democracy*. As to the third part of this book, it heads overseas, covering contemporary leaders in particular, many of the least democratic among them endorsed by Trump.

For the Afterword, I've analyzed the likely front-runners for the next presidential race as the Democratic party settles on a candidate to oppose Trump in 2020. Former Republican party boss Mark Hanna quipped in 1895: "There are two things that are important in politics. The first is money and I can't remember what the second one is." In actuality, aside from the monies earned by fundraising, the other main currency in politics consists of the emotions candidates elicit. Anybody who intends to face Trump must seek to counter his playbook of stoking grievances while leveraging fear.

Research shows that our emotions "turn on" when something matters to us. The situation here is getting dire. Presently, less than a third of Europeans and North Americans say it's essential to live in a democracy, and almost one fourth of millennials reportedly don't favor democracy.[13] If, in some small way, this book helps us as citizens to focus less on venal, transactional interests and more on emotion-infused values that involve better understanding and respecting others, then it will have served the common good. While somebody of Abraham Lincoln's caliber doesn't come around every day, hoping for the best leaders possible is a worthwhile quest.

April 2019

PART 1

U.S. Presidents and Their Relative Greatness

ORIENTATION

Presidents and Their Personalities

Plenty has been written about America's presidents, and most of it focuses on *what* they did while in office. The focus here, however, isn't on what presidents have done, but instead on *who* they were (or are, if they're still alive). In other words, personalities, rather than policy decisions, are the focus of this opening part of *Two Cheers for Democracy*.

Presidential biographies aside, rigorous, intimate evaluations comparing presidents are rare. In fact, I only know of one, called *Personality, Character, & Leadership in the White House: Psychologists Assess the Presidents*.[1] Published a decade and a half ago, its claim to fame is that nearly 120 experts on various U.S. presidents participated in a study by completing a psychology questionnaire rating the personality traits of the president(s) whom they felt qualified to judge. Presidents who weren't rated by at least three experts were excluded from the final results. In the end, 30 of our now 44 presidents were comparatively assessed, and the book contains a wealth of in-depth analysis.

The main measure of personality used for that study is known as the Five Factor Model, or the Big 5. While most Americans are more aware of the Myers-Briggs system, with its two opposing sets of traits, the Big 5 trait model is the only model backed by substantial research in the field of psychology. As part of being held in greater critical esteem, the Big 5 adds a crucial, fifth factor that Myers-Briggs overlooks: neuroticism.

In simplest terms, neuroticism refers to the fact that people aren't all that emotionally stable. More poetically, I link *neuroticism* to Napoleon Bonaparte's comment that fire, water, air, and earth aren't enough to explain the universe; *mud is the fifth element*.[2] Besides the personality traits of Openness (to experience), Conscientiousness, Extraversion, and Agreeableness, add Neuroticism to the picture if you want to fully grasp the mercurial, often unstable nature of human nature.[3]

Openness (to experience)	Conscientiousness	Extraversion	Agreeableness	Neuroticism
Fantasy	Competence	Warmth	Trust	Fear
Aesthetics	Order	Gregariousness	Straight-forwardness	Angry Hostility
Feelings	Dutifulness	Assertiveness	Altruism	Depression
Actions	Achievement Striving	Activity	Compliance	Self-consciousness
Ideas	Self-discipline	Excitement Seeking	Modesty	Impulsiveness
Values	Deliberation	Positive Emotions	Tender-mindedness	Vulnerability

THE BIG 5 FACTOR MODEL: EACH TRAIT'S FACETS

Facets are the specific, unique aspects of a broader personality trait. Those parts make the whole. For instance, Openness is really about creativity and the degree to which people are curious and use their imaginations to explore new ideas and possibilities in life. In turn, Consciousness is in essence about being industrious and orderly, Extraversion about being enthusiastic and assertive, Agreeableness about being compassionate and polite, and Neuroticism about being volatile and having a tendency to withdraw from people and situations.

Traits are important. But while I will cite each president's top two personality traits as a point of reference in Part 1, the method utilized throughout *Two Cheers for Democracy* is facial coding. My goal is to see if there's an emotional relationship or formula that predicts presidential greatness. Put another way, which emotions, characteristically felt, may either enable or impair a president's ability to do well in office?

Naturally, in a study covering a time span of over two centuries, there are confounding factors that could affect the results. Regarding facial expressions and the emotions they convey, those factors include:[4]

- A struggle to find enough images, especially of the Founding Fathers and other early presidents. By relying on portraits, and the occasional sculpture or medallion embossed with a president's likeness, a minimum of 30 different images were usually found for each president.

- A need to account for changes in decorum over time. To sit for a portrait in 1820 was a grand occasion, an opportunity for a president to convey the dignity, the gravitas, of their high office. In contrast, in 1976 Americans elected a president who preferred to be called Jimmy instead of James (Carter), in order to make himself look friendlier and more approachable.

WHAT EMOTIONS MEAN

As emotions are the building blocks of life, and this book, why not provide a handy summary? Laid out here in simplified terms is how each emotion shows on people's faces, what the emotion means (the causes or motivations underlying it) as well as the good and bad behavior it inspires. Note that while some facial expressions signal a single emotion (e.g., pursed lips, anger), other expressions may signal two or more emotions (e.g., knitted eyebrows, anger, fear, and sadness). When multiple emotions may be involved, where to put the interpretative emphasis depends on what else the face may be exhibiting then, as well as the leader's emotive patterns over time.

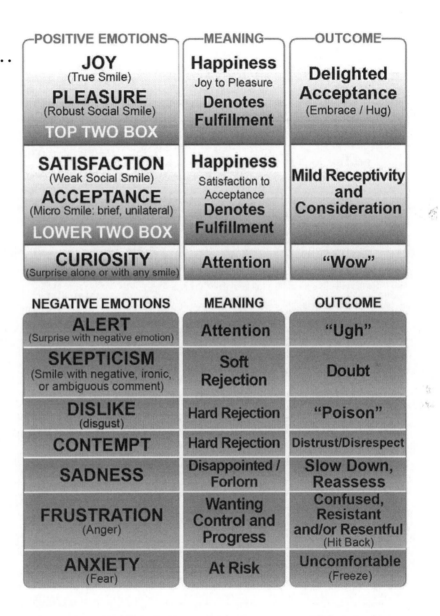

POSITIVE EMOTIONS	MEANING	OUTCOME
JOY (True Smile) **PLEASURE** (Robust Social Smile) TOP TWO BOX	**Happiness** Joy to Pleasure **Denotes Fulfillment**	**Delighted Acceptance** (Embrace / Hug)
SATISFACTION (Weak Social Smile) **ACCEPTANCE** (Micro Smile: brief, unilateral) LOWER TWO BOX	**Happiness** Satisfaction to Acceptance **Denotes Fulfillment**	**Mild Receptivity and Consideration**
CURIOSITY (Surprise alone or with any smile)	**Attention**	**"Wow"**

NEGATIVE EMOTIONS	MEANING	OUTCOME
ALERT (Surprise with negative emotion)	**Attention**	**"Ugh"**
SKEPTICISM (Smile with negative, ironic, or ambiguous comment)	**Soft Rejection**	**Doubt**
DISLIKE (disgust)	**Hard Rejection**	**"Poison"**
CONTEMPT	**Hard Rejection**	**Distrust/Disrespect**
SADNESS	**Disappointed / Forlorn**	**Slow Down, Reassess**
FRUSTRATION (Anger)	**Wanting Control and Progress**	**Confused, Resistant and/or Resentful** (Hit Back)
ANXIETY (Fear)	**At Risk**	**Uncomfortable** (Freeze)

- A need to account for changes in technology. To sit still for a laborious portrait painting is entirely different than being in a photograph taken on-the-fly. With the introduction of the Brownie camera by Eastman Kodak in 1900, the task of capturing a president's image was utterly transformed.

- A need to recognize advances in dentistry. By inauguration day, George Washington was down to a single tooth. So he wasn't exactly inclined to smile broadly (even if the customs of the day had been different).

- A need to account for the rise of advertising and the influence of mass media. Besides advances in photography, motion pictures and television are both a factor here. Greater self-consciousness and a desire—or even need—to smile more became part of the presidential repertoire by the early 20th century.

As a result of these potential confounds, to compare the presidents more fairly over time it became necessary to normalize the facial coding results by era. I grouped the presidents into three eras: 1789-1845 (George Washington to John Tyler), 1845-1933 (James K. Polk to Herbert Hoover) and 1933-today (Franklin D. Roosevelt to Donald Trump). By doing so, I could account for how the era in which the presidents lived was likely to influence their propensity to smile. As a specific example, no U.S. president showed a broad smile of the type I call a joy or pleasure smile until Polk, our 12th president.

THE OVERALL RESULTS

Regarding the earlier study involving personality traits, the results are striking. Compared to ordinary Americans, U.S. presidents score above average for Extraversion and Neuroticism, and below average for Agreeableness. But when the Big 5 traits were used to predict presidential greatness, only two traits had a fairly strong correlation to success in the White House: .32 for Openness (to experience) and .17 for Extraversion.

Correlation to Greatness

Using my methodology, up to seven emotions are correlated with greatness and potentially worth citing. Those that seem to enable greatness consist of the first and third strongest forms of happiness, which I call joy and satisfaction, along with anger, the single most pervasive emotion among presidents. As for which emotions seem to impair or derail a president's potential for greatness, it seems that sadness, disgust, contempt, and fear have that affect.

Three other emotions are not able to predict performance well at all: surprise, and the other two levels of happiness, namely, acceptance and pleasure. So they will only be mentioned briefly. The accompanying chart summarizes, per emotion, how strongly it correlates to predicting presidential greatness, and on a scale from one to five stars how frequently it gets displayed on the faces of presidents.

Overall, the emotions of joy, sadness, disgust, and contempt correlate at a higher level with presidential greatness than what the previous research study found with Extraversion. All four of those emotions have either a positive or inverse (negative) correlation above a .17 level.

Enables Greatness			Impairs Greatness			Non-Factors		
Emotion	Correlation	Frequency	Emotion	Correlation	Frequency	Emotion	Correlation	Frequency
Joy	.28	★	Sadness	(.23)	★★½	Surprise	.09	★★
Satisfaction	.14	★★	Disgust	(.19)	★½	Acceptance	.07	★★
Anger	.12	★★★★★	Contempt	(.18)	★½	Pleasure	.03	★
			Fear	(.15)	★★½			

In addition, what predicts presidential greatness even better than the .32 correlation found by previous research between presidential performance and Openness is a formula that combines being more emotionally negative than positive, primarily due to anger, with also being able to *avoid* sadness. In everyday lingo, grouchy presidents can be great, so long as they're not also "sad-sacks," too despondent or otherwise emotionally erratic to handle their duties well. When negative emoting is linked to a low level of sadness, the correlation to presidential greatness reaches .34, which is pretty rock-solid ground. After all, we're talking about trying to predict something as complex as human nature amid all the countervailing influences and stress involved when you occupy the White House.

During the discussion to follow here in Part 1, I will be framing the results using two sets of rankings. The first references which emotion a president best qualifies for, given that it's both an emotion that they feel often and that they feel it to the degree that is unique and differentiates them from their fellow presidents. I'll call this a president's *stand-out emotion* for short. (The uniqueness element is vital because, given the frequency of anger, almost every president would otherwise have that as their single most characteristic emotion.)

The second set of rankings includes how the presidents have been ranked by presidential scholars, from #1 to #44 based on their performance in office, taking into account the

WHICH EMOTIONS CORRELATE TO GREATNESS (OR FAILURE)

This charts show how strongly emotions predict presidential success. A score of .50 would be phenomenal, especially in cases like this where human behavior is involved and the researcher doesn't have direct access to the people involved. So realistically, anything about a level of .15 is definitely worth talking about. Anger is a special case, given how frequently that emotion gets shown—by people in general, and certainly by presidents who ambitiously fought to reach The White House.

duration of their stay in office and the severity of the issues they faced. For my purposes, I focused on whether each president is considered a top-tier president (ranked #1-#15), a middle-tier president (#16-#30) or a bottom-tier president (#31-#44). In discussing the presidents by tier, I'll include details from their lives that both reflect and help to explain why their respective stand-out emotions are so central to their lives.

As to order, I'll be moving through first those emotions that enable success. Then I'll address those emotions that correlate to a lack of presidential greatness instead. Finally, those emotions that don't seem to relate to either success or failure will be more briefly covered.

Top-Tier Presidents		
President	Greatness	Stand-Out Emotion
16 Abraham Lincoln	95	Sadness
01 George Washington	93	Surprise
32 Franklin D. Roosevelt	89	Acceptance
03 Thomas Jefferson	81	Anger
26 Theodore Roosevelt	81	Disgust
33 Harry S. Truman	75	Surprise
34 Dwight D. Eisenhower	74	Satisfaction
44 Barack Obama	71	Joy
36 Lyndon B. Johnson	69	Surprise
40 Ronald Reagan	69	Fear
28 Woodrow Wilson	67	Surprise
04 James Madison	64	Anger
42 Bill Clinton	64	Pleasure
02 John Adams	63	Acceptance

Middle-Tier Presidents		
President	Greatness	Stand-Out Emotion
07 Andrew Jackson	62	Sadness
35 John F. Kennedy	62	Satisfaction
05 James Monroe	61	Contempt
41 George H. W. Bush	61	Fear
25 William McKinley	55	Acceptance
11 James K. Polk	54	Fear
18 Ulysses S. Grant	53	Sadness
06 John Quincy Adams	52	Sadness
27 William Howard Taft	52	Joy
22 Grover Cleveland	51	Anger
38 Gerald Ford	47	Anger
39 Jimmy Carter	45	Acceptance
08 Martin Van Buren	44	Satisfaction
19 Rutherford B. Hayes	42	Fear
30 Calvin Coolidge	42	Anger

Bottom-Tier Presidents		
President	Greatness	Stand-Out Emotion
21 Chester A. Arthur	40	Acceptance
43 George W. Bush	40	Fear
23 Benjamin Harrison	38	Anger
20 James A. Garfield	37	Sadness
37 Richard Nixon	37	Sadness
31 Herbert Hoover	33	Pleasure
10 John Tyler	31	Fear
12 Zachary Taylor	31	Contempt
13 Millard Fillmore	28	Contempt
17 Andrew Johnson	25	Disgust
29 Warren G. Harding	25	Disgust
14 Franklin Pierce	23	Satisfaction
09 William Henry Harrison	19	Contempt
15 James Buchanan	15	Surprise
45 Donald Trump	12	Sadness

PRESIDENTS DESIGNATED BY GREATNESS AND THEIR STAND-OUT EMOTIONS

The ranking of presidents in terms of their presidential greatness score was done by the 170 members of the American Political Science Association's Presidents and Executive Politics section. The stand-out emotions were identified, in turn, by facially coding typically 40-50 portraits or photographs of the presidents during their adulthood and especially, when possible, while they were in office.

EMOTIONS THAT ENABLE SUCCESS

JOY

What the Results Reveal

This study's findings suggest that, of all the levels of happiness, it's the most intense, rapturous level of happiness that plays the largest role in presidential success. The positive correlation between the two is .28, indicating that joy has the second strongest relationship with greatness. (Only stronger is the combination of negative emoting predominating along with a low level of sadness.) An infrequent emotion, joy seems to enable success when it happens, but it doesn't happen much. Despite its rarity, what is the case in favor of joy among U.S. presidents? It could well be that this most expansive version of happiness indicates a willingness to be broad-minded and highly creative when tackling the issues of the day.

Third, should we be surprised that the two leaders to be showcased here, Obama and Taft, also qualify as extraverts based on what previous research by psychologists has concluded? If stereotypes hold true, then the characteristics of an often bubbly (or joyful) and outgoing (extraverted) person fit together.

Three Levels of Greatness

Greatness – Top Tier

Alone in the top tier for greatness is Barack Obama, having apparently achieved the caliber of leadership he aspired to realize. This is a man who ran for office with the

	Greatness	Joy Rank	2nd Emotion	Top Trait	2nd Trait
Obama	8th	2nd	Contempt	Extraversion	Conscientiousness, Agreeableness (tie)
Taft	22nd	1st	Acceptance	Extraversion	Neuroticism

The five U.S. presidents who qualify as showing the most joy relative to the other presidents are, in rank order from first to fifth: William Howard Taft, Barack Obama, Woodrow Wilson, Theodore Roosevelt, and John F. Kennedy. Of them, only Taft and Obama will be discussed here, because the other three presidents have other stand-out emotions that distinguish them the most.

From these five names, you can already see the first pattern: Democrats (slightly) prevail in terms of joy. Second, all but Taft are from the latest era, after mass media made having an infectious smile caught on camera a definite plus.

JOY AS PRESIDENTS' STAND-OUT EMOTION

As will be true of the other charts like this to follow, what's listed here are the qualifying presidents' greatness rank (as assigned by political science scholars), the rank or degree to which this stand-out emotion characterizes a president over and above his fellow presidents, plus each president's other, second strongest stand-out emotion (also based on facial coding), and finally each president's top two traits (as assessed by psychology scholars).

BARACK OBAMA

44th President 2009-2017
(Democrat)
A full, true smile that you can believe in occurs
when the muscle around the eye constricts,
causing a twinkle in the eye and often crow's
feet. A grin alone isn't as powerful a signal of
happiness. In Obama's case, his joyful smile
would decrease in frequency as gray hair
emerged and the travails of being president
increasingly took their toll.

slogan "Change we can believe in," the chant "Yes We Can,"
and a campaign poster with a single word— "Hope" —
emblazoned above an image of the sun rising over America.
I was in the small crowd huddled inside a room in Des
Moines, Iowa, the night that Obama won the Iowa caucuses.
What I remember the most isn't his victory speech. Instead,
it's how Obama only briefly waved to the audience and only
briefly flashed his big, trademark smile, as if he didn't want
to boast or fake exaggerated ecstasy about having successfully taken his first step to the White House that evening.

The day after Obama became president-elect, Alice
Walker wrote an open letter in which she advised him "to
cultivate happiness" for himself and not become like the
other "men in the White House" who "soon become juiceless
and as white-haired as the building," with "smiles so lacking
in joy that they remind us of scissors."[1] Walker's concern
was well-founded. Obama did become more disappointed,
even bitter, about the stubborn partisanship he experienced
in the nation's capital, although his tendency to flash smiles
of true joy never entirely evaporated.

On a happier note, what's fascinating about Obama's
rise from being a state legislator to president in four years is
that he won by projecting a message of hope and promised
change. He didn't get elected because of his experience or
proven expertise.

The Audacity of Hope was the title of one of Obama's
previous books, and it played out in why he won the Nobel
Peace Prize almost immediately upon taking office: for being
himself.[2] None of this is to suggest that Obama was perfect.
Instead, it's to demonstrate the importance of emotion,
and how Obama's joyful smile fit so perfectly on Inauguration Day 2009 when he spoke of a country mired in a Great
Recession and yet having "chosen hope over fear."[3]

Greatness – Middle Tier

While he scored as number one for joy in this study, William Howard Taft certainly didn't find it in being president. Instead, he joins the ranks of those who considered the day when they left the White House among the happiest days of their lives. It's hard to be great at something that you don't enjoy. "Politics when I am in it makes me sick,"[4] Taft once said. Upon leaving office, he added, "I have proven to be a burdensome leader . . . . I am entirely content to serve in the ranks."[5] Of course, within the ranks in Taft's case meant attaining his dream job: becoming the Chief Justice of the U.S. Supreme Court after having been president. Nobody else has ever held both posts. "I love judges, and I love courts," Taft gushed. "They are my ideals," representing "what we shall meet hereafter in heaven under a just God."

Though he was obviously capable, Taft could nevertheless easily be pegged as a big softie. When Taft and Teddy Roosevelt became political foes, Taft burst into tears, telling a reporter, "Roosevelt was my closest friend." Taft took losing the White House in stride, having been pushed to take the job in the first place by both his dad and wife.

When he wasn't focused on the law, Taft's passions lay elsewhere. He was the first president to play golf and the man who created the tradition of the seventh-inning stretch at baseball games. Taft probably loved baths, too, until he got stuck in one and it took six men to pull him out. Taft wasn't big, he was h-u-g-e. Since he weighed 332 pounds as president, it's possible that only the cow that Taft kept on the White House grounds was bigger than he was. A joke around town was that "Taft is a real gentleman. He got up on a streetcar and gave his seat to three ladies." When Yale University offered Taft the Kent Chair of Constitutional Law after his presidency, he replied that a sofa of law would be even better.

WILLIAM HOWARD TAFT

27th President 1909-1913
(Republican)
When he wasn't miserable, Taft was utterly happy. A belly laugh translates in this case to a smile so broad and relaxed that Taft's eyes close.

SATISFACTION

What the Results Reveal

Second after joy in terms of predicting presidential greatness is satisfaction: the middle-of-the-road level of happiness. It has a positive .14 correlation to success, though its frequency is modest. What is it about this mildly upbeat form of happiness that causes it to be advantageous in securing greatness? One plausible explanation is that satisfaction follows in the wake of joy, with both forms of happiness likely to help presidents maintain their emotional equilibrium while in office.

These five presidents top the satisfaction list: John F. Kennedy, Franklin Pierce, Abraham Lincoln, Martin Van Buren, and James Monroe. All of them will be discussed shortly, except Lincoln, whose stand-out emotion is sadness despite his top five status here. In Honest Abe's place is Dwight Eisenhower. While the man known as "Ike" didn't make the top-five list for any of the emotions, satisfaction is the emotion that distinguishes him the most.

As for patterns, in this case, some do emerge. The clearest trend is that in every instance where the presidents' traits have been identified, Extraversion accompanies satisfaction. That's hardly a big revelation. To be happy is to reach out, typically. More eye-opening is that the two presidents with a scornful secondary emotion (contempt in Eisenhower's case, disgust in Van Buren's case) are also seen as Conscientious. Perhaps scorn caused these two presidents to temper the comfort of happiness in a way that made them more dutiful and organized. Last, it's not a pattern as it applies only to Pierce. But I find it intriguing to wonder if the oscillation between satisfaction and fear as Pierce's two stand-out emotions may have contributed to Neuroticism being his defining trait.

SATISFACTION AS PRESIDENTS' STAND-OUT EMOTION

Satisfaction and Extraversion go hand-in-glove here. Note that only Kennedy feels another level of happiness, namely pleasure, as a secondary emotion. These other presidents are all more on the grim side.

	Greatness	Satisfaction Rank	2nd Emotion	Top Trait	2nd Trait
Eisenhower	7th	8th	Contempt	Conscientiousness	Extraversion
Kennedy	16th	1st	Pleasure	Extraversion	Openness
Van Buren	27th	2nd	Disgust	Conscientiousness	Extraversion
Pierce	41st	3rd	Fear	Neuroticism	Extraversion

Three Levels of Greatness

Greatness – Top Tier

Dwight Eisenhower stands in contrast to the other two presidents in the satisfaction chart whose secondary emotions are "negative" by having a better, higher greatness ranking. This leads one to explore why he is the exception. A look into Ike's life suggests that the explanation may involve his ability to learn to curb his hostile feelings in order to keep them from being detrimental.

What's the evidence? Eisenhower had an aloof, mean-spirited father, who thought nothing of whipping his six sons with a leather harness to discipline them. Eisenhower, in turn, showed plenty of anger during his childhood. Most famous is the time when, as a six-year-old boy denied the chance to go trick-or-treating on Halloween, a young Eisenhower responded by punching a tree so hard—and repeatedly—that his hand turned bloody.[1] As an emotion, contempt has an element of anger to it. At the same time, though, smirks also bear some physical resemblance to smiles, and it was to smirking that Eisenhower gravitated in his adult life when either not happy or trying to be amused by a situation he found himself in.

Put another way, somewhere along the way Eisenhower became "Ike": the guy with the nice, luminous smile and a sense of humor. That quality became invaluable in The White House, as it was in military service that involved navigating (at close quarters) the huge, vexing egos of commanders like Douglas MacArthur, George Patton, Bernard Montgomery, and Charles de Gaulle.

DWIGHT D. EISENHOWER

34th President 1953-1961
(Republican)
"I'd like Ike (to smile more)" was never an official campaign slogan. Well it might have been. While Eisenhower qualifies for the satisfaction category, his smiles were typically at the low end of that level of happiness, whereas Kennedy's smiles were at the high end instead.

JOHN F. KENNEDY

35th President 1961-1963
(Democrat)
Left to his own devices, Kennedy could
be as happy-go-lucky a president
as we've had. His back was bad, but
there was never anything wrong with
Kennedy's smile.

Greatness – Middle Tier

John F. Kennedy, the man who replaced Eisenhower in office, is really a very different guy. Degrees of happiness become the point of discussion when it comes to JFK. Regarding joy, pleasure, and satisfaction, Kennedy qualifies for the respective top-five list for all three of those levels of happiness. Still, it's mid-level happiness, namely satisfaction, which defines him best. After all, that would be very much in keeping with how Kennedy saw himself: as a balancing act, an "idealist without illusions."[2]

Happiness can make a person delightful company but can also lead to a certain sloppiness in handling circumstances. To describe Kennedy as Open (to experience) is an understatement. Only Thomas Jefferson, John Quincy Adams, and Abraham Lincoln score higher on that trait according to previous research, followed by Bill Clinton and Kennedy in a tie.

It's with Clinton that the greatest similarities exist, in fact. Much could be made here of Kennedy's extramarital sex life, from a habit of skinny-dipping in the White House pool with secretaries nicknamed Fiddle and Faddle to an affair with the girlfriend of a mob boss. Discrete judgments weren't Kennedy's strong suit. During World War Two, he had an affair with a former Miss Europe, who counted among her "friends" Nazi bigwigs.[3] If some of this laxity spilled over into matters like having been a "fool" to listen to his advisors advocating for the Bay of Pigs, who should be surprised? That Kennedy did well as a president in being open-minded attests to his voracious reading habit, a willingness to devour information in order to learn how best to address a challenge.

To wrap up the middle tier here, let's consider Martin Van Buren. Yes, he was a kind soul. The writer Washington Irving characterized Van Buren as "One of the gentlest and most amiable men I have ever met with."[4] Was our eighth president also profligate? Perhaps so. Certainly, his opponents liked to describe him that way.[5]

During the Panic of 1837, "Martin Van Ruin" could be seen traveling through the muddy streets of the capital in a fancy green coach driven by men in fancy uniforms. His coat had a velvet collar, his gloves were made from soft leather. From there, the opposition took its cues and ran head-long into rumor. Surely, Van Buren dined using a golden spoon, bathed in a tub of cologne, and slept in a bed worthy of Louis XV. Whatever his actual merits as a president, as a candidate for re-election Van Burden couldn't survive such mockery.

Greatness – Bottom Tier

With a greatness rank near the bottom of the barrel, Franklin Pierce obviously struggled in office. What was his problem? No doubt alcoholism had a lot to do with Pierce's inability to succeed as president. Though he fought valiantly in the Mexican War, Pierce was mocked by his opponents as the "Hero of Many a Well-Fought Bottle."[6] There is more than booze, though, that explains our fourteenth president. Undermining Pierce's satisfaction was fear, his other main emotion. Lacking self-confidence, Pierce "endeavored to be gracious and accommodating to all who sought [favors]."[7] The bottom line is that Pierce serves as a cautionary tale of why happiness, despite its often-beneficial nature, can't be counted on as a sure-fire sign of presidential greatness.

MARTIN VAN BUREN

8th President 1837-1841
(Democrat)
Van Buren's mouth doesn't betray much of a smile in this case. The smile's existence and extent is to be found more, instead, in the degree to which his cheeks are raised.

FRANKLIN PIERCE

14th President 1853-1857
(Democrat)
This image doesn't show a guy saying "cheese". But it's a healthy enough smile all the same from Pierce, especially given the earlier, pre-TV era in which he served.

ANGER

What the Results Reveal

Anger is important as a factor in predicting presidential greatness. While it only has a positive correlation of .12 to presidential greatness, its prevalence as an emotion goes a long way to explaining why the single strongest correlation to success involves a combination of more negative emoting alongside a low level of sadness. In fact, anger accounts for nearly half of all presidential emoting on average, vastly exceeding the frequency of joy and satisfaction combined.

Yes, happiness alone isn't enough to guarantee success in The White House. Some "fire" has to go along with the balm of joy and satisfaction. It's a yin-yang proposition, which is where anger enters the picture. Of all of the so-called negative emotions, compared to sadness, disgust, contempt, and fear, anger alone predicts greatness. Maybe that's true because this emotion can signal a desire to control one's circumstances and make determined progress toward achieving a goal.

	Greatness	Anger Rank	2nd Emotion	Top Trait	2nd Trait
Jefferson	5th	8th	Acceptance	Openness	Conscientiousness
Madison	12th	2nd	Satisfaction	Conscientiousness	Agreeableness, Openness (tie)
Cleveland	24th	3rd	Contempt	n/a	n/a
Ford	25th	1st	Contempt	Extraversion	Conscientiousness
Coolidge	28th	7th	Disgust	Conscientiousness	Neuroticism
B. Harrison	32nd	5th	Acceptance	Conscientiousness	Neuroticism

ANGER AS PRESIDENTS' STAND-OUT EMOTION

Most of these presidents aren't so great, but they are generally marked by Conscientiousness.

As for the five U.S. presidents most given to anger relative to other presidents, they are Gerald Ford, James Madison, Grover Cleveland, Franklin D. Roosevelt, and Benjamin Harrison. Of them, only Roosevelt won't be discussed here. That's because acceptance qualifies as FDR's stand-out emotion. Instead, both Calvin Coolidge and Thomas Jefferson get added here because, although they don't land on any of the top five lists, anger emerges as their single most distinguishing emotion.

From this list of the angriest presidents, what patterns emerge most clearly? First is that of these presidents, Jefferson, Madison, and Harrison all balance anger with happiness as their second, most characteristic emotion. In contrast, Cleveland, Ford, and Coolidge double down with a second, negative, scorning emotion (contempt or disgust). Of those two tendencies, it certainly seems like balancing anger with happiness works better in The White House, if these men's greatness rankings are any indication.

Anger can be expressed by having the eyes narrow, reducing a person's field of vision. Suffering from "tunnel vision" is always a risk with anger. In contrast, happiness is a more expansive emotion. As a result, it makes sense that the two best-performing presidents on this list—Jefferson and Madison—have in common both some level of happiness as their secondary stand-out emotion and Openness as one of their top two personality traits, according to previous research.

Three Levels of Greatness

Greatness – Top Tier

Of the two top-tier angry presidents, Thomas Jefferson reigns supreme. Beyond his well-known accomplishments, what might be some clues that help identify and explain his anger streak? The single clearest link is that a motivation for anger is a desire to make progress, and as necessary eliminate any unjustified barriers in your way.

Inspired by the Declaration of Independence that he penned, Jefferson wanted "this ball of liberty" to "roll around the world."[1] Therefore, Jefferson strongly supported the French Revolution (despite its violent excesses) because only then could the world "be better than as it now is." Jefferson opposed slavery, and he resigned from George Washington's cabinet to protest what he saw as the threat of a burgeoning monarchy. Ready to let states disobey any federal laws they opposed, Jefferson was, in essence, one of the great free spirits of his or any era.

THOMAS JEFFERSON

3rd President 1801-1809
(Democratic-Republican)
Jefferson could be pugnacious.
With a taut, straight lower left
eyelid and a mouth so firmly set
that a bulge appears below the
lower lip, he appears here more
than ready to fight on.

While Jefferson's anger seems to have been embedded into his values, with James Madison it's possible that anger had its roots in needing to defend himself. At five feet four inches and weighing all of 100 pounds, Madison remains our smallest president ever: memorably described as being "no bigger than a half piece of soap." Did our fourth president have a Napoleonic complex? If so, Madison managed to make it more than merely something personal. By leading America into the War of 1812, he proved to be a little man capable of standing up to the world's only super-power by fighting England to a stand-still.

• •

JAMES MADISON

4th President 1809-1817
(Democratic-Republican)
With his eyebrows lowered and his right, lower eyelid especially taut with anger, Madison stares out at viewers of this portrait with a hard, resolute stare. Lips pressed firmly together complete the picture of a guy who wouldn't take no for an answer.

Greatness – Middle Tier

These next three presidents all combine anger with a scorning emotion (contempt or disgust) as their secondary emotion. Of them, Grover Cleveland was the most obviously given to a quick temper and to speaking bluntly. Cleveland didn't like to schmooze, and he was frugal enough that as president he turned down the idea of spending $10,000 to distribute seed grain as aid to drought-stricken Texas farmers. Earnest to a fault, Cleveland was known as Grover the Good. When *The New York Times* endorsed him for president in 1884, the newspaper gave three reasons for supporting him: "1. He is an honest man. 2. He is an honest man. 3. He is an honest man."[2]

• •

GROVER CLEVELAND

22nd and 24th President 1885-1889; 1893-1897
(Democrat)
You don't get to be the only president to serve non-consecutive terms by avoiding a struggle. Here, the massive wrinkle between Cleveland's eyebrows reinforces the grim determination shown by his gun slit of a left eye.

Some of Gerald Ford's aides would later describe him as touchy and temperamental, but a good man overall.[3] Born Leslie Lynch King, Jr., Ford took his stepfather's last name when his mom remarried, valuing his adoptive father as a man of far greater integrity than his birth father. As to Ford's adult years, one of the downsides of anger is that it can make a person seek single-minded, straightforward answers. None were available amid the recession of the mid-1970s, when Ford took to wearing a WIN button ("Whip Inflation Now") as if the economy merely required a little cheerleading in order to improve. Not always viewed by others as up to the job of being president, Ford once indirectly admitted to his limitations as a leader by characterizing himself as "a Ford, not a Lincoln."[4]

. . . .

GERALD FORD

38th President 1974-1977
(Republican)
"I'm not having much fun handling the job," Ford might well have been thinking as this photograph was taken. As to his feelings, lowered eyebrows and lips firmly set indicate the presence of anger.

Often rigid, Calvin Coolidge would quickly repay any loan, down to the penny, and was parsimonious with his words, too. What was Silent Cal's single most famous remark? The hostess of a party told Coolidge, "You must talk to me, Mr. President. I made a bet today that I could get more than two words out of you." His reply: "You lose." Coolidge cut the federal budget nearly in half during his time in office through steps like having government workers be issued only one pencil at a time. When the Great Depression came on the heels of his leaving office, Coolidge admitted to friends that he had spent his presidency "avoiding the big problems."[5]

. . . .

CALVIN COOLIDGE

30th President 1923-1929
(Republican)
Besides the taut left lower eyelid, the bulge of skin right below Coolidge's lower lip also marks him as truly angry. The upside-down smile caused by an upwardly thrusting chin doesn't help Coolidge look very content, either.

BENJAMIN HARRISON

23rd President 1889-1893
(Republican)
Smoldering would be one way to
describe Harrison's expression. The
eyebrows are firmly set, the eyes
narrow and piercing, and the mouth
with lips so tightly pressed together
that our twenty third president is a
million miles away from a smile.

Greatness – Bottom Tier

Who's the very last president to be covered in this section of *Two Cheers for Democracy*? It's time to meet Benjamin Harrison. Called the "human iceberg" behind his back,[6] Harrison came across as diligent, aloof, and suffering from so much confidence that it bordered on arrogance. Like Coolidge and Cleveland, Harrison didn't like to engage in "small talk" on the job and couldn't tolerate the inefficiency he found other people guilty of. Clearly, being the grandson of the country's ninth president and the great grandson of one of the signers of the Declaration of Independence wasn't enough of a heritage to ensure success in Harrison's case.

EMOTIONS THAT IMPAIR GREATNESS
SADNESS

What the Results Reveal

All in all, this study's findings suggest that nothing tends to harm presidents' odds of being successful in office more than their exhibiting large amounts of sadness. In feeling sad, whether due to isolation, regrets or a sense of hopelessness, the "blues" seep in and seem to reduce the odds that a president will be an effective leader.

The great exception to sadness being a problem is Abraham Lincoln's presidency. Otherwise, a link between elevated levels of sadness, Neuroticism, and mediocrity in office looms large. With a negative -.23 correlation to success, sadness has the strongest negative link to presidential greatness. Nor is sadness a rare emotion. It ties with fear for being the third most prevalent emotion presidents feel, thereby casting a long shadow.

Of the five U.S. presidents who qualify as showing the most sadness relative to the other presidents, only John Tyler won't be discussed now. That's because fear, more so than sadness, is Tyler's stand-out emotion. In addition, James Garfield is joined by John Quincy Adams and Andrew Jackson in this discussion. While all three men don't land on any of the top five lists, sadness is in each case their distinguishing emotion.

Two entries are immediately noteworthy. Although low amounts of displayed sadness tend to correspond to presidential greatness, the top-rated and lowest-rated presidents both appear here: Lincoln and Donald Trump, respectively. Adding in these two presidents' second most uniquely characteristic emotion and their top two personality traits, what may psychologically account for the disparity in greatness when it comes to comparing Lincoln and Trump?

SADNESS AS PRESIDENTS' STAND-OUT EMOTION

In terms of greatness, there's Lincoln, maybe Jackson, and then a big gap. As a trait common to many of these presidents, Neuroticism definitely puts in an appearance here. Only Lincoln and Nixon offset sadness with a level of happiness as their secondary emotion, with Lincoln trumping Nixon with both a higher greatness ranking and a higher level of happiness (satisfaction, as opposed to mere acceptance).

	Greatness	Sadness Rank	2nd Emotion	Top Trait	2nd Trait
Lincoln	1st	3rd	Satisfaction	Openness	Neuroticism
Jackson	15th	8th	Anger	Extraversion	Neuroticism
Grant	21st	2nd	Fear	Extraversion	Agreeableness
J. Q. Adams	23rd	6th	Fear	Neuroticism	Openness
Nixon	33rd	4th	Acceptance	Conscientiousness	Neuroticism
Garfield	34th	13rd	Anger	n/a	n/a
Trump	44th	1st	Disgust	Extraversion	Neuroticism

One key explanation may be that Lincoln offsets sadness with its direct opposite emotion, happiness (in the form of satisfaction). That emotional balancing act may have helped Lincoln, in addition to having as his top trait Openness: the trait with the highest correlation to presidential success. In contrast, Trump's second stand-out emotion is another "negative" emotion, disgust. Meanwhile, our current president's degree of Openness is so lacking that it rivals Conscientiousness for being his weakest, least characteristic trait.[1]

Three Levels of Greatness

Greatness – Top Tier

When it comes to Abraham Lincoln, while you might think you already know everything that there is to know about him, here are a few quotes and details that may surprise you as well as simultaneously confirm Lincoln's unique mix of sadness and happiness. Yes, he had empathy for others, sometimes expressed by a wry, trenchant sense of humor: "Whenever I hear anyone arguing for slavery, I feel a strong impulse to see it tried on him personally." And, yes, Lincoln could be morose. Fate wasn't always kind, so it's no wonder that Honest Abe was also Sad Abe. Lincoln's mother died when he was nine. His first romantic love died of typhoid. And when his son Willie died, it would become the only instance of a child dying in The White House.

It would have been easy to be bitter. But sadness combined with happiness made Lincoln remarkably resilient. "If elected, I shall be thankful; if not, it will be all the same," he said in campaigning for office his first time.[2] It was ever so with Lincoln; he was always ruefully coping with whatever he faced. Four days before his death, Lincoln told a crowd gathered to celebrate winning the Civil War: "We shall sooner have the fowl by hatching the egg than by smashing it." If sadness taught Lincoln anything, surely it was to have patience.

ABRAHAM LINCOLN

16th President 1861-1865
(Republican)
The creased cheeks, lowered eyebrows, and especially the downturned left corner of his mouth are all signs of Lincoln's abiding sorrow.

Old Hickory grew up as an orphan and came to his inauguration dressed in black, mourning his wife, who had died three months earlier. Losing his mom, dad, and wife may account for much of Andrew Jackson's sadness. Even so Jackson was feisty, unlike Lincoln, for whom anger was a rare emotion. What deeply marked Jackson? That would be both the bullet he carried near his heart from a duel fought to protect his wife's honor, and the scar across his face from a British officer slashing Jackson for refusing to clean his boots after Jackson was taken prisoner during the Revolutionary War.[3] Sadness seems to have mostly spurred Jackson on to anger, rather than slowing him down to contemplate what had gone horribly wrong.

ANDREW JACKSON

7th President 1829-1837
(Democrat)
A disheveled mess here, Jackson has strongly arched inner eyebrows pulled hard together (notice the wrinkles across the forehead and between the eyebrows). The decline of the right mouth corner seals the deal: Jackson is despondent.

Greatness – Middle Tier

In seeking admiration from his father in vain, Ulysses S. Grant was set to launch into a life-long desire to receive praise from other people instead. Hoping to prove himself, Grant failed many times over. Whether as a farmer, wood seller, rent collector, railroad owner, or leather merchant, he couldn't make ends meet. No wonder he feared flunking out of West Point after his dad arranged for him to attend there.[4] Grant's wife, Julia, protected her husband's self-esteem and without her nearby, Grant would often resort to heavy drinking. Fortunately for the Union army men under his command during the Civil War, Grant's wife and children almost always accompanied him to battle.

ULYSSES S. GRANT

18th President 1869-1877
(Republican)
The raised, inner left eyebrow and the eyebrows pulled together, and down, suggest Grant's downcast state. The sagging mouth corners merely confirm it.

In John Quincy Adams' case, you have got to wonder if living up to his Founding Father's legacy didn't prove to be too much for him. John Adams' son was prone to be self-abusive, often working 15 hours a day or more. When he died, this ex-president was serving in the U.S. House of Representatives where, after a stroke, colleagues carried him to the Speaker's Room. Always high-minded, the leader nicknamed Old Man Eloquent was "generally miserable" and had few friends.[5] Of course, it didn't help that Adams wouldn't put his own supporters into his Cabinet, believing that to do so wasn't fair.

JOHN QUINCY ADAMS

6th President 1825-1829
(National Republican)
The sagging left mouth corner and the raised chin are both relatively subtle expressions. But the way Adams' eyebrows undergo a gravitational pull that pinches them inward is pronounced and a clear sign of a man suffering from a pensive, brooding nature.

Greatness – Bottom Tier

Prior to entering politics, Richard Nixon acquired the nickname Gloomy Gus while attending Duke University's law school. Sadness is Nixon's quintessential emotion. Was it the early death of two brothers that set him down the path to sadness? Or was a former aide right in theorizing that "as a young person, he [Nixon] was hurt very deeply by somebody he trusted. . .. He never got over it and never trusted anybody again."[6] Certainly, Nixon kept to himself. "A major public figure is a lonely man," he told an interviewer. "You cannot enjoy the luxury of intimate personal friendships." At the White House, Nixon ran his administration as if from a distance, disliking personal encounters.

RICHARD NIXON

37th President 1969-1974
(Republican)
Even without the lowered gaze, Nixon reveals sadness due to lowered eyebrows and the sag in the lower right corner of his mouth.

Raised in modest circumstances, James Garfield was a conflicted soul. On the one hand, Garfield saw himself as "destiny's child, marked out for some special purpose." On the other hand, while in office Garfield suffered from nightmares in which he ran around naked and lost.[7] Which version of Garfield should we believe: the self-confident version or the one wracked with doubt? On balance, given that sadness is Garfield's most characteristic emotion, the latter wins. That verdict suits the fate of Garfield, whose tenure in office was the second shortest ever. For three months, doctors couldn't locate the assassin's bullet near his spine, and it was their unsterilized fingers and instruments that were the single, most direct cause of his death from blood poisoning.

- -

JAMES GARFIELD

20th President 1881-1881 (Republican) Later in life Garfield would have a full beard that obscured his expressions. Here, the dour downturned corner of his mouth and the brooding, hunched eyebrows already signal his emotional future. Note that alongside Garfield is his wife, Lucretia, on the couple's wedding day.

Last, we come to Donald Trump. Sure, it's tough when the mantra you hear growing up is "Be a killer, be a winner" (instead of "I love you").[8] But beyond a hard-driving father he couldn't entirely please or impress, what else might explain Trump's sadness? Like Nixon, yes, Trump had a brother die young, but they weren't that close. Could it simply be that extreme narcissism means that this "very stable genius" (as he describes himself) is doomed to feel endlessly let down because he can't secure universal acclaim?

While Trump has touted being even more popular with Republican voters than Abraham Lincoln ever was, it's actually Andrew Jackson, also prone to sadness, with whom Trump has more of an affinity.[9] Indeed, Jackson is the predecessor that Trump so favors that in decorating The White House, he put Old Hickory's portrait in the Oval Office. In contrast, it's harder to picture Trump and Lincoln being especially alike. Lincoln tops the list of greatness, and his advisers were a team of accomplished rivals. Trump is dead last on the greatness list, and considers his advisers "fools" whose advice he often responds to by sitting back in a chair, arms crossed, scowling with disappointment.[10]

- -

DONALD TRUMP

45th President 2017- (Republican) Disgruntled to disappointed is about the range of Trump's sadness. Downcast eyes, and eyebrows pinched together are part of the story here. But the key to Trump's sadness, visually, remains the corners of the mouth sagging at the same time that an upward chin thrust results in an upside-down smile.

DISGUST

What the Results Reveal

Disgust signals that something isn't right. A person, idea, behavior, or situation might literally or metaphorically "stink," causing a president's instinctive urge to be to back away. In national politics, at least in the old days before cable TV newscasters helped to make "compromise" a dirty word, moving closer together and finding consensus was how most presidents got things done. As a result, it isn't too surprising to find that, overall, disgust has a negative correlation to presidential success. You can't "clean something up" if your main instinct is to step *back* and avoid a problem rather than step *up* to tackle it.

Nevertheless, there is one stellar example of a reform-minded president who did both: felt revulsion *and* confronted the problems the country faced. That person is Theodore Roosevelt. He's in the minority, given that disgust has a negative correlation of -.19 regarding presidential success.

In rank order from first to fifth, these are the presidents most given to disgust: Warren Harding, Andrew Johnson, James Monroe, Bill Clinton, and Theodore Roosevelt. Of these, two presidents won't be discussed here, Monroe and Clinton, because contempt and pleasure, respectively, are their stand-out emotions. With only three presidents in the spotlight here, it's hard to speak in terms of patterns, but one seems possible: disgust and Extraversion match up for two of these presidents.

DISGUST AS PRESIDENTS' STAND-OUT EMOTION

The marvel in this case is that Roosevelt has the exact same top two emotions as Trump—but in reverse order, along with totally different results in terms of greatness ranking. May the mysteries of human nature never cease.

	Greatness	Disgust Rank	2nd Emotion	Top Trait	2nd Trait
T. Roosevelt	4th	5th	Sadness	Extraversion	Conscientiousness
Harding	39th	2nd	Anger	Extraversion	Agreeableness
A. Johnson	40th	3rd	Contempt	n/a	n/a

Three Levels of Greatness

Greatness – Top Tier

Sitting atop Mount Rushmore and fifth in the ranks of the greatest presidents ever is Theodore Roosevelt. Much disgusted him. Here is the guy who the reform-minded, "muck-racking" journalists of the day, at least initially, found to be their greatest ally. In Roosevelt, we have somebody who attacked the financier Jay Gould for being "part of that most dangerous of all dangerous classes, the wealthy, criminal class." No doubt Roosevelt wore it as a badge of honor to be labeled by his critics as a "goo-goo" (meaning someone committed to *good government*).[1]

Yes, Roosevelt was a moralist and, therefore, prone to disgust. In heading to college, Roosevelt had been told by his father, "Take care of your morals first, your health next and finally your studies." In turn, the man often referred to as TR pointedly said, "It is of no use to preach to [children] if you do not act decently yourself." It would be wrong, though, to believe that this president only felt disgust in regards to politics and morality. More broadly, he also felt instinctive disgust for anybody who didn't exhibit vitality. To be bored or act sluggishly met with Roosevelt's disapproval.

There are numerous and legendary examples to demonstrate this point. Roosevelt advocated for the "strenuous life." Not only did this most famous of the Rough Riders storm up San Juan Hill and then, later, become a sportsman rancher out west in Medora, North Dakota; he loved to declare, "Get action, do things . . . be somebody." Sure, TR also said, "Speak softly and carry a big stick" (citing an African proverb)—but who really believes that this guy ever, ever spoke *softly*?

TR was both Phi Betta Kappa and a boxer at Harvard University. So it wasn't an aberration for him to spar with boxing champion John L. Sullivan in the White House gym. An imperialist through and through, Roosevelt objected to Colombia asking for more money in exchange for letting the Panama Canal be built. His vow: "Warn these cat-rabbits that great through our patience has been, it can be exhausted." When told a recent appointee had voted against him, costing him a victory in a Supreme Court case against a railroad company, Roosevelt retorted, "I could carve a better judge out of a banana."[2] (Should you hear an echo of Donald Trump in that last example, you're not alone.)

Almost nothing could stop Roosevelt, not even his mother and wife dying on the same day. When a would-be assassin shot Roosevelt in Milwaukee during the 1912 campaign, he went on to give a 50-minute speech without changing his blood-stained shirt until he was taken to a local hospital after leaving the stage.

THEODORE ROOSEVELT

26th President 1901-1909
(Republican)
Not someone ever accused of being
tepid, this is Roosevelt yet again
giving it his all. The wrinkled nose
and the lifting of the upper lip signal
a double dose of disgust.

In Warren G. Harding, we have a man in over his head. "I'm not fit for this office and never should have been here," he confessed at one point. On another occasion, he said, "I don't know what to do or where to go. I know somewhere there is a book that will give me the truth, but hell! I couldn't read the book."[3] Maybe Harding felt revulsion for the mendacity of the men who joined his cabinet and caused the Teapot Dome scandal. But it wouldn't have required a stretch of the imagination to see our twenty ninth president as surrounded by like-minded types. Harding enjoyed playing poker and once gambled away a whole set of the White House's china. Booze was illegal during his administration, but Harding drank anyway, along with members of his cabinet. Although one of his appointees fled the country to avoid indictment and another committed suicide, Harding never did clamp down, earning the nickname Wobbly Warren.[4]

WARREN G. HARDING

29th President 1921-1923 (Republican)
Harding's face bears the stamp of disgust (and anger). Note the upper lip subtly flared.

Forget Harding. With Andrew Johnson, the story is if anything, even worse. A poor boy made good, Johnson forever after harbored resentment (expressed as disgust) for the prejudice he felt subjected to by those in the upper classes. As a white supremacist, Johnson's life-long support for underdogs would, however, run smack up against his lack of care of, or support for, African-Americans after the Civil War ended. When Congress retaliated against Johnson for his leniency toward ex-Confederates, how did he respond? The president hit the road to give speeches, sometimes drunkenly, often antagonizing his audiences. "Let them impeach and be damned,"[5] he bitterly said, and escaped losing office by merely one vote, hardly a ringing endorsement.

ANDREW JOHNSON

17th President 1865-1869 (Democrat)
Johnson is looking as turbulent as his administration was. Disgust is evident in the raised upper lip, amid a welter of other emotions being expressed (fear and anger foremost among them).

CONTEMPT

What the Results Reveal

Contempt has its upside. A smirk mingled with a smile might signal confidence that you really *are* superior to people and circumstances you feel are beneath you. Then again, contempt also tends to isolate people. You see yourself as above others, so it becomes too easy to dismiss their opinions as unworthy of consideration. Pretty soon, a contemptuous president can star in a latter-day version of Hans Christian Andersen's "The Emperor's New Clothes." You know, the story about the king who parades about naked in public because nobody dares to tell him that the clothes the weavers had made aren't magically invisible; they're simply non-existent. The king has been had, with his vanity not allowing him to recognize reality.

Based on the evidence here, it's clear that contempt isn't the sign of a successful president. Given a negative -.18 correlation to success in office, contempt places second behind only sadness in raising the odds of failure. Smirk a lot, fail a lot: that's the basic plot line. About the only saving grace contempt offers is that it's rare. Contempt ties not only with disgust but also with joy and pleasure for being the least common emotion presidents exhibit.

Want another indication that contempt is problematic? In rank order from first to fifth, the five presidents most given to contempt are Millard Fillmore, James Monroe, Gerald Ford, William Henry Harrison, and Barack Obama. Of these, only Obama is a top-tier president. And once you remove Obama and Ford from the list of presidents to be discussed here (because other emotions better distinguish them from their fellow presidents), the results look even worse. Let's add Zachery Taylor because he's not on any top-five list but comes closest for contempt. Now the results become downright miserable. After all, regarding the *second* worst of the presidents I'm about to cover, namely Fillmore, a Yale University history professor has joked: "to discuss . . . Millard Fillmore is to overrate him."[1]

The contempt these leaders felt toward others could, Monroe aside, easily be directed at themselves in turn. Quite honestly, three of these four presidents shouldn't be looking *down* at others. They should instead realize that they weren't, even for a moment, considered for a spot atop Mount Rushmore. Based on their own less-than-great greatness rankings, they should figuratively speaking be craning their necks to look *up* at their peer group instead.

	Greatness	Contempt Rank	2nd Emotion	Top Trait	2nd Trait
Monroe	18th	2nd	Disgust	n/a	n/a
Taylor	35th	6th	Anger	n/a	n/a
Fillmore	38th	1st	Acceptance	Conscientiousness	Agreeableness
W. Harrison	42nd	4th	Fear	n/a	n/a

CONTEMPT AS PRESIDENTS' STAND-OUT EMOTION

Looking for a great president here? After Monroe, you'll be looking for a long time.

JAMES MONROE

5th President 1817-1825
(Democratic-Republican)
When the upper left corner of
the mouth goes into a tight, little
upward tug, it's a smirk. That
movement and a slightly raised
upper lip means time-to-own-it,
Mr. Monroe: you're displaying
contempt.

Three Levels of Greatness

Greatness—Middle Tier

Let's start with James Monroe, the one saving grace on this list of presidents prone to contempt. Quite honestly, when I started analyzing Monroe's facial expressions and detected the prevalence of contempt, I thought my eyes were deceiving me. Of Monroe, Thomas Jefferson said: "He is a man whose soul might be turned wrong side outwards without discovering a blemish to the world."[2] Candid, disarming, warm, steady, affable, thoughtful, unpretentious; those were among the adjectives I encountered when first reading about Monroe. *Did I have him pegged wrong?* Why, this president even presided over what became known as the Era of Good Feelings because, like only George Washington before him, Monroe ran unopposed for office (a feat surely never to be repeated).

Slowly, though, another side of our fifth president emerged. Monroe could also be thin-skinned, sensitive to perceived slights. After being recalled as our ambassador to France for not staying neutral in the conflict between the French and the British, Monroe fiercely denounced Washington. When offered the governorship of the Louisiana Territory by Jefferson, his friend and mentor, Monroe turned the post down as utterly beneath him.

Yes, Monroe could behave like a spoiled child, "operating as he did with such an elevated sense of his own integrity" that he "couldn't easily adjust when old friends failed to approve his conduct."[3] In short, Monroe wasn't so perfect after all. Monroe could be wonderful—or he could be indiscreet and honest to the point of naiveté. Here was somebody whose smirks signaled passive-aggressive, bottled-up disdain for others who hadn't also given fifty years of service to their country.

Greatness—Bottom Tier

Those who are left after Monroe aren't much to write home about. Oddly enough, two of the three presidents on the contempt list were a team of sorts. Millard Fillmore was Zachary Taylor's vice president and assumed the presidency thanks to Taylor receiving terrible medical advice. Here's the story in brief. Taylor gets violent stomach cramps after eating heavily at a Fourth of July event. What's the solution? *Why not try a mercury compound to induce bleeding and blisters!* Five days later, Taylor is dead, and his replacement is a guy who Taylor took an immediate disliking to upon first meeting him.

Why is Fillmore held in such historical disrepute? A good reason could be that Fillmore gave up his convictions in favor of expediency. Personally opposed to slavery, he signed into law a bounty hunters' right to grab fugitive slaves as part of the so-called Compromise of 1850, and strictly enforced it. Personally opposed to the anti-immigrant, anti-Catholic, and anti-Irish stance animating the Know-Nothing Party, Fillmore nevertheless accepted the party's nomination for president in 1856. As for why Fillmore felt so much contempt, most likely it had to do with the looming Civil War and Fillmore's condescending despair: "May God save the country, for it is evident that the people will not."

MILLARD FILLMORE

13th President 1850-1853
(Whig)
It's hard to look past Fillmore's harsh stare, but do so and you'll also notice the raised upper lip and especially the smirk on the left side of Fillmore's mouth. Both of those facial muscle activities are reliable signs of contempt.

As for the man Fillmore replaced, Zachary Taylor also definitely felt superior to others. Famous for helping to win the Mexican War, Taylor was a forerunner of how General Douglas MacArthur would disobey Harry Truman's orders during the Korean War. Not only did Taylor offer the enemy a brief armistice against the express wishes of President James Polk, he also didn't stay put when told that he shouldn't march his troops further south, into battle. Who knows if Taylor would have carried through on his threat to hang Southern leaders (starting to urge succession) in the run-up to the Civil War? History took a different course. The general ate too much and perished, end of story.

ZACHARY TAYLOR

12th President 1849-1850
(Whig)
What's the difference between a smile and a smirk? In this example, that would be nothing more than how the narrowing of Taylor's lip on far-left side signals the utmost self-confidence.

Speaking of generals who died in office brings us, next, to William Henry Harrison. Why did he feel lots of contempt? Was it being born into the planter aristocracy? Was it being a general? After all, Dwight Eisenhower was likewise prone to contempt. (That said, it's hard to call smirking a pattern characteristic of generals when Ulysses S. Grant's *least* frequent emotion was contempt. All we can say with certainty is that Harrison gave a two-hour-long inauguration speech during a cold rain, without wearing a coat, and died 31 days later of pneumonia. Going from giving the longest speech to having the shortest presidency ever sure sounds like pride-cometh-before-a-fall to me.

WILLIAM HENRY HARRISON

9th President 1841-1841
(Whig)
See Harrison smirk: along the left side of his mouth, note the tightened lip corner that rises a little. Also evident, a small dimple in the adjacent cheek and an asymmetrically raised upper lip.

FEAR

What the Results Reveal

Survival is the bottom line in politics, as in life. Because of this reality, it's no wonder that fear matters. With a negative -.15 correlation to presidential success, yes, it's true that fear is in fourth place as an emotion that hurts a president's odds of doing well in office. Even so, fear ties with sadness for being the third most common emotion presidents feel. It's this high degree of prevalence that lends fear weight as an emotion. Overall, sadness and fear are almost three times as common as contempt and disgust, the other two emotions most likely to undermine a president's performance.

Fear serving as a harbinger of struggling in the White House makes sense. It's an emotion that flickers ever stronger as people move from feeling uncomfortable to experiencing utter danger. Allies and followers alike look to leaders to gauge how they're handling uncertainty and the risk of harm. The presidents who can't cope with the pressure very well will, over time, shake everyone's confidence in what the outcome will be.

FEAR AS PRESIDENTS' STAND-OUT EMOTION

These greatness results reveal that feeling fear neither assures, nor prevents, a president from being successful in office. Symptomatic of fear's ambivalent impact is that half the time here, fear corresponds to Extraversion as a fearful president's leading trait; but the other half of the time, it's Neuroticism arising instead. Note how Bush '43 is characterized by both those traits!

	Greatness	Fear Rank	2nd Emotion	Top Trait	2nd Trait
Reagan	9th	1st	Pleasure	Extraversion	Agreeableness
G. H. W. Bush	17th	5th	Anger	Neuroticism	Extraversion
Polk	20th	4th	Surprise	Neuroticism	Conscientiousness
Hayes	29th	2nd	Satisfaction	n/a	n/a
G. W. Bush	30th	7th	Surprise	Extraversion	Neuroticism
Tyler	37th	3rd	Sadness	n/a	n/a

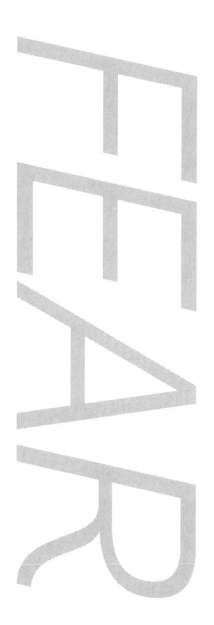

The five U.S. presidents who qualify as showing the most fear relative to other presidents are in rank order from first to fifth: Ronald Reagan, Rutherford B. Hayes, John Tyler, James K. Polk, and George H. W. Bush (Bush '41). All five are discussed here. In addition, George W. Bush (Bush '43) will be covered because while he doesn't land on any of the top five lists, fear is his stand-out emotion.

From this list of the fearful presidents, what results emerge most vividly? For starters, only the lone top-tier president here—Reagan—isn't also defined by having Neuroticism as one of his top two personality traits. Whatever fear he felt didn't "warp" his personality or hinder his abilities in office.

Two other results also stand out. Yes, it figures that surprise would emerge as the second most common emotion for Polk and Bush '43. That's because fear and surprise are both reactive, notice-your-surroundings type of emotions, which show in similar ways on people's faces. In addition, it's impossible to overlook Bush '41 and Bush '43 both making this list, and sharing the same top two traits (in reverse order). Clearly, in this case the apple didn't fall far from the tree. Their affinity is greater than that of either the original father and son presidential example, the Adams family, or the Harrisons, where the grandfather's contempt was replaced by the grandson's penchant for anger.

Three Levels of Greatness

All alone here in the top tier for greatness is Ronald Reagan. Identifying this beloved-by-many president as fearful will be controversial and disputed by some of his supporters. But I'm a Marxist, a Groucho Marxist based on his famous line to Margaret Dumont: "Who are you going to believe, me or your own eyes?" So as a facial coder, I'll stick by what I saw and turn to Regan's biography for further support.

The plausibility of Reagan being characterized by fear starts with his childhood years.[1] Reagan's dad was an alcoholic shoe salesman. There were week-long benders, embarrassment galore, and a poor family that moved almost every year. Friendships came and went, collateral damage as it were. But apparently Reagan didn't mind. Later in life, he would recall his youth as being "as sweet and idyllic as it could be." From that remark, you can already see evidence of Reagan's second most characteristic emotion: strong happiness (pleasure).

Then again, you should also see our fortieth president's remark for what it surely is, in part, namely denial: a coping mechanism. It isn't a stretch to put Reagan into the same camp as other children of alcoholics, people whose strategy is to adopt "a happy face" and act like nothing's wrong.

Distancing himself from his own experiences by sugar-coating them was one way that Reagan coped. It seems that another was to distance himself from others. When an official biographer made that same observation, Reagan objected and called his life an open book. The biographer's reply? "Yes, Mr. President, but all the pages are blank."

Other people were even more direct. Three of Reagan's four children portrayed him in memoirs as emotionally distant, with his son Ron claiming that he had never *once* had a real conversation with his dad. Reagan's wife Nancy likewise admitted that her husband was a mystery to her.

Perhaps because Reagan's fear was offset—or buoyed—by pleasure, he's the exception here. No other president on this list joins him in the top tier. Might he have done even better in terms of his greatness ranking if not for the assassination attempt? Who knows? Certainly, both his mental and physical abilities began to decline afterwards. When exactly Alzheimer's set in is anybody's guess, but someone with better odds of knowing would be Reagan's Chief of Staff Howard Baker. Baker got to be so concerned about Reagan's mental state that he considered invoking the 25th Amendment in order to remove Reagan from office. The fear so evident on Reagan's face later in life could well be due, in part, to Alzheimer's.

RONALD REAGAN

40th President 1981-1989
(Republican)
A pensive Reagan reveals fear in the way his eyebrows are raised and pinched together, and especially in how the left side of his mouth slides wide.

GEORGE H. W. BUSH

41st President 1989-1993
(Republican)

Full of shy ambition, witness
paradoxical Bush '41: the eyebrows
are slightly raised and yet bunched
together, too; moreover, he smiles,
but with a nervous twitch.

Greatness—Middle Tier

With George H. W. Bush, the question becomes: where did his sense of duty come from? The credit goes mostly to his mother, Dorothy. She wanted her son to be both fiercely competitive and, at the same time, neither boastful nor self-promoting. That's a tricky line to walk. Another uneasy, odd juxtaposition in life came years later when Bush found himself—the epitome of a Connecticut, blue-blooded Yankee—newly married, working in the oil industry in Odessa, Texas, and for a brief while stuck in housing that meant sharing a bathroom with a mother-daughter team of prostitutes.[2]

Maybe such oddity helps to explain the strange, even kind of endearing awkwardness that was Bush '41. A former Democratic Chairman, Robert Strauss, might have said it best: "George is a damn good guy, but he doesn't come through well. It's a case of choking. It takes eleven hours to get George ready for an off-the-cuff remark."

A decorated World War Two pilot, Bush was hardly a wimp. And yet stirring acts of defiance were few and far between. Alongside Patrick Henry's "Give me liberty, or give me death," doesn't this declaration by Bush look pale: "I do not like broccoli. And I haven't liked it since I was a little kid and my mother made me eat it. And I'm president of the United States, and I'm not going to eat any more broccoli." No wonder cartoonist Garry Trudeau joked that Bush had put his manhood into a "blind trust" while serving as Reagan's vice president.

Our forty first president's counterpart on this list is James K. Polk. They're almost equal in the greatness rankings, and share Neuroticism as their primary personality trait. Most of all, they both felt a duty to serve their country. In Polk's case, you could even argue that duty killed him. Sworn in as the country's youngest president to date, Polk survived leaving the White House by only three and a half months. Long days on the job may have done him in. Polk's work ethic was all the more remarkable considering his legacy of poor health dating back to his childhood.

How do you square Polk's record as the president of Manifest Destiny with his being prone to fear? The answer lies in being a classic over-achiever. Should you doubt me, trust Polk's own words, for he wrote with pride in his diaries about how "the meager boy, with pallid cheeks, oppressed and worn with disease" had accomplished so much.[3] Fear doesn't mean that you're going to freeze. Freeze, flight or flee are all possible reactions to fear, which means that fear can be motivating. Not only did Polk wage war on Mexico, but in challenging England for the land north of California, Polk's motto was that America must either gain all the land above the fifty-fourth parallel, "or fight."

JAMES K. POLK

11th President 1845-1849
(Democrat)
A wary Polk is what we have here.
His eyes are wide, alert to danger; the
eyebrows hunched together, with a
crease between them; and the left side of
the mouth is ever so slightly wider.

GEORGE W. BUSH

43rd President 2001-2009
(Republican)
The considerable forehead wrinkles
give away the game. They're caused
by raised eyebrows that accompany
open, searching eyes and a slightly
unsettled smile. By the way, yes,
of course it's Bush holding forth at
the podium.

Greatness—Bottom Tier

After his younger sister died early in life, to cheer up his mother, George W. Bush (Bush '43) would often play the clown. Sometimes, that role has proved to be deliberate later in life as well. In a mischievous way, he's said: "You can fool some of the people all the time, and those are the ones you want to concentrate on." At other times, Bush playing the clown seems to be more of a self-inflicted role. For example, note his saying of critics: "They misunderestimated me." From bouts of heavy drinking and carousing as a young man to less successfully following in his father's footsteps, there's always been something about Bush '43 that seems a little off-kilter. He swaggers when he walks, but stumbles when he speaks. He's a former fighter pilot who never proved his worth in combat, unlike his valorous dad.

Family matters plagued Rutherford B. Hayes. For starters, Hayes never knew his father, who died three months before his birth. Then, especially as a young man, Hayes feared he might go insane (a condition that plagued relatives on both sides of his family tree).[4] Whether that scenario always loomed somewhere in the back of Hayes' mind, no one can say for sure. Observers saw him grow into an affable, easy-going fellow who, like Bush '43, often liked to poke fun at people and turn everything possible into a joke.

RUTHERFORD B. HAYES

19th President 1877-1881 (Republican)
Where does Hayes betray feeling scared? His right eye is wide, as if warily scanning the horizon for trouble, and the eyebrow above it is hunched.

For John Tyler, laughter didn't come easily. Nicknamed "His Accidency," Tyler became president when William H. Harrison died of pneumonia soon after his inauguration, leaving Tyler as a man without a political home. He was a Democrat turned Whig, only to be expelled from the Whig party and have almost his entire cabinet resign in protest against his policies. What was the basic problem? Tyler feared that slavery might be abolished, and, in fact, he would get elected to the new Confederate Congress in Richmond after leaving the White House. What was likely Tyler's most memorable statement? Sounding like Thomas Jefferson—in reverse—he declared that "Life and liberty are captivating sounds, but they often captivate to destroy."

JOHN TYLER

10th President 1841-1845 (Democratic-Republican)
Yes, Tyler's left eyelid is raised and taut. But besides anger, there's fear here, too, in eyebrows pulled together at the same time that Tyler's mouth is pulled slightly wider.

EMOTIONS THAT QUALIFY AS NON-FACTORS

Out of the ten emotions I considered, there are three that didn't seem to have enough of a correlation to presidential greatness, pro or con, to be worthy of much discussion here. They are surprise, acceptance, and pleasure. In brief, I'll discuss the presidents who qualify as having one of these three emotions as their stand-out emotion, and a synopsis of how, in autobiographical terms, each of these emotions most clearly applies to each president in turn.

SURPRISE

Why might surprise qualify as a non-factor emotion, unlikely on its own to either help or hurt a president's odds of success in the White House? The answer may involve the nature of surprise itself. Surprise is an inherently neutral emotion because it functions as a *pre-emotion*. This kind of reaction happens super quickly, in under a second. Surprise is really about getting focused, paying attention, than it is anything else. Next, the judgment comes. Is this new, mysterious thing that just happened a positive or negative development? Does curiosity or wariness hold sway?

Those two competing impulses of curiosity or wariness are likely at play in the five presidents distinguished by the frequency with which they show surprise. In rank order from first to fifth, they are Harry S. Truman, James Buchanan, George Washington, Lyndon B. Johnson, and Abraham Lincoln. For two of these presidents, Truman and Johnson, their second most distinguishing emotion is acceptance: a low-grade version of happiness. Let's put them in the curiosity camp. Meanwhile, Buchanan, Washington, and Lincoln belong in the wariness camp. Their second most distinguishing emotions are, respectively, contempt, disgust, and sadness. Note that as sadness is more prominent for him, Lincoln is replaced here by Woodrow Wilson. That's because while Wilson doesn't appear on any top-five lists, surprise is his stand-out emotion, followed by joy.

What follows is a quick look at each of these presidents, one after the other.

SURPRISE AS PRESIDENTS' STAND-OUT EMOTION

From the high greatness ranking for most of the presidents here, you might swear that surprise is obviously the key to presidential success. But widen the picture beyond the presidents most prone to surprise, and the correlation to greatness falls off—hence surprise is a non-factor emotion.

	Greatness	Surprise Rank	2nd Emotion	Top Trait	2nd Trait
Washington	2nd	3rd	Disgust	Conscientiousness	Neuroticism
Truman	6th	1st	Acceptance	Extraversion	Conscientiousness
L. Johnson	10th	4th	Acceptance	Extraversion	Neuroticism
Wilson	11th	6th	Joy	Conscientiousness	Neuroticism
Buchanan	43rd	2nd	Contempt	Conscientiousness	Neuroticism

A land surveyor as well as a military officer before becoming president, George Washington was working in professions where having your eyes wide open was a relevant skill. Terrain wasn't all Washington liked to observe. Aside from uniforms, Washington also paid attention to his attire and that of the women who caught his eye at social functions.[1] Something of a dandy, the leader of the world's first democracy in 1,800 years was both fonder of fashion than most people realize, and happy to marry Martha, among the prettiest and wealthiest widows in America.

• •

GEORGE WASHINGTON

1st President 1789-1797
(Independent)
While no stranger to anger, too, this is classic Washington: gathering information with a field of vision aided by having his eyes wide and his eyebrows sky high.

The later stage of Harry S. Truman's life was all about surprises. Along with FDR's death in 1945, making him president, there was of course his upset of the Republican candidate Thomas E. Dewey in 1948. In signing-off on the Marshall Plan, Truman said, "I don't believe in little plans. I believe in plans big enough to meet a situation which we can't possibly foresee now."

• •

HARRY S. TRUMAN

33rd President 1945-1953
(Democrat)
A wide-eyed look combined with raised eyebrows are all evidence of Truman's characteristic surprise.

If any of the presidents characterized by surprise favor the curiosity, opportunity-seizing aspect of this emotion, it's Lyndon B. Johnson. Idealistic parents who struggled financially made LBJ just that much more eager to succeed. With a definite preference for dating rich girls, LBJ met Lady Bird for the first time ever and then proposed to her the very same day.[2]

....

LYNDON B. JOHNSON

36th President 1963-1969 (Democrat)
The massive forehead wrinkles that perpetual wariness can cause are fully on display here on Johnson's face. Raised (and knitted) eyebrows deliver this look.

"It is not men that interest or disturb me primarily; it is ideas. Ideas live, men die." That's the logic Woodrow Wilson favored. So you can imagine why he often had problems getting people to warm up to him. "He thinks he is another Jesus Christ come upon the earth to reform men," French president Georges Clemenceau wryly observed.[3]

....

WOODROW WILSON

28th President 1913-1921 (Democrat)
You might call Wilson lots of things, but never a slacker. The raised left eyebrow and the commanding gaze are quintessential Wilson.

After all of these lively, successful characters, what do we have left in the surprise category? That would be a total loser: James Buchanan, a man who was literally both near-sighted and far-sighted at the same time and said that the country's "prospects are daily brightening" on the eve of the Civil War.[4]

. . . .

JAMES BUCHANAN

15th President 1857-1861 (Democrat)
Looking the worse for wear, Buchanan appears with cocked eyebrows and eyes wide (as if to survey the damage his time in office was causing).

	Greatness	Acceptance Rank	2nd Emotion	Top Trait	2nd Trait
F. Roosevelt	3rd	5th	Anger	Extraversion	Openness
Adams	14th	8th	Surprise	Neuroticism	Conscientiousness
McKinley	19th	3rd	Fear	n/a	n/a
Carter	26th	2nd	Joy	Conscientiousness	Neuroticism
Arthur	31st	1st	Sadness	n/a	n/a

ACCEPTANCE AS PRESIDENTS' STAND-OUT EMOTION

Acceptance seems to lend itself to either Conscientiousness or Neuroticism. Or at least that's true of Adams and Carter. As usual, FDR is in a class by himself by not fitting the pattern those other two presidents' traits suggest.

ACCEPTANCE

In facial coding terms, acceptance means the slightest of smiles. With presidents, this minimal form of happiness is as common as all the other, more robust, forms of happiness put together. Therefore, acceptance qualifies in this study as presidents' second most frequent emotion overall and is potentially important—except it isn't. The correlation to presidential greatness is only .07, making acceptance a non-factor. It seems as if a wan smile leads to wan results in terms of acceptance correlating to presidential greatness.

The five U.S. presidents who exhibit acceptance most often, relatively speaking, are in rank order from first to fifth: Chester A. Arthur, Jimmy Carter, William McKinley, Franklin D. Roosevelt, and Millard Fillmore. Of them, only Fillmore won't be discussed here because contempt is an emotion that defines him better. In addition, John Adams is added because while he doesn't land on any of the top five lists, acceptance is his stand-out emotion. As for patterns, there aren't any. These five presidents have different, varying secondary emotions, and no clear pattern for the traits is possible given the unavailability of information in a pair of cases.

Here's a quick look at each of these presidents.

Franklin D. Roosevelt could be genuinely jocular and jaunty. But the real, essential FDR, emotionally speaking, is best expressed by the slightest of smiles. In trying to ingratiate himself while in college at Harvard University, FDR was remembered as being "like a dog whose tail wagged too much."[1] He wouldn't make that mistake again.

. . . .

FRANKLIN D. ROOSEVELT

32nd President 1933-1945
(Democrat)
For a president in the age of modern mass media, this qualifies as quite a modest smile from Roosevelt.

If not for a happy marriage to Abigail, John Adams might not have been happy at all. Plenty of colleagues agreed with Adams that vanity was his "cardinal folly." As a result, they went around behind his back calling Adams by his principal physical attribute: His Rotundity.

. . . .

JOHN ADAMS

2nd President 1797-1801
(Federalist)
"Okay, sure I'll smile (a little)," Adams seems to be telling us. (Is that also a smirk evident along the left side of the mouth? It certainly is.)

Understatement made William McKinley and his habit of displaying a ghost of a smile a perfect fit. To get a sense of McKinley's warm but subdued personality, you need only to read accounts of his death. After getting shot while on an official visit to Buffalo, McKinley's message was, "Don't let them hurt him" to halt the throng rushing to attack his assassin.[2] Upon his death, his parting words to assembled friends consisted of a gentle, "Good-bye, *good-bye all.*"

· ·

WILLIAM MCKINLEY

25th President 1897-1901
(Republican)
With eyes staring ahead, McKinley would appear at least vaguely menacing if not for the slight but definite smile playing upon his lips.

In Jimmy Carter, Americans elected a guy who smiled broadly. They voted out of office a guy whose frosty smiles could barely hide his stubbornness. Said one person of Carter, he "reminds me of a South Georgia turtle. He doesn't go around a log. He just sticks his head in the middle and pushes and pushes until the log gives way."[3]

· ·

JIMMY CARTER

39th President 1977-1981
(Democrat)
Carter came to office with a beaming smile. Before long, determination and worry took precedence over happiness and the smiles grew more subdued and even grim.

Several presidents didn't enjoy being in office and found other ways to extract some happiness from life. In Chester A. Arthur's case, that meant being a gourmand and becoming the first president to hire a valet. But most of all, he liked fishing. In an echo of Greta Garbo's famous line, "I just want to be left alone," Arthur said, "I may be President of the United States, but my private life is nobody's damned business."[4]

CHESTER A. ARTHUR

21st President 1881-1885
(Republican)
Now you see it, now you don't: welcome to Arthur's ghost of a smile.

PLEASURE

This study's findings indicate that pleasure is, in statistical terms, a non-factor in predicting presidential greatness. In fact, no emotion plays a smaller role than pleasure does in determining a president's likelihood of success. For starters, analyzing the relationship between pleasure and success on the job reveals only a measly .03 correlation between pleasure and success. Furthermore, like joy, pleasure is one of the two least common emotions that presidents show on their faces.

Why might joy correlate to greatness, but not pleasure? The answer may be that joy has also been called a "true" smile, suggesting greater authenticity. Both joy and pleasure are intense forms of happiness, involving big smiles. But pleasure lacks the additional, hard-to-fake way the corners of the eyes crinkle when experiencing joy. In a world where politicians engage in lots of grip-and-grin, staged photographs, perhaps joy enables more trust, which translates into more success on the job?

The five U.S. presidents who show the most pleasure relative to the other presidents are, in rank order from first to fifth: Herbert Hoover, John F. Kennedy, Bill Clinton, Ronald Reagan, and Franklin D. Roosevelt. Of these five, only Hoover and Clinton are discussed here, as the others have already been covered regarding their own stand-out emotions.

Here's a quick look at both Clinton and Hoover.

PLEASURE AS PRESIDENTS' STAND-OUT EMOTION

Pleasure aside, these two presidents couldn't be much more different. As the chart shows, they have nothing else in common. Whereas Hoover might fetch his dog as a companion, Clinton would be more likely to ask: "Where's the party?"

	Greatness	Pleasure Rank	2nd Emotion	Top Trait	2nd Trait
Clinton	13th	3rd	Disgust	Extraversion	Openness
Hoover	36th	1st	Acceptance	Conscientiousness	Neuroticism

Maybe Bill Clinton's greatness ranking could have been higher if he was a little different. The First Lady in the presidential-portrait-as-novel, *Primary Colors,* certainly thinks so. Almost everyone assumes it's really Hillary Clinton speaking these words to her husband: "You could have been such a great president if you weren't such an undisciplined shit." Clinton's biological father was a "lady-killer" married four times by the age of 30.[1] Clinton's high school jazz trio was named Three Blind Mice. Let's just agree that self-denial was never a big part of Clinton's story.

BILL CLINTON

42nd President 1993-2001
(Democrat)
Clinton's ability to offer up a smile and a laugh is legendary. There's nobody better when it comes to making whomever he's greeting feel like they're the only person in the room just then.

Herbert Hoover saved more people from hunger through his humanitarian efforts after World War One than anybody ever, and he was nominated for the Noble Peace Prize *five* times. Yet, he's also the guy who declared, "If a man has not made a million dollars by the time he is forty, he is not worth much."[2] All told, Hoover will primarily go down in history for advocating self-reliance during the Great Depression, leading to jokes like, "What's an empty pocket turned inside out? Why, that's a Hoover flag."

HERBERT HOOVER

31st President 1929-1933
(Republican)
Having gained fulfillment (and happy about it), Hoover wasn't always quick to understand its absence in other people's lives. By the time Hoover left office, what are the odds that his faithful dog was the closest thing Hoover had left in terms of a political ally?

AN EXTRA TWIST

As suggested by this book's title, *Two Cheers for Democracy*, how democracy works isn't always pretty—or fair. Article II of the U.S. Constitution merely stipulates that presidential eligibility is a matter of being a natural born citizen, at least 35 years of age, and with 14 years of residency in America. In practice, however, who was legally able to vote was inevitably a huge, corresponding factor in who was elected to the White House.

Originally, only about 6% of the American populace could vote: property-owning, tax-paying, white males. By 1828, all non-property holding white males had gained suffrage. For the rest of society to join them would take an awfully long time. In 1870, non-white men and freed male slaves officially gained the vote, only to soon, in effect, lose that option again in southern states until the passage of the Voting Rights Act of 1965. Others didn't fare a whole lot better. In 1887, Native Americans first secured the right to vote. In 1920, women joined them. Not until as late as 1943 did Chinese immigrants also, finally, acquire voting rights.

Therefore, it's hardly surprising that the occupants of the White House have looked the way they have: entirely a cast of white men, until Barack Obama came along. Nevertheless, First Ladies have certainly had a role in how America is governed and, like "First Men," have been ranked by experts regarding their own relative greatness, i.e., degree of influence.[1] Listed here are the stand-out emotions of the top ten most influential First Ladies, compared to each other, and in comparison to the stand-out emotions of their husbands.

On top, #1, for greatness among the First Ladies is Eleanor Roosevelt, who relieved her own sadness about a dysfunctional marriage by spending her time speaking out about racism and sexism, alongside holding meetings with labor leaders. She was the first First Lady to hold her own press conferences. She also had her own newspaper column, and later became the U.S. delegate to the United Nations. As an active advisor to her husband, Eleanor Roosevelt was similar to other First Ladies like Abigail Adams, Rosalynn Carter, and Hillary Clinton, who all also gave advice on a wide array of issues or even took a role in their husband's administrations. Joy is the stand-out emotion for our thirty second First Lady, an outcome that aligns with how joy enables presidential greatness.

Some of the other emotional results are likewise intriguing. When not serving as advisors, First Ladies have often adopted a favorite cause. Jackie

TOP TEN MOST INFLUENTIAL FIRST LADIES

Of these ten First Ladies, Eleanor Roosevelt isn't just first by influence: she seems to have found the most joy in the role that defined much of her adulthood. Hillary Clinton and Dolley Madison are the next most upbeat here. Four couples are perfectly matched, emotionally speaking: the Adams, Clintons, Johnsons, and Carters. The Madisons, Obamas, and Fords are the least similar emotionally, as couples.

White House Couple	Her Stand-Out Emotion	His Stand-Out Emotion
Eleanor (& Franklin) Roosevelt	Joy	Acceptance
Abigail (& John) Adams	Acceptance	Acceptance
Jacqueline (& John F.) Kennedy	Surprise	Satisfaction
Dolley (& James) Madison	Satisfaction	Contempt
Michelle (& Barack) Obama	Dislike	Joy
Hillary (& Bill) Clinton	Pleasure	Pleasure
Lady Bird (& Lyndon B.) Johnson	Surprise	Surprise
Betty (& Gerald) Ford	Satisfaction	Anger
Martha (& George) Washington	Anger	Surprise
Rosalynn (& Jimmy) Carter	Acceptance	Acceptance

ELEANOR ROOSEVELT

32nd First Lady, 1933-1945
(Democrat)
What a physically handicapped
Franklin Roosevelt couldn't
do—get around and see people
freely—his wife was only too
happy to do, repeatedly. Here's
the foremost of the First Ladies
out enjoying herself visiting our
troops overseas.

Kennedy's open-eyed curiosity certainly pushed her to promote the arts as well as to restore and refurbish the White House. Lady Bird Johnson's wide-eyed affinity for surprise might have helped her to spot the opportunity to protect the environment and engage in national beautification projects. Meanwhile, Michelle Obama's disgust for people's bad habits no doubt helped to motivate her Let's Move! campaign in favor of more physical activity and healthier school lunches to combat childhood obesity.

Who is unexpectedly missing from this top ten list? To some the notable absence might be Nancy Reagan; for others, Edith Wilson, who stepped in for her husband after a stroke partially paralyzed him. Pleasure and satisfaction were these two First Ladies' respective stand-out emotions. As for Melania Trump, no one is sure to what degree, if any, she influences her husband's administration. What is easier to deduce is that acceptance is her stand-out emotion. The sad joke could be made that she's had to accept (or tolerate) a lot when it comes to her husband's reported affairs with both a porn star and a centerfold model around the time of giving birth to her son Barron.

Even if Edith Wilson, in effect, ran the White House for a while, it's striking that America has never officially had a female president. By now, seventy nations have been led by a woman, including currently Bangladesh, Chile, Liberia, and nine European countries—but not the U.S., at least not so far.[2] With almost a quarter of all members of Congress being female, the largest amount ever, maybe that time isn't so far off. Four female Democratic candidates for president in 2020 are analyzed , along with the rest of the field, in the closing section of this book.

PART 2
U.S. Presidential Debates, Emotionally X-Rayed

ORIENTATION

Eloquence Rarely Matters Much

For over fifty years now, televised presidential debates have been the political equivalent of a heavyweight boxing match. From 1960 through 2016, thirty-three debates have been staged, drawing audiences of as great as 80 million viewers.[1] In theory targeted mainly at "undecided voters," these debates have arguably been decisive in determining the winner of every U.S. presidential election ever held involving them. But is that an accurate claim?[2] And if even approaching the truth, what's been the key to victory? Great oratory? Controversial issues clearly and honestly explained? In reply to all of those questions, don't bet on the answer you might have expected.

Election	Winner	Lead Prior to First Debate	Lead After the Last Debate	Difference
1960	Kennedy	-1%	+2%	+3%
1976	Carter	+12%	+6%	-6%
1980	Reagan	0%	+3%	+3%
1984	Reagan	+16%	+18%	+2%
1988	Bush '41	+8%	+10%	+2%
1992	Clinton	+18%	+12%	-6%
1996	Clinton	+20%	+19%	-1%
2000	Bush '43	-8%	-11%	-3%
2004	Bush '43	+8%	+8%	0%
2008	Obama	0%	+2%	+2%
2012	Obama	+6%	-3%	-9%
2016	Trump	-3%	-5%	-2%

DOES WINNING THE DEBATES MATTER?

The three candidates who most benefited from the debates was Kennedy in 1960, who pulled ahead; and Reagan in 1980 and Obama in 2008 because they were merely even with their respective opponents before the debates began. Bush '43 in 2000, Obama in 2012, and Trump in 2016 all won despite losing ground during the debates.

Let's start with whether presidential debates are decisive. The media loves the "horse race" aspect of presidential campaigns, of which the debates are always treated as key moments. What do we find if we compare the polling data, on average, prior to the first debate with where the polls stood soon after the last debate? And how did the momentum shift correspond to who eventually won? Allowing for the reality that, of course, the debates weren't the only factor during the time period between the two sets of poll data, the correlation is weak.

What we see is basically a coin flip. In twelve campaigns to date in which debates were held, the candidate who "won" the debates (based on polling trends) also won the national election in six of twelve cases: basically a coin flip. In other words, winning the debates provides no lock on winning the election. Nor on the other hand does losing the debates mean you can't win The White House.

As to what may influence undecided voters watching the debates, don't fool yourself into believing that facts and logic dictate. One-liners, jokes, and especially blunders matter a whole lot more. "Stump the Chump" is a game that can be played both on the debate stage and at home. As amusingly illustrated back in the day by Jay Leno's "Jaywalking" episodes on *The Tonight Show*, voters aren't really the informed electorate that those who run the country's policy think tanks might prefer. To what degree do citizens lack basic knowledge? A lot. Consider these findings:[3]

- 75% of Americans can't name all three branches of government.

- 60% of Americans don't know which countries we fought in World War Two.

- 50% of American college graduates don't know how long the terms of U.S. Representatives and Senators are.

- 20% of Americans believe the right to own a pet is enshrined in the First Amendment of the U.S. Constitution.

- 10% of American college graduates think Judith Sheindlin, television's "Judge Judy," is a member of the U.S. Supreme Court.

Are the last two bullet points funny? Yes, but I'm not here to shoot fish in a barrel. All of us are far simpler than we might imagine. For one thing, people are very visually oriented and susceptible to having faith that a tall person can literally "see over the horizon" better than a short person. What's the joke in corporate circles? *Diversity in senior management is a short, white guy.* Surely, we must at some subliminal level trust in tall leaders to have a better vantage point. How else to explain results like the greater success ratio for taller candidates in U.S. presidential debates.

Now, seven of twelve isn't a decisive trend, but add the tie in 1992 and you're talking about a trend that holds up two-thirds of the time. Who prevails? Typically, it's been the candidates attuned to the reality that TV is a visual medium, and that their faces play a key part in achieving the ultimate goal: an ability to connect emotionally with voters. Observing the debates in 1976, Norman Cousins noted in *Saturday Review* that "When the camera burrows into a man's face, the fact that some wrinkles may be covered up by pancake makeup is not as important as the visibility of the emotions that come to the surface. The strength of the TV debater derives less from what is hidden than what is impossible to conceal."[5]

Election	Taller Candidate	Other Candidate(s)	Winner
1960	Kennedy	Nixon	Kennedy
1976	Ford	Carter	Carter
1980	Reagan	Carter / Anderson	Reagan
1984	Reagan	Mondale	Reagan
1988	Bush '41	Dukakis	Bush '41
1992	Bush '41/Clinton (tie)	Perot	B. Clinton
1996	B. Clinton	Dole	B. Clinton
2000	Gore	Bush '43	Bush '43
2004	Kerry	Bush '43	Bush '43
2008	Obama	McCain	Obama
2012	Romney	Obama	Obama
2016	Trump	H. Clinton	Trump

TALLER CANDIDATES OFTEN PREVAIL

Two-thirds of the time, the taller or equally tall candidate has won the election. The average height difference is a little over three inches, with Trump having had the biggest height advantage: ten inches. But is Trump really America's third tallest President ever? His 2012 driver's license states his height at 6'2", but his 2018 White House physician's report increased that to 6'3".[4]

Talking points are fine, but *feeling points* are even more important. In ambiguous situations—like a debate—where voters as viewers are trying to decide which candidate they like and trust most, one seminal study suggests that 55% of what constitutes "true" communication signals (that voters rely on) comes from the face, 38% from the voice, and merely 7% from the words.[6]

1960: JOHN F. KENNEDY VS. RICHARD NIXON

Background

Before I suggest a winning emotional formula based on correlating facial expressions and post-debate poll results from 1960 through the 2016 election, let's make a pit-stop first. If ever there were a campaign cycle in which visuals, including facial expressions, were decisive, 1960 would be it.

That year brought us three first-time events in U.S. presidential campaigning: the first presidential debate ever held, the first televised debate, and the first presidential debate remembered for a blunder by one of the candidates. In August, Richard Nixon had badly injured his knee and spent two weeks in a hospital. He showed up for the first debate with a temperature of 102, twenty pounds underweight, pale, and sporting a five o'clock shadow. Nixon then compounded his sickly status by refusing to wear any make-up after John Kennedy had refused make-up. What Nixon didn't know was that his younger opponent then had make-up secretly applied anyway.

What the general public remembers is that Nixon looked like death warmed over. What presidential historians remember is that Nixon won the first debate—insofar as radio listeners were concerned. Only those who watched the debate on TV saw Nixon as the loser.

Emotionally, the first four presidential debates in 1960 also retain a distinct story line that involves a glaring error. The journalist Theodore White, author of the famous campaign series *The Making of the President*, bears responsibility.[7] Yes, White got one part right: Nixon was indeed "glowering and occasionally haggard-looking" (though "occasionally" is in itself a faulty qualifier). But to say "Kennedy was calm and nerveless in appearance" compared to Nixon being "tense, almost frightened" is to miss the boat.

In reality, the taller, more handsome, and happier Kennedy was also the more anxious of the two candidates across all four debates. So, to three other first-ever events in 1960, we need to add a fourth: that year also saw our first debate analysis error by a political pundit.

A DISHEVELED NIXON

Clowns wear better-fitting suits than this when performing in a circus. Could Nixon's sleeves be any more wrinkled than on display here?

The Famous Opening Debate

Because it was the first debate ever and looms large in lore, and because after the first debate Kennedy moved ahead of Nixon in the Gallup Poll and never relinquished his newfound lead, this debate must be discussed all on its own. Did Nixon look terrible? Absolutely. Compounding Nixon's weight loss and failure to have make-up applied is that he didn't buy a different suit. The one he wore on the air on September 26th was so ill-fitting that Nixon's arms looked several inches too short to fill out the sleeves, while his pale, thin neck swam inside his dress shirt's collar.

But enough about image: what did the two candidates' facial expressions and general body language reveal that evening? Let me start by puncturing the myth that Kennedy wasn't nervous. The single most reliable sign that somebody is nervous is when their mouth pulls wide. Kennedy's facial muscles gave that sign not once, but twice within the first minute of the debate and yet again shortly thereafter. Then, yes, that one particular, mouth-pulled-wide "Yikes!" expression of fear by Kennedy subsided. It would only occur twice more—when Kennedy was discussing Africa and Russia, topics on which the much-traveled Nixon had the advantage.

THE MYTH: A FEARLESS KENNEDY

The myth is that Kennedy felt no fear. The pinched, raised inner eyebrows, along with the mouth pulled ever so slightly wide to the left, suggest otherwise.

To what degree did Nixon look "tense, almost frightened," as White famously claimed? The answer is that Nixon was more nervous during the first debate than during any of the other three, but the amount of anxiety he revealed was less than half of what Kennedy displayed. More accurate is, if by "tense", White meant not only tightly *stretched* but also *taut*, rigidly stiff facial muscles. Truth be told, Nixon showed *ten-fold* more anger than Kennedy on-air that evening. But since Kennedy's level of displayed anger was unusually low for U.S. presidential candidates on stage across the years, it wasn't Nixon's anger that got him into trouble emotionally on September 26th.

The fatal problem that exacerbated Nixon's illness, weight loss, and ill-fitting clothes was sadness. Frankly, he looked forlorn out there on stage. Only Bob Dole during his second debate with Bill Clinton in 1996—and trailing badly in the polls—showed more sadness than Nixon did during the first debate in 1960.

Nixon is famous for loving the movie *Patton*, in which George C. Scott proclaims that "Americans love a winner and will not tolerate a loser." By showing so much sadness, Nixon gave off a vibe of being lonely and bereft of hope: a loser. Several times, Nixon's eyes shut (probably a vestige of having been sick), and his eyebrows sometimes knit together in a sign of sadness, anger, and fear. Even worse—since people tend to remember the opening, high point, and then the end of an experience—is how the debate concluded. Nixon's last notable expression was his eyebrows again knitting together in consternation as he alluded to his having grown up poor and downtrodden compared to the far wealthier and ultimately victorious Kennedy.

NIXON LOOKING WEARY

With eyes closed and a right cheek raised in a wince, Nixon appeared sad and forlorn. A left eyebrow slightly raised in a sign of surprise and fear is largely beside the point given Nixon's predominant emotions of sadness and anger that evening.

The Other Three Debates

Not only does facial coding reveal that Kennedy was nervous during the first debate, I have an ace in the hole when it comes to having the inside scoop. Clint Hill, a relative of mine, is justifiably honored for having tried to save Kennedy's life by clamoring aboard the President's limousine after the President was shot in Dallas in 1963. I've met Clint on several occasions in San Francisco, where he now lives. From being the Secret Service agent assigned to Jackie Kennedy, to broader duties that included serving under five Presidents from Dwight Eisenhower to Gerald Ford, Clint has, to say the least, a unique vantage point on American presidential history. In being told of my findings from the first debate, Clint wasn't at all surprised. Within the Kennedy clan, it was well-known that their candidate was as nervous before the first debate as he was elated afterwards.

Emotion Displayed	Kennedy > Nixon (Debate 1)	Nixon > Kennedy (Debate 1)	Kennedy > Nixon (all 4 debates)	Nixon > Kennedy (all 4 debates)
Skepticism				
Satisfaction	★★★			
Fear	★★★		★★★	
Pleasure	★★			★
Joy				
Anger		★★★		★
Sadness		★★★		
Disgust	★			
Contempt				
Surprise	★		★★★	

During the remaining debates, Nixon had his missteps and odd moments. For instance, given his wife's name (Pat), it's likely some observers were amused at Nixon's expense when he said: "America can't stand pat." Nevertheless, he retired the ill-fitting suit and looked less morose. The amount of sadness that Nixon had displayed during the first debate would subsequently decline by two-thirds, and in the second debate Nixon was instead forceful and assertive (more anger) while devoid of fear.

In addition, Nixon got the better of Kennedy over time in terms of feeling more at ease. Nixon's use of skeptical smiles to disarm Kennedy's attacks doubled and stayed high throughout the remaining debates. Eventually, Nixon even learned to smile more often on stage, vastly surpassing Kennedy's level of happiness in the third debate and almost matching Kennedy smile-for-smile in the fourth and final debate. For his part, after a particularly dour performance in the second debate, Kennedy relaxed and enjoyed himself more on stage. But his anxiety (matched by surprise) never went away and stayed at levels far greater than what Nixon betrayed.

1960 DEBATES: EMOTIONAL PROFILE

Almost radiant with happiness compared to Nixon in debate 1, Kennedy didn't sustain that advantage. Instead, fear and its related emotion, surprise, define Kennedy the most here. After a rocky start, Nixon was the more assured candidate on stage after the first debate, making a mix of the two most common emotions (happiness and anger) the basis of what the viewers saw at home.

Overall, what's most striking about the 1960 debates compared to the debates that followed was how informed, articulate, and devoted to making persuasive, rational arguments the two candidates were. Both men spoke quickly and well, and neither man showed much if any contempt toward the other.

Spooked by Nixon's first-debate debacle, Lyndon B. Johnson in 1964—as well as Nixon in 1968 and 1972—refused to agree to any presidential debates (televised or otherwise). Only when Gerald Ford was losing in the polls in 1976 did agreement come to resume the debates. By then, besides the events being televised in color instead of black-and-white, more emotionally-oriented appeals to voters had come out of the closet. At first a little, then over the years a lot more sophisticated in their demeanors, presidential candidates would never again clearly wipe sweat off their faces as Nixon did during his second debate with Kennedy.

NIXON HITTING STRIDE

Another myth: Nixon wasn't ever emotionally adept. A fast learner, he would soon learn to smile more and easily held his own on stage after the first debate.

What's the Winning Formula?

Over the course of twelve campaign cycles featuring U.S. presidential debates, it might make sense to assume the happier, more upbeat candidate won, right? Wrong. Remember how gaining ground in the polls taken before versus after the debates didn't have better than a 50/50 correlation to victory on Election Day? It's even worse here. In only one-third of the elections, four of twelve, did the sunnier, more emotionally upbeat candidate on stage go on to win the general election.

That winning the debates or coming across as more optimistic doesn't matter might seem to herald the end of the discussion. After all, why investi-

Election	Happier Candidate	Other Candidate(s)	Winner
1960	Nixon	Kennedy	Kennedy
1976	Ford	Carter	Carter
1980	Reagan	Carter / Anderson	Reagan
1984	Mondale	Reagan	Reagan
1988	Dukakis	Bush '41	Bush '41
1992	Perot	Bush '41, Clinton	B. Clinton
1996	B. Clinton	Dole	B. Clinton
2000	Bush '43	Gore	Bush '43
2004	Kerry	Bush '43	Bush '43
2008	McCain	Obama	Obama
2012	Obama	Romney	Obama
2016	H. Clinton	Trump	Trump

BEING MORE POSITIVE ISN'T CRUCIAL

"Hope sells" is a business maxim. But in presidential debates, projecting optimism about the American dream isn't a sure ticket to The White House. In fact, the opposite is closer to being true.

gate what's insignificant? In truth, there is still a way forward in determining whether some kinds of emotional displays or tendencies give a candidate an advantage or not. The solution is to focus not in general terms across all the debates but, instead, focus specifically debate by debate, identifying rises and falls in the polls taken after each one and identifying what helped or hurt.

Taking that route, there are 14 debates that proved most notable. Maybe the lead changed, with somebody else now ahead after a debate. Or candidates got a bounce or "stopped the bleeding" in a way that put new life into their campaigns. Using a threshold of at least a 4% swing in the polls after a debate, these 14 results didn't always lead to victory but point to real momentum shifts.

Election	Debate	Benefactor	Opponent(s)	Swing
1960	1st	Kennedy	Nixon	4%
1976	1st	Ford	Carter	10%
1980	2nd	Reagan	Carter	9%
1984	1st	Reagan	Mondale	4%
1988	2nd	Bush '41	Dukakis	4%
1992	1st	Perot	Bush '41, Clinton	8%
1992	3rd	Bush '41	Clinton, Perot	6%
1996	2nd	Clinton	Dole	4%
2000	3rd	Bush '43	Gore	8%
2004	1st	Kerry	Bush '43	8%
2004	3rd	Bush '43	Kerry	9%
2008	1st	Obama	McCain	8%
2008	2nd	McCain	Obama	5%
2012	1st	Romney	Obama	6%

Run the numbers and now we've got something worth talking about. There are emotional patterns here that, on balance, may signal how a candidate's chances improve. The patterns emerge from taking into account the margin of difference, per emotion, between how much that emotion gets shown in debates where candidates did well in the polls after those debates, versus how much that emotion was shown by candidates who "lost" those debates (based on the polling results afterwards). The bigger the difference between a "winning" and "losing" emotion and its impact on a candidate's standing in the next poll, the more that particular emotion gets more stars in my chart regarding which emotional displays help (and hurt) candidates most.

14 NOTEWORTHY DEBATES

These are the debates where, at times, nearly as much as a tenth of America seemed to have changed their perceptions of the candidates. One of these 14 debates, the first Kennedy-Nixon debate, has already been covered. As you go on through Part 2, the emotional profiles for the other 13 key debates will be highlighted similarly to what you see here. That way, if you're the kind of person who's not that much "into" charts, you can focus on those results in particular and skip over the other, less important debate results—sticking mostly with the story of each election cycle.

Emotion Displayed	Volume/Frequency	More Helps	More Hurts	No Difference
Skepticism	★★★	★★★★		
Satisfaction	★★	★★★★		
Fear	★★	★★★		
Pleasure	★	★★		
Joy	★		★★★	
Anger	★★★★		★★	
Sadness	★★		★★	
Contempt	★			★
Disgust	★			★
Surprise	★			★

(Left-side row group labels: HELPS — Skepticism, Satisfaction, Fear, Pleasure; HURTS — Joy, Anger, Sadness; NO IMPACT — Contempt, Disgust, Surprise)

WHICH EMOTIONS PROVE TO BE MOST IMPACTFUL

Skepticism, satisfaction, and pleasure—all variants of happiness, including skepticism, which is expressed by flashing a smile while making an ironic comment—are among the keys to success on stage. Oddly enough, expressing more fear than a rival is a pattern that also fits winning candidates. Want to hurt your chances as a candidate? Then show joy or resort to displays of sadness or anger. Along with surprise, the scorning emotions of disgust and contempt prove to be non-factors, not helping or hurting candidates on the debate stage. Note that correlation factors aren't given in this case, unlike in parts 1 and 3 of this book, because the sample size (14 debates, 30 individual candidate debate performances in all) is a little too small of a sample to be trying to make firm projections.

Let's start with the four types of emotional displays that aid candidates showing them often during a debate, or at least more often than their opponents. Those emotions consist of:

- *Skepticism*: This is an essential springboard to emotional success on stage. Think of it as wielding a smile like a knife, though really more like a butter knife. Skepticism means softening an ironic or sarcastic remark on stage with an "I doubt you" smile. The three instances among these 14 key debates where skepticism was especially advantageous for the debate winner consist of George W. Bush against Al Gore in 2000 (debate 3), Ronald Reagan against Jimmy Carter in their 1980 debate, and George W. Bush against John Kerry in 2004 (debate 3).

- *Satisfaction*: This is a mild, middle-of-the-road display of happiness. The smile is broad but doesn't rise to the level of a grin. The three debates were this was most notably an advantage for the better-performing candidate was Bill Clinton against Bob Dole in 1996 (debate 2), John F. Kennedy against Richard Nixon in 1960 (debate 1), and Mitt Romney against Barack Obama in 2012 (debate 1).

- *Fear* is the wild card here. I for one can't say that I expected fear to prove *helpful* to candidates. Indeed, I'm still not sure it actually is.

Maybe expressions of fear are okay, even helpful, because "gotcha" questions from the moderator or media panel may strike the audience as unfair, and therefore the voters watching the debate at home on their TV sets unconsciously start rooting for the candidate showing fear then. Or maybe Americans simply empathize with anyone who feels stage fright because fear of public speaking routinely gets cited in surveys as Americans' #1 fear. I don't know, I'm speculating here about how voters may intuitively respond to seeing candidates express fear. In contrast, when I consider fear from the debaters' perspective, I feel like I'm on more solid ground. Yes, the pattern linking fear and success might be coincidental or it might mean that, once again, conventional wisdom isn't so wise and the downside of fear has been over-rated. After all, in my work doing professional and NCAA Division I sports consulting, it's not fear but, rather, sadness that I've found to be the greatest, most reliable and consistent threat to athletes performing well. Fear can often help get the "engines roaring." Whatever the cause, expressions of fear are counterintuitively shown more by the winner, rather than the losers, of specific debates, with John McCain against Barack Obama in 2008 (debate 2), Ronald Reagan against Walter Mondale in 1984 (debate 1), and John F. Kennedy against Richard Nixon in 1960 (debate 1) being the clearest examples.

- *Pleasure*: This is when the smile lifts the cheeks substantially. In terms of happiness, pleasure is only half as effective as skepticism and satisfaction in aiding a candidate during a debate. Easily the two most notable instances of this emotion aiding the winning debate performer both involve the 2004 debates, with John Kerry benefitting

in the first debate and George W. Bush in their third debate.

What emotional displays, by contrast, harm candidates' chances of winning the debate? There are three detrimental emotions, discussed here in descending order of importance:

- *Joy*ful smiles—where there's a twinkle in a candidate's eyes—fall into this category. Maybe the dignity of the presidency is perceived at being at risk, making this strongest, most intense level of happiness a little too over the top in trying to "sell" hope on TV. Whatever the reason, displays of joy appear to be harmful to a candidate's performance on stage. The three clearest examples of this pattern consist of John Kerry against George W. Bush in 2004 (debate 3), Walter Mondale against Ronald Reagan in 1984 (debate 1), and Bill Clinton in comparison to George H. W. Bush in 1992 (debate 3).

- *Anger*: This is a very prevalent emotion—only skepticism comes close in terms of its frequency on a debate stage. Anger may help candidates to the degree they look determined to, for instance, enact progress on behalf of the country. But too much anger, too strongly felt, is all in all slightly harmful to a candidate's chances. The three instances where excessive anger was problematic based on it characterizing more strongly the losing debate performer consist of Jimmy Carter against Ronald Reagan in 1980 (debate 2), Richard Nixon against John F. Kennedy in 1960 (debate 1), and Barack Obama against John McCain in 2008 (debate 2). Right behind that last example was Gerald Ford against Jimmy Ford in 1976 (debate 1).

- *Sadness*: "Always sell hope" is the motto of business. Sadness is bad for sales. As early as Joe McGinnis's book *The Selling of the President*, about Roger Ailes helping Richard Nixon win in

1968, the idea of the candidate as a product has made good "packaging" an urgent matter. The three strongest examples to support this pattern consist of Richard Nixon against John F. Kennedy in 1960 (debate 1), Bill Clinton in comparison to Ross Perot in 1992 (debate 1), and Bob Dole against Bill Clinton in 1996 (debate 2). On the other hand, sadness used to express empathy can, arguably, be a virtue if selectively employed.

Finally, there are three emotions that don't seem to be a factor either way. In other words, they neither help nor hurt a candidate's chances; they're neutral in terms of their impact:

- *Contempt*: This is the other scorning emotion, along with disgust. Since contempt often shows in conjunction with a smile, contempt can signal confidence. More often, however, contempt can be taken as a sign of off-putting arrogance.

- *Disgust*: Best to be avoided is this version of a scorning emotion. Apparently, voters don't like the idea that something smells or tastes bad, metaphorically speaking. Think of disgust as the direct opposite of singing the praises of the American Dream.

- *Surprise* is another non-factor, maybe either because it happens so quickly that TV audiences don't notice or because the reaction that follows being surprised matters more.

Now, let's see how these emotional patterns come into play. With the original Kennedy versus Nixon trial run behind us, it's now time to move through the other, subsequent election cycles that have featured debates.

1976: JIMMY CARTER VS. GERALD FORD

Background

While Nixon's suit was ill-fitting, Gerald Ford's was ill-conceived. Actually, it wasn't the suit so much as it was the vest Ford wore under his suit, transforming the ensemble into a three-piece suit. A snug fit, the vest made the President resemble a dressed-up, small-town banker or Rotary Club leader. The way the ex-college football player gripped the podium during all three debates with Jimmy Carter was perhaps even worse. All told, the image that came to my mind while facially coding these debates was of Ford as a mighty grizzly bear turned costumed circus animal.

Ford had bigger problems than his wardrobe, however. He'd pardoned Nixon to put an end to the Watergate scandal and its aftermath. Every day on my walk to high school in 1976, I would pass a rusted old Ford pickup truck with its tailgate spray-painted with the message: "I sure wish Nixon would pay off this FORD."

In contrast, it was as if Carter hadn't even heard of Washington, D.C., let alone ever been there. At least he came off that way. The guy with the big, "aw, shucks," peanut-eating grin had slept on people's pull-out beds in Iowa while emerging seemingly out of nowhere to win the Democratic nomination. What viewers got treated to in these debates (if "treat" is really the operative verb) was enough earnest sincerity to make the then-popular TV show *The Waltons* look downright snarky by comparison.

Was anybody truly adept on stage in 1976? The answer would be, no. Exhibit A would be how the two candidates responded to having the sound system malfunction for an agonizing, bewildering 27 minutes during the first debate. How did the candidates adapt? Not at all. Ford and Carter remained stock still behind their respective podiums throughout the delay!

FORD CAGED BY HIS PODIUM

Some candidates practically hide behind their podiums. But Ford looked more like he was ready to grab his podium and give it the old heave-ho in order to free himself from all the stage-craft nonsense holding him back.

Emotion Displayed	Debate 1 Highlights (more than rival)	Debate 2 Highlights (more than rival)	Debate 3 Highlights (more than rival)
Skepticism			
Satisfaction	★ - Ford	★★★ - Ford	★★★ - Ford
Fear		★ - Carter	★ - Carter
Pleasure			
Joy	★★★ - Carter		
Anger	★★ - Ford	★ - Ford	★★ - Carter
Sadness	★★ - Carter	★ - Carter	★ - Carter

(Rows grouped: HELPS = Skepticism, Satisfaction, Fear, Pleasure; HURTS = Joy, Anger, Sadness)

1976 DEBATES: EMOTIONAL PROFILE

While Carter was feeling plenty joyful early on, a surging Ford came to feel to contempt for his challenger from Georgia. Both men were so earnest on stage that skepticism all but eluded them, giving neither candidate an advantage over the other in that regard.

Ford's Performances

The rap on Ford was that he wasn't very bright. In *Saturday Night Live* skits, Chevy Chase made it worse by transposing mental bumbling into a physical lack of grace. Was confusion and awkwardness the cause of Ford's surprisingly frequent displays of low-grade anger (especially in debate 1)? Whatever the explanation, his anger level was noticeable. On stage, Ford predated other, subsequent presidential debate performers like John Kerry and John McCain, who would also allow nearly *half* of their emoting during debates to involve anger. Indeed, a recap of Ford's monotonous emoting during the debates in 1976 would go something like this: annoyed, annoyed, annoyed, semi-happy, annoyed. Okay, I exaggerate— but not by much. Along with increasing his amount of smiling after the first debate, anger remains the other big trend for Ford in these debates.

Even more telling is that Ford was the only candidate who didn't show *any* surprise at all while on stage. A hallmark of surprise is that your eyes go wide. A surprised person is taking in information by looking around, observing what's happening and making the necessary adjustments.

The first debate had gone well for Ford, or at least well enough that the infrequent polling of that era suggested that Ford could overcome the advantage Carter held. Voters were seemingly starting to forgive him for the Nixon pardon, for instance. During the second debate, however, the candidate least given to surprises (namely, Ford) created one of the biggest debate surprises ever. Asked by *The New York Times* reporter Max Frankel about conditions in Eastern Europe, Ford adamantly said: "There is no Soviet domination of Eastern Europe and there never will be under a Ford administration."

In disbelief at what he was hearing, Frankel couldn't help but *giggle*—which Ford seemingly didn't notice—while asking the President a follow-up question meant to

give him the opportunity to retract or at least amend his answer. Ford didn't take the hint. Instead, the President maintained his position by giving the example of three Eastern European countries he'd recently visited (Yugoslavia, Romania, and Poland), insisting they were "independent" and "autonomous" countries. Yes, that was true of Yugoslavia. But hadn't Ford ever heard of the Iron Curtain?

Ford's big blunder would utterly overshadow another, smaller misstep during that same debate. In discussing the country's agricultural policies, Ford told America: "It's our responsibility that we get rid of the farmer."

The blunders weren't fatal per se. Ford nearly came back to win the election despite Carter's massive early lead in the national polls. But when I tested a group of eligible voters' emotional responses to some 25 or so different famous moments from various presidential debates—great one-liners, gaffes, and stark looks—nothing generated more of a reaction than Ford's plodding, dogmatic, and ill-advised answer, reinforced by his full-steam-ahead follow-up.

Carter's a Little Better

Carter was a worthy presidential debate opponent for Ford. That isn't a compliment. Like Ford, the Carter of 1976 was prone to anger (especially in the third debate), hardly experienced surprise, and smiled more broadly but less frequently than his Republican counterpart. Where Carter had a slight edge over Ford involves a little more sadness when appropriate. Now, I know that I just said that one of Richard Nixon's weaknesses was exhibiting sadness, and all in all sadness hurts candidates on stage during debates. But the difference in this case is that Nixon's displays of sadness merely augmented his bone-weary look during the first debate in 1960. They suggested a lack of vitality.

In comparison, some of Carter's most subtly adroit moments, emotionally speaking, involved expressions of sadness. One time, his eyes crinkled in pain at

FORD'S EASTERN EUROPEAN BLUNDER

The journalist was incredulous on hearing Ford's answer. Note the eyebrows arched in utter surprise, and the almost leering grin. At some level, the President must have known he'd just "stepped in it." Eyes narrowed in anger and pursed lips suggest resentment. As to Carter, he could hardly believe his good luck. This is what a true smile looks like: eyes crinkled with delight, accompanied by a huge grin.

the thought of the soldiers still missing in action in Viet Nam, their families unable to have any closure for the distress they continued to suffer. Another time, Carter winced, causing his cheeks to wrinkle as he discussed the comparatively high level of African-American unemployment.

On the other hand, Carter also winced during the third debate. The topic was now his foolish *Playboy* magazine interview confession about having experienced "lust in his heart." Surely knowing this was his version of Ford's Eastern Europe blunder, Carter winced, then his eyebrows knit together in consternation about how best to atone for his remark. A slightly derisive, ironic smile—aimed at himself and his folly for giving the interview—followed.

Fully one tenth of Carter's emoting on stage during the first debate had consisted of enthusiastic, maybe even over-

the-top joyful smiles. According to polling done afterwards, Carter had "lost" that debate, consistent with the formula's finding that displays of joy are problematic for a candidate. In the third debate, joy and even happiness in general was largely absent. Instead, Carter responded to the stress he felt with lots of anger and more than a little self-pity as Nixon-like forlornness enveloped a candidate at risk of losing an election that was once easily his.

CARTER TRYING TO HOLD ON

The tables had turned. With the media pouncing on his *Playboy* interview, Carter looked grim and literally downcast (eyes averted). For Ford, this expression was as much amusement as he could muster.

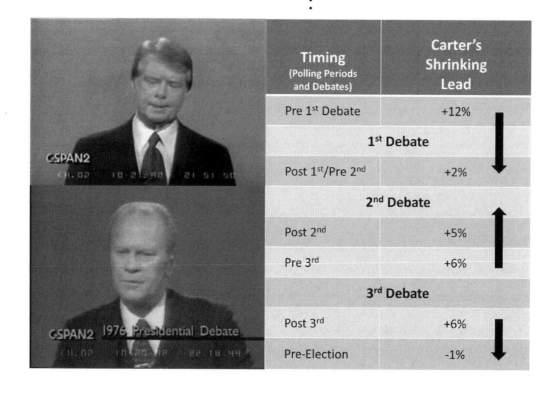

Timing (Polling Periods and Debates)	Carter's Shrinking Lead
Pre 1st Debate	+12%
1st Debate	
Post 1st/Pre 2nd	+2%
2nd Debate	
Post 2nd	+5%
Pre 3rd	+6%
3rd Debate	
Post 3rd	+6%
Pre-Election	-1%

1980: JOHN ANDERSON VS. RONALD REAGAN, JIMMY CARTER VS. RONALD REAGAN

Background (Why a 3rd Party Challenger?)

Lost in the fog of time, it might seem crazy to recall why John Anderson (a Republican member of the U.S. House of Representatives from Illinois) ran as an independent candidate for President in 1980. Basically, the answer is that Ronald Reagan was viewed as a right-wing warmonger by more than a few people, while Jimmy Carter had worn out his welcome. In time, Reagan would emerge as the icon of the modern Republican party. Meanwhile, Carter might nowadays win the most votes as laudatory ex-President, thanks to his efforts on behalf of Habitat for Humanity and other good causes. But during the 1980 campaign, none of that was evident.

1980 DEBATES: EMOTIONAL PROFILE

Why favor an emotion on stage that either doesn't help you or even hurts your chances, like Anderson did by emphasizing contempt and Carter by emphasizing anger? Meanwhile, Reagan managed a skillful blend of satisfaction and skepticism, holding his rivals at bay.

	Emotion Displayed	Anderson > Reagan (Debate 1)	Reagan > Anderson (Debate 1)	Carter > Reagan (Debate 2)	Reagan > Carter (Debate 2)
HELPS	Skepticism		★★		★★
	Satisfaction		★★★		★★★
	Fear	★★★			
	Pleasure				
HURTS	Joy			★	
	Anger		★	★★★	
	Sadness		★★		★

Anderson Bellows

You may think that having been a member of Congress for nearly two decades would have taught Anderson a thing or two about how to conduct himself during a debate. But you would be wrong. Of all the candidates covered here, not one was more bereft of happiness than Anderson. Besides a lack of smiling and generally failing to emote, what most characterized Anderson's single debate performance, against Reagan, was how the Republican-turned-Independent rushed through his answers, speaking at an unwaveringly high-decibel level.

Loud, fast-talking, and given to speaking like a monotone technocrat, Anderson emerged as a scold. Berating U.S. army expenditures as "boondoggles" was but one example of his tendency to deride most everything going on in America.

Fortunately for viewers' sake, Anderson participated only in the first debate: the one that put him face-to-face against Reagan, with Carter absent, due to his refusal to join a three-way debate. Then the tone-deaf scold was gone. How could Anderson have done so poorly after being known as a good orator in Congress? Odds are his performance was a classic case of stage fright. A key statistic in Anderson's case is that no candidate for the White House ever betrayed a greater amount of fear on stage relative to his other emoting than this guy. In other instances, fear proved okay for candidates to show, but not here. It would seem that getting this moment in the limelight was simply too big for Anderson to handle adeptly. He bellowed on and on, lacking all composure.

Carter Struggles

With Anderson kept off stage for the second debate, thanks to sinking poll numbers, Carter and Reagan went at it *mano a mano*. How was the Carter of 1980 different from the candidate who took the stage against Gerald Ford in 1976? The greatest single change was that Carter's level of irritation spiked in 1980, up by a third more than before. Anger had already been a mainstay for Carter, who in 1976 exhibited it at levels well above what is typical of U.S. presidential candidates during debates.

In 1980, though, anger dominated, accounting for nearly two-thirds of Carter's emoting tendencies. Who was the warmonger? With Reagan revealing less than half as much anger as Carter, the argument against Reagan's candidacy could be readily turned on its head for any viewer who went by the candidates' expressions alone.

Unhappy and looking worn-down—even outright grim—Carter fluctuated among expressions like knitting his eyebrows, pressing his lips together, or glaring with wide-eyed hostility during Reagan's responses. How to handle the Iranian hostage crisis invited the first of those three typical looks. The notion of repealing the minimum wage invited the second look. Reagan's assertion that racial tension wasn't a feature of American life during his childhood elicited the third type of anger. All in all, Carter wasn't ready for Reagan to re-imagine American history so blatantly. Confronting what he no doubt considered to be a liar, Carter couldn't help but stare Reagan down.

While mocked by pundits afterwards for saying his daughter, Amy, had told him the gravest threat facing the world was nuclear war, Carter's biggest mistake during the debate was actually failing to exhibit more happiness. In talking about America's "exciting future," for instance, Carter didn't manage to smile. Even skeptical smiles didn't put in an appearance. Carter had in essence gone from being fairly upbeat to resolutely grim in a four-year span and paid the price accordingly.

Reagan Smiles, Shrugs and Jabs

One of Reagan's most memorable debate moments didn't occur while facing Carter. It came during the "warm-up" debate against Anderson instead. For his closing remarks, Reagan heralded America as "a nation which is for all mankind a shining city on a hill." The Gipper delivered this no-doubt planned, set-piece with his characteristic combination of a smile, followed by a display of lips taut with determination. In that way, pride—a mixture of happiness on accomplishing a goal, joined by the anger that made it possible—gets signaled.

Reagan mostly left what his supporters would consider his "best stuff" for the debate with Carter. With Anderson, as one of the two Republicans on stage born in Illinois, Reagan was fully capable. While Anderson bellowed, Reagan spoke at times as softly as if he were huddled around a campfire with friends. But fairly genial jokes, like comparing government spending to a child whose allowance needs to be cut, became more biting and personal with Carter as Reagan's foil. Next to Anderson, Reagan smiled modestly and often. Beside Carter, Reagan upped his number of skeptical smiles delivered while making a sarcastic remark, of which the single most famous example became: "There you go again."

Reagan's debate with Carter featured a reference to "the misery index" (the unemployment rate added to the inflation rate). And there was of course the question: "Are you better off now than you were four years ago?" Carter countered by invoking the "voodoo economics" critique of Reagan's plans originated by Reagan's newly-minted running mate and former rival: George H. W. Bush. In response, Reagan offered a dismissive, shrugging smile and a chin pulled up in disgust, anger, and disappointed, condescending sadness, as if Carter were a boxer whose strongest jab hadn't landed. *You're pathetic* Reagan seemed to convey nonverbally, an unspoken message that stuck on election day.

THE BROTHERS GRIMM BATTLE THE GIPPER

With lips either zipped-up or pursed in anger, Anderson and Carter weren't exactly selling hope. Narrowed eyes and lowered eyebrows—with a crease between them—made Carter look like a far cry from the more easy-going guy who had won election in 1976. Eager to soften his cold-war warrior image long enough to triumph, Reagan knew to smile.

1984: WALTER MONDALE VS. RONALD REAGAN

Background

Even before he took on Ronald Reagan, Walter Mondale was in trouble in 1984. For a former Vice President to struggle to win his own party's nomination wasn't a promising start. Indeed, it wasn't until he stole the signature line from a then popular Wendy's TV commercial that Mondale found his footing. "Where's the beef?" Mondale asked on stage during a debate against his Democratic challenger Gary Hart in Atlanta, thus saving his primary campaign. But when it came time to face Reagan, no salvation emerged.

Mondale Semi Holds His Own, Until He Doesn't

Mondale had the strangest way of taking down a debate opponent: smiling radiantly. Joy is the highest level of happiness, an expression whereby a huge smile joins with eyes that twinkle with delight. No candidate who has gone through a series of U.S. presidential debates ever displayed more joy than Mondale did, and with less success as a result of it. Carter's former Vice President was the proverbial happy camper while quoting Will Rogers. Ditto while saying "I like President Reagan."And yet again, oddly enough, Mondale was filled with joy while vowing to raise most people's taxes to cover the yawning federal deficit Reagan's tax cuts had created.

During the first debate, Mondale also showed pleasure at times. Perhaps the most notable instance came when Reagan tried his old line, "There you go again," assuming he'd have the same luck with it that he'd had against Carter. Mondale was ready. "You remember the last time you said that?" he quizzed the President. "Mm-hmm," was all Reagan managed to say. Then Mondale reminded him and the TV audience that it came in response to Carter's warning that Reagan would try to cut Medicare if elected (something Reagan, in fact, did propose once he took office).

Overall, however, Mondale wasn't all that successful on stage—especially during the start of both debates. Each time, Mondale couldn't resist his mouth pulling wide with fear in anticipation of a tough evening. Most of Mondale's hand gestures were halting, and he often looked downright shy. A case in point is the first debate, a performance that cost Mondale 4% with voters based on polling done afterwards. For a while during that debate, nearly every one of the former Vice President's answers was followed by his looking down at the podium as if whatever notes he had taken could somehow, miraculously, enable victory.

Apparently, it didn't hurt Mondale's (non-existent) chances to reveal fear. His opponent was showing it, too, for one thing. But joy and fear put together in one candidate is a weird combination. And in truth, while Mondale looked like a spooked owl at times during the first debate, that was nothing compared to the second debate. He vacillated bizarrely, showing joy, sadness, and disgust.

Moreover, long hours on the campaign trail had reduced him to being the second coming of Richard Nixon on stage for his first debate with John Kennedy. The deep, dark circles beneath Mondale's eyes were everything Reagan could have wanted. Those circles served to undercut the public's concern that Reagan was the (only) candidate here too old for the job of being President. Those circles were also the perfect set-up for Reagan unleashing his zinger: "I am not going to exploit for political purposes my opponent's youth and inexperience." What was Mondale's response? He laughed, with joy, at a great line well-delivered, even though weeping would have made more sense. Any hope Mondale had of winning was now gone.

A JOYFUL LOSER, AN OFTEN BEFUDDLED PRESIDENT

Mondale made losing look like fun. In contrast, with the early stages of dementia possibly settling in, Reagan often looked lost. Unfocused eyes and the faint vertical wrinkles between the eyes all help to convey his unease.

Emotion Displayed	Mondale > Reagan (Debate 1)	Reagan > Mondale (Debate 1)	Mondale > Reagan (Debate 2)	Reagan > Mondale (Debate 2)
HELPS				
Skepticism	★★			
Satisfaction		★		
Fear		★★★		★★★
Pleasure	★★			★★
HURTS				
Joy	★★★		★★★	
Anger				★★
Sadness			★★	

1984 DEBATES: EMOTIONAL PROFILES

Relentless campaigning left Mondale dead tired and yet incongruously smiling like crazy on stage. Reagan stepped it up in the second debate, with pleasure off-setting the anger he showed while making sure he crossed the finish line.

Reagan Salvages Victory

Was Reagan, in turn, unflappable and always in command during his pair of debates with Mondale? Hardly. Reagan had been slightly more nervous during his "for-all-the-marbles" debate with Jimmy Carter in 1980 than he was on stage with John Anderson. Now, Reagan's anxiety soared. In facing Mondale, Reagan's fear level climbed to twice the amount shown against Carter in 1980 and eclipsed Mondale's own considerable anxiety.

For Reagan, the first debate was the worst, with fear exceeding one-third of all his on-stage emoting. The man was clearly uncomfortable. His mouth pulled wide, he gulped. From the budget gap to whether the "war on drugs" was really, truly working, Reagan looked disarmed and lost at sea. Was all that fear an early sign of Reagan's forthcoming battle with Alzheimer's? Or did it have more to do with a shaky knowledge of what was going on in his administration? Nobody can say for sure, though it occurs to me that in this case Reagan's notable fear might have made voters feel sorry for the guy in battling old age. If so, then in that way fear may have benefitted Reagan's re-election chances.

During the second debate, Reagan's susceptibility to fear diminished slightly. In place of some of his previous trepidation, Reagan increased the amount of anger on display but not too an overwhelming extent. The result was a candidate who seemed to have a little more spine, which wasn't hard to do.

Of all the debaters in this study, Mondale showed less anger on stage than all but two candidates ever: John F. Kennedy and Michael Dukakis.

Then came Reagan's long, meandering, closing remarks about the beauty of driving along the coastal highway in California. Where he was headed with his shiny-highway-by-the-sea remarks not even Reagan knew, most likely. The clock ran mercifully out, and Reagan was free to relish his triumphant zinger about not exploiting his opponent's relative youthfulness.

How good was the joke meant to relieve fears of Reagan having become a doddering old man? Very, very good. In my test of people's emotional responses to some 25 or so different famous moments from past presidential debates, Gerald Ford's blunder regarding Eastern Europe was the most engaging, hence the most memorable. But none of those moments had the positive, heart-warming appeal of the zinger that Reagan had promised his aides would help carry him to victory.

1988: GEORGE H. W. BUSH VS. MICHAEL DUKAKIS

Background

This was the year Gary Hart was supposed to win the Democratic nomination. Early in the election cycle, with Hart holding a commanding lead in national polls and his seven rivals far behind, the race was characterized as Hart and "the Seven Dwarfs." Then, after reporters heard rumors of Hart's womanizing, the Democratic hopeful told them, "Follow me around," and added that they would be "very bored." A short time later, Hart was photographed aboard a yacht named *Monkey Business* with a woman named Donna Rice, formerly the girlfriend of rock star Don Henley.

The scandal gave the diminutive Michael Dukakis his chance to shine, but Dukakis had problems of his own. His chief of staff, John Sasso, was the Massachusetts governor's fixer. While Dukakis could fancy himself running a squeaky-clean administration, the word in Boston was that you could always take the back staircase up to Sasso's office. When Sasso had to resign from Dukakis's campaign because of distributing a video revealing Joe Biden's plagiarism of a speech by a British politician, the loss was just as bad for Dukakis as Robert E. Lee losing Stonewall Jackson during the Civil War. Suddenly, Dukakis— nicknamed Zorba the Clerk for his reticent, technocratic style—began to flounder.

Of course, George H. W. Bush wasn't without problems, either. This was the patrician candidate who had been taken to school in a limousine at the height of the Great Depression. During the 1988 Democratic National Convention, Texas state treasurer and future governor Ann Richards had mocked him: "Poor George, he can't help it. He was born with a silver foot in his mouth." The Texas agriculture commissioner Jim Hightower piled on, calling Bush someone who was "born on third base" but thought he "had hit a triple." Which of these two men, Bush or Dukakis, could better handle the debates was anybody's guess.

	Emotion Displayed	Bush > Dukakis (Debate 1)	Dukakis > Bush (Debate 1)	Bush > Dukakis (Debate 2)	Dukakis > Bush (Debate 2)
HELPS	**Skepticism**		★★★	★★	
	Satisfaction		★		★★★
	Fear	★★		★	
	Pleasure	★			★★★
HURTS	**Joy**				
	Anger	★★			
	Sadness	★★★		★★	

Debate #1: A Pair of Deer

Did Bush like to debate? No way. Early in the first of these candidates' two debates, Bush asked if it was time to "unleash our one-liners." Next, he suggested that Dukakis's previous answer was about "as clear as Boston harbor." During both debates, the amount of fear Bush showed was more than even Dukakis's and twice as much as what candidates have shown on stage, on average, across the various election cycles. Bush's eyebrows rose in implying the artificiality of debates, in calling Dukakis a "card-carrying member of the ACLU," and in insisting his position on abortion hadn't changed but, rather, simply "evolved" over time. The good news for Bush is that since fear proves to link up with success in debating, this tendency of Bush's wasn't a hindrance for him in triumphing in post-debate polls.

Whatever campaign manager Lee Atwater thought could win the race, Bush was at least trying to do. But the truth of the matter was that Bush never liked to debate, and anger and sadness especially were a part of Bush's debate performance. Clearly, the Vice President regretted employing tactics that Atwater, years later on his deathbed, would apologize for in acknowledging the campaign's "naked cruelty." In general, Bush came across as more concerned than aggressive, hence eyebrows knitted in a sign of anger, sadness, and fear.

For his part, Dukakis got the better of the first debate. With skeptical smiles, the Democratic candidate undermined the Vice President's supposed

foreign policy expertise, while linking him to Ronald Reagan's policies at home. Still, there were indications of the trouble ahead. Was he some kind of buttoned-up yuppie? Asked if he cared about people, Dukakis insisted he did and was merely "a little calmer than some" in showing it. Any wife who has ever, by chance, complained that talking to her husband "is like talking to a brick wall" couldn't have been impressed.

Debate #2: Shaw's Shot

CNN anchor Bernard Shaw was an ex-Marine and, being a black man, might have gone after Bush (and Atwater) for their strategy of making voters wonder if Willie Horton was Dukakis's de facto running mate. Who was Horton? He was a convicted felon, an African-American serving a life sentence for murder. Horton became part of a weekend furlough program established before Dukakis became Massachusetts's governor. Granted a weekend furlough in 1986, Horton didn't return on schedule and was later recaptured and charged with assault, armed robbery, and rape.

Again, Shaw might have taken aim at Bush but instead challenged Dukakis, asking him whether he might support the death penalty should his wife, Kitty, be raped and murdered. Dukakis's legalese answer about being a lifelong opponent of the death penalty because there's "no evidence that it's a deterrent" immediately became the single most famous, cold-fish moment in U.S. presidential debate history. No discernible emotional response was forthcoming in reaction to Shaw's startling question.

A SCORNFUL DUKAKIS, A PONDEROUS BUSH

With a mouth that tended to curl into expressions of disgust, Zorba the Clerk (Dukakis) didn't come across pleasantly. Fortunately for Bush, his pensive nature, knitted eyebrows and all, went relatively unnoticed by comparison.

10/13/88

BERNARD SHAW
CNN Anchor

1988 Presidential Debate

C-SPAN

C-SPAN

THE QUESTION

Shaw's question about rape and the death penalty didn't stun Dukakis. Instead, it seemed to leave him totally unaffected, and that was the problem: Mr. Spock of *Star Trek* fame on TV is one thing; Mr. Spock in the White House is something else entirely.

Sixteen years earlier, in 1972, another New Englander, the Democratic candidate Ed Muskie, had looked teary-eyed after *The Manchester Guardian* wrote a story attacking his wife. But Muskie denied it, claiming the moisture was from snowflakes caught in his eyelashes. Why the evasion? The answer is that in the ethos of that era, looking strong was everything. Muskie may have lost the nomination due to that very moment in New Hampshire, and now for exactly the opposite emotional reason—no visible concern—Dukakis was doomed. Even self-righteous anger wasn't part of Dukakis's style, any more than was true of John F. Kennedy before him. Indignation in response to such a hypothetical event didn't happen, leaving Dukakis looking like a zombie and not a very good husband, either.

Instead, Dukakis smiled more during the second debate, as if to counter Bush's description of him as "the ice man" during the initial debate. By discarding skepticism, a weapon that by comparison Bush used a lot more of during the second debate, Dukakis unilaterally disarmed. Bush was home safe, though his repeating on stage that evening a pledge of "no new taxes" would come back to haunt him four years later.

1992: GEORGE H. W. BUSH VS. BILL CLINTON VS. ROSS PEROT

Background (Why a 3rd Party Candidate, Again?)

Any third-party candidacy is inherently a critique of the two-party system. But whereas John Anderson had initially run in the Republican primaries in 1980, before registering as an independent, in 1988 Ross Perot wasn't having anything to do with either party. A fervent Viet Nam war supporter, Perot wasn't a likely Democratic party supporter or a fan of "draft-dodger" Bill Clinton. As for the Republican party, Perot had likewise fallen out with it over issues ranging from the federal budget deficit to the Iran-Contra scandal. That George H. W. Bush had ultimately reneged on his promise not to raise taxes ("Read my lips") made the Texas businessman all the more inclined to enter the race.

Perot Feels Shut Out

It's an easy emotional trajectory to follow. During the first of the three debates in 1992, Perot was upbeat. He practically buried Bush and Clinton beneath an avalanche of joyful and skeptical smiles. Nobody was enjoying Perot's biting witticisms more than himself. His opponents were knaves. The difference between potato chips and computer chips was beyond them. Perot would host electronic town hall gatherings and be responsive to America's rightfully frustrated electorate. Why not? After all, he was the candidate who was "all ears"! So what if he

3RD DEBATE 1992: EMOTIONAL PROFILE

Perot and Clinton often battled for being the most joyous during these debates, but Perot was out of the gate first with that tendency. Given the recession going on, Clinton played the empathy ("I feel your pain") card—especially in the first debate when Bush was ill at ease and busy grousing about having to be on stage. In other words, based on the emotions that have historically proven helpful to candidates during debates, none of them was exactly "nailing it" (though Clinton came the closest). Perhaps that's why no candidate "won" more than a single debate, with Perot gaining an advantage the first time around, Clinton the second, and Bush as a result of the third and final debate.

	Emotion Displayed	Debate 1 Highlights (more than rivals)	Debate 2 Highlights (more than rivals)	Debate 3 Highlights (more than rivals)
HELPS	Skepticism	★ - Perot	★ - Bush	
	Satisfaction			★ - Bush
	Fear	★★ - Bush		
	Pleasure			
HURTS	Joy	★★★ - Perot	★★★ - Clinton	
	Anger	★ – Bush	★ - Clinton	
	Sadness	★★★ - Clinton		

PEROT AS FEISTY MUNCHKIN, BUSH CHECKS HIS RETIREMENT WATCH

Perot was a fun, mad-as-hell Munchkin who turned stale repeating himself. Bush didn't allow his audience to grow weary and tune out. He did that on his own, daring to glance impatiently at what proved to be his retirement watch.

didn't have experience in government? With Perot in The White House, lobbyists in Washington, D.C. would become so obsolete they would only be found in The Smithsonian.

On and on, Perot went. The second and third debates were more of the same from the Texas tycoon, and yet less enjoyable for him. Politics had caught up with Perot. His amusing as well as spot-on complaint at the start of the second debate that, with NAFTA, there would be this "great sucking sound" of American jobs headed for Mexico, was his last big hurrah on stage.

Some questions Perot didn't seem to understand. At other times, the candidate who was "all ears" interrupted the moderator to talk some more about himself. In the end, Perot only smiled while plugging his campaign infomercials. Otherwise, he could be caught glaring at his two opponents and even mild-mannered PBS moderator Jim Lehrer. It was as if Perot was trying his best to imitate either a crabby Munchkin from *The Wizard of Oz* or else Elmer Fudd, the hapless, frustrated cartoon character bent on killing Bugs Bunny.

Bush Has Had Enough

Compared to his debate performances in 1988, Bush was more relaxed. The sky-high levels of fear on display in the previous campaign subsided, after the first debate, to a more manageable level. In 1992, Bush's problem, emotionally, wasn't fear. (After all, as already, repeatedly noted by now, fear can actually be okay.) Instead, the problem for Bush was his almost complete lack of happiness. He simply didn't want to be out campaigning. It wouldn't be until about halfway through the second debate that Bush would notoriously look at his wristwatch to see how much longer he had to stay on stage, but the emotional signals were evident from the start.

In the first debate, Bush was cranky as hell. Every negative emotion emerged. Perot's and Clinton's criticisms elicited a curled upper lip response time and again, and challenges to the country's fiscal policies caused Bush to take a page from Gerald Ford's underwhelming debate playbook by balling one of his hands into a fist.

The second time on stage wasn't much better. Slipping into frequent expressions where his inner eyebrows lifted or knitted together, the President often came across as perplexed, tired, and forlorn. The second debate was the first ever, town-hall format (Clinton's idea) and yet Bush rarely moved toward the voters assembled along the edges of the stage. Worst of all, he actually glanced at his wristwatch not once but *twice* before the debate was over. During the third debate, yes, Bush finally remembered to smile, but was still only somewhat energetic. People were "only hearing how bad things are," Bush complained, as if he somehow expected his opponents would appreciate his efforts in The White House.

Clinton Triumphs

What's the perfect debate expression, especially for a challenger? I would suggest that it's serene, purposeful anger. Clinton was capable of broad grins of joy and pleasure. But he also matched those displays of upbeat, can-do optimism with looks of anger that equaled—but didn't exceed—the levels candidates normally show during a debate. Clinton's tell-tale hand gesture became a fist topped by a thumbs-up signal, frequently accompanied by a smile.

In those ways, I'd suggest, Clinton was often able to offset the liabilities of joy and anger by putting them together. The outcome was Clinton creating what I call The Golden Blend.

Clinton wasn't about to be Michael Dukakis. Challenged, he would let his resentment become evident through either pursed lips or a raised eyelid drawn straight and taut. Debate by debate, as he became more certain of beating Bush, Clinton became more assertive. Overshadowed by Perot in the first debate, Clinton came into his own during the second, town-hall style debate. There, he stalked Bush, looming over the President's shoulder, fully in camera view, while Bush fielded questions. Most of all, Clinton managed to combine optimism with both (slightly angry) assurance and tremendous empathy.

In the opening debate, Clinton had said, "I've seen heartbreak" and winced plenty of times to display sadness. In being the opposite of forlorn and solitary in nature, such usage of sadness works. Then in the second debate, Clinton proved to be utterly solicitous of the feelings of especially women in the audience. What was the net result? A network television camera panned to one young woman in attendance—who looked like she was about to swoon.

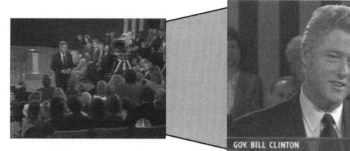

CLINTON'S TOWN HALL COMMAND PERFORMANCE

The format was Clinton's idea (and Bush was naive enough to accept it). When Clinton wasn't visually stalking the incumbent, he was in cahoots with enamored audience members.

If there is any mystery with this set of debates, it's why Clinton didn't also go on to "win" the third debate. Maybe it's because Bush's endeavors to tar Clinton for his record as Governor of Arkansas were treated as disgraceful attempts to dishonor Clinton's home state, causing Clinton to flare up with some disgust. Certainly, happiness in whatever form wasn't a distinguishing feature of Clinton's third debate performance. No matter the reason, although viewers judged Perot the winner, Bush, as a more realistic alternative to Clinton, benefitted the most from that evening's debate, leaving Clinton to hold onto a narrower lead in the polls than before.

1996: BILL CLINTON VS. BOB DOLE

Background

One of the peculiarities of politics in America is just how often a party gives its nomination to somebody who can't possibly win. During his 1956 presidential campaign, for instance, the Democratic nominee Adlai Stevenson heard a woman say, "You have the vote of every thinking person," to which Stevenson replied: "That's not enough, madam. We need a majority!" Indeed, that was the problem as Stevenson went down in defeat to Dwight Eisenhower.

Could Bob Dole fare any better in 1996? With the economy roaring and Dole having all the freshness of yester-year's news headlines, it was all but impossible to imagine a scenario in which the Republican nominee would take The White House from Bill Clinton. So, with all the high spirits of a man walking the plank, Dole mercifully enough for all involved joined with Clinton in limiting the debates in 1996 to merely two outings on stage.

Part of what would make these debates so soporific was that they were filmed more poorly than any debates since 1960's debates between John F. Kennedy and Richard Nixon. Most of the few zoom-in, close-ups that happened were of Clinton, and the cameras captured the candidates from a side angle as Clinton and Dole gave their opening remarks. Whose idea this was, I don't know, but I assume Dole was the more responsible party because being telegenic wasn't exactly among his foremost qualities.

OVER VAST DISTANCES, DOLE'S JOURNEY AS CAPTAIN AHAB

If the camera isn't your friend, why not keep it a million miles away from you? That was surely Dole's idea. Eventually, the camera snuck in closer and Dole's quest to harpoon the Great White Whale—known in this case as the White House— was shipwrecked on dour, grim expressions nobody found welcoming.

Highlights Such as They Were

Their first time together on stage, Clinton was far happier than Dole, who could only manage dour remarks. For example, when Dole jabbed at Clinton, calling him "a great talker" and saying "Yes, *you're* better off" now (as opposed to the country at large), Clinton didn't feel compelled to do more than laugh off those attacks. Why bother when most everything, including the age discrepancy between the two candidates, weighed heavily in his favor? During the campaign, Dole fell off a stage in California and on another occasion made reference to a recent no-hitter thrown by a pitcher for the "Brooklyn" Dodgers, despite the team having moved to Los Angeles 38 years ago.

In the first debate, therefore, Clinton needed to go no further than to suggest that some of Dole's ideas reminded him of those golden-oldie hit records sold on TV. In contrast, Dole was uneasy and grim before turning sadder and much angrier during the second, final debate. While the looks of fear may not have been debilitating, the anger and sadness displays were—especially when combined, as they so often were. Ronald Reagan had poked fun at Democrats by calling them the party of "doom and gloom." But here was Dole, doing his best imitation of Captain Ahab: the gloomy, obses-sive skipper in Herman Melville's *Moby Dick* who would rather go to his death trying to harpoon a great white whale than relinquish his goal.

You're "tearing me apart" were Dole's most searing, personal words directed at Clinton in the first debate. Rivaling that comment for peculiarity was the Republican nominee mistakenly asserting "all you've got going for you is fear" near the debate's conclusion. Clearly, emotional equilibrium was in short supply for Dole that night.

The second debate resembled the later rounds of a boxing match in which both fighters are tired (of it) and engage in lots of clinches that the referee tries to break up. Even a still fairly ebullient Clinton had had enough, with his happiness eroding some as disgust occasionally crept into Clinton's emoting. For his part, Dole's most memorable moment came when he demanded to know: "Where's the outrage?" in response to Clinton's conduct in office. Dole might as well have been saying, "Where are the votes I need?" None of it made any difference. Casting a glowering and foreboding presence on stage, Dole came across as downright Nixonian, even a little pathetic, as he invoked the sufferings his family had endured in rural, small-town America.

Emotion Displayed		Clinton > Dole (Debate 1)	Dole > Clinton (Debate 1)	Clinton > Dole (Debate 2)	Dole > Clinton (Debate 2)
HELPS	Skepticism		★	★	
	Satisfaction	★★★		★★★	
	Fear		★★★		★★★
	Pleasure	★★★		★★★	
HURTS	Joy				
	Anger				★★★
	Sadness		★★		★★★

1996 DEBATES: EMOTIONAL PROFILE

Clinton specialized in pleasure and satisfaction, Dole in doling out forlorn grievances. Guess who won? Not even his growing distaste for Dole's petulant witticisms did much to dampen Clinton's enthusiasm for getting re-elected.

2000: GEORGE W. BUSH VS. AL GORE

Background

Welcome to the Supreme Court deciding an election! That was but one anomaly in a strange race that, for debate purposes, kicked off with James Fallows declaring in *The Atlantic* that "Al Gore is the most lethal debater in politics."[8] Along with John F. Kennedy being supposedly unflappable during his first debate with Richard Nixon, little else said by a pundit related to a debate has ever been so inaccurate.

When the series of three debates held between George W. Bush and Gore were over, such was his misery that Vice President Gore likely found himself wishing he'd never entered politics at all. Whatever approach he tried, he couldn't slay an opponent who had utterly failed to distinguish himself at Harvard Business School and whose heavy drinking earlier in life inspired the tale, whether true or not, that his wife Laura Bush finally had to tell him it was "Jim Beam or me."

Timing (Polling Periods and Debates)	Gore	Bush	Who Ahead (Gore's lost ground)
Pre-Debate 1	49%	41%	Gore + 8%
1st Debate			
Post-Debate 1	51%	40%	Gore +11%
Pre-Debate 2	45%	45%	Tie
2nd Debate			
Post-Debate 2	45%	45%	Tie
Pre-Debate 3	44%	47%	Bush +3%
3rd Debate			
Post-Debate 3	40%	51%	Bush +11%

THE AIR GOES OUT OF GORE'S BALLOON

After the first debate, Gore actually experienced a slight surge in the polls—which didn't last long, once the critiques of his initial debate performance started to pour in. As for the second debate, it might look like Gore held his own but actually, again, shortly thereafter his polling numbers began to slump, never to recover. The third debate outcome was more a matter of Gore "burying his dead" than anything else, as only once before Election Day did Gore ever even pull close to Bush in the polls.

Emotion Displayed	Debate 1 Highlights (more than rival)	Debate 2 Highlights (more than rival)	Debate 3 Highlights (more than rival)
Skepticism	★ - Gore	★ -Bush	★★★ - Bush
Satisfaction	★★ - Bush		★★★ - Gore
Fear	★★ – Gore	★★★ - Bush	
Pleasure		★ - Bush	★ - Bush
Joy			
Anger		★ – Gore	
Sadness	★ - Bush	★★ – Gore	★ - Gore

(HELPS: Skepticism, Satisfaction, Fear, Pleasure. HURTS: Joy, Anger, Sadness)

2000 DEBATES: EMOTIONAL PROFILES

Gore tried to turn on the charm in the third debate, showing plenty of satisfaction, but by then it was too late to save himself. The amount of harmful sadness he revealed during the second debate already signaled his fate. Bush was more affable in the first debate, before turning to a heavy dose of skepticism to puncture Gore's attempts at happiness and generally ward off his challenger.

Fiasco #1

Basically, Gore laid it on thick during the first debate. There was mock fear shown in offering his infamous "lock box" analogy about protecting Social Security from getting raided by other politicians to pay for their pet projects. There were some skeptical smiles offered up to condemn Bush's proposed tax cuts and his siding with Big Oil against environmentalists. Most telling of all, however, there was Gore's putrid combination of sighs, snorts, chuckles, and contemptuous smirks. In that way, Gore came across as the heavy in this debate, literally looking like a stuffed shirt, while also talking loudly and forcefully interrupting his opponent at times.

Did Bush win the first debate, or did Gore lose it? For most of this exchange, Bush failed to distinguish himself. Yes, he looked uneasy discussing fiscal matters, including when his mouth pulled wide with fear at the prospect of handling a future crisis. But mostly, Bush came across as affable and slightly goofy, thanks to moments like a dumb laugh mid-way through the debate. Only a strong, late surge, chastising Bill Clinton for his involvement with Monica Lewinsky while showing flashes of disgust, was at all commanding. Otherwise, the debate came down to Gore just hanging himself.

Fiasco #2

No doubt feeling shamed on learning the response to his first debate performance, Gore put away the lock box analogy, the snorting, the sighing, and most of his dismissive remarks. Half an hour into the second debate, Bush recognized how much more subdued Gore was and joked about the event being a "love fest." While feeling chastened and therefore kind of a sad sack for the evening, Gore became even more derisive and scornful of Bush than before. The Democratic challenger's displays of contempt were no less common than in the first debate. At one point, Gore gave Bush such a "You've got to be kidding" look that I could have sworn he despised the guy through and through. From global warming to racial profiling by the police, the evening became what Gore was against more than what he was for.

Meanwhile, Bush couldn't quell his nerves. In no other debate in 2000 or 2004 was Bush more nervous than during this second debate. From foreign affairs to how to talk about gun rights and other social issues in ways that would attract independent voters, Bush didn't look comfortable. His one saving grace was to make fun of himself, noting his reputation for being able to "manage a syllable or two."

GORE'S SIGHS ARE THE STORY

Sometimes Gore was busy sighing, at other times he evinced great scorn for his opponent. His problem: the voters emotionally aligned with the person being scorned.

Fiasco #3

Having tried sighs, then faux humility, with the third debate Gore attempted charm. This time he smiled more, talked more gently and sought to show more empathy in keeping with the town hall format in which scores of voters ringed the stage, waiting to feel like they had been heard. Despite his best attempts, though, Gore never could escape the shadow of coming across as a stiff bureaucrat.

When Gore sought to identify with voters' sorrow and angst, the effect was more like Clinton Lite replacing Gore Heavy. More characteristically, the Vice President was prone to saying "under my plan" as if those were compelling words. Far worse was the moment early on when Gore seemed to be stalking Bush on stage in a pale imitation of Clinton doing likewise during the second town hall debate of 1992. That time worked, as if Clinton was casting a shadow over the older Bush. This time, the younger Bush looked startled at first, only to quickly become amused by Gore's attempt to intimidate him.

In contrast, this was Bush's best debate in 2000. He got the audience on his side by offering his reading glasses to a woman struggling to ask her question. In between bouts of nervous, even awkward laughter, a chummy Bush casually (almost flippantly) greeted one voter by saying "Hi", thanked another voter for the question being raised, and almost played host by being ready to hand over his microphone to yet another voter if that would make things easier.

Nothing about Bush's performance the third time around was superb, but his comfort level had improved markedly. Broader smiles were evident, and he resorted to diffusing Gore's criticisms with more skeptical smiles—peppered with dismissive disgust—than during the previous two debates. Imagine the two men going to battle based on that old likeability question, "Whom would you rather have a beer with?" On those terms, Bush was going to beat Gore hands down as the far more approachable candidate.

BUSH UNFAZED BY GORE STALKING HIM

All Bush had to do, in emotional terms, was let his opponent fall on his own sword. So Bush stepped back and grinned, leaving viewers to wonder why his space was being invaded by the Vice President.

2004: GEORGE W. BUSH VS. JOHN KERRY

Background

A little luck never hurts in trying to win The White House (or retain it). The favor the Republicans gave Bill Clinton in 1996 by running the bitter, prickly Bob Dole—with his barbed-wire sense of humor—was repaid in full in 2004 when the Democrats ran another stiff candidate from Massachusetts. (How is it that Michael Dukakis hadn't been enough of a warning?)

George W. Bush was on the ballot again as only the fourth President ever, to date, to have "won" the election without taking the majority of the popular vote. All of the others, from John Quincy Adams to Rutherford Hayes and Benjamin Harrison, had served only a single term in office. Might Bush succumb to that pattern? Given how poorly both the economy and the Iraq War had fared under his command, there was reason to wonder. Being a war-time President post 9/11 was going to have to count for a lot.

The Disaster

Being sequestered for nearly four years in The White House can exact a toll directly relevant to a debate: you haven't heard anybody refuse to accept your judgment of the issues, right to your face, in an awfully long time. You're rusty, out of practice. Speaking at carefully choreographed campaign rallies full of handpicked attendees is no substitute for a spirited, prolonged debate. The version of Bush that took the stage for the first time in 2004 was in trouble right from the start, regardless of whatever he said. There was some sadness evident, as in *I really don't want to be here.* That sank him for sure. But

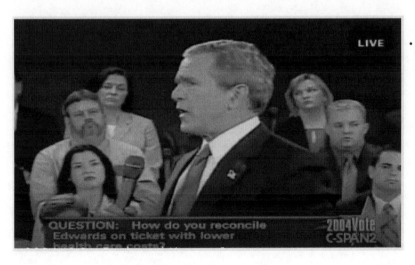

QUESTION: How do you reconcile Edwards on ticket with lower health care costs?

BUSH AS IMPERIAL COWBOY

Isolated in the White House and accustomed to staff genuflecting, Bush was petulant and peeved on stage. Karl Rove tried to spin it otherwise, but everybody could see Bush's negativity about having to go through election rigmarole again. Wouldn't a coronation just be so much nicer?

in addition, there was also contempt. Before the first debate was over, Bush would have displayed five times more disdain than was normal of candidates in presidential debates.

Bush betrayed contempt when John Kerry said the Iraq War had been a "colossal mistake." Being compared unfavorably to his father, who had the "wisdom" not to go all the way to Baghdad, caused Bush to smirk again. Yet another smirk erupted as Bush delivered the news to voters that being President entails "hard work."

For his part, Kerry was mostly upbeat (though he showed fear when Bush raised the issue of his flip-flop U.S. Senate votes regarding support for the Iraq War). And that was enough. Kerry had plenty of material to work with: if it wasn't Iraq, how about Bush having looked into Vladimir Putin's eyes and seen a man he could trust?

Afterwards, the Democrats pounced. The next day, the party posted a "Faces of Frustration" video to highlight Bush's miserable performance on stage. Bush's so-called

"brains" (advisor Karl Rove) did all he could to refute the charge, saying he'd seen the President plenty mad before and that the guy on stage wasn't angry. But the spin didn't take hold. Bush had gotten angry enough on stage that a tell-tale bulge had formed below the middle of his lower lip at times. Nevertheless, the bigger story was Bush's contempt. As a sign of arrogantly disrespecting others, it's hardly a charming emotion. Much of the footage the Democrats used in their video showed contempt more often than anger.

Thus the Democrats missed an opportunity to paint Bush throwing a truly imperial temper tantrum on national TV. Images of contempt mingled with anger are even less charming and could have made for a devastating attack ad. As it was, Democratic operatives seized on an emotion (anger) that Kerry showed almost as often as Bush did during the first debate, and that he would show more frequently than Bush during the next two debates.

Emotion Displayed	Debate 1 Highlights (more than rival)	Debate 2 Highlights (more than rival)	Debate 3 Highlights (more than rival)
Skepticism	★ - Kerry	★★ – Bush	★★★ - Bush
Satisfaction	★ - Kerry		
Fear		★★★ - Bush	
Pleasure	★★★ - Kerry	★ - Bush	★★★ - Bush
Joy			★★★ - Kerry
Anger		★★★ - Kerry	★ - Kerry
Sadness	★ - Bush	★★★ - Bush	★★ - Bush

2004 DEBATES: EMOTIONAL PROFILES

Kerry strode the stage smiling in the first debate, while Bush scorned his opponent. From there, Bush improved by showing more pleasure, in addition to also wielding more skepticism in the later debates. Fortunately for him, Kerry was busy delving into anger and joy and basically lost his way.

A Reprieve

Did Kerry back off in the two subsequent debates? Not entirely. In fact, in the second debate he made the opposite mistake: he pressed his case too hard. Not since Gerald Ford's first debate against Jimmy Carter in 1976 had voters seen a more consistently angry candidate on the debate stage. Indeed, if anything, Kerry's anger was even more persistent than Ford's. So an historic spike in contempt by Bush in the first debate was then followed by an equally disturbing burst of anger being shown by Kerry.

In that way, Bush's emotional mistake gave way now to the Democratic challenger manhandling the second debate. Lips firmly pressed together amid condemning the President for the "rush to war" was but one example of the nonverbal signals coming from Kerry. On another occasion, the decorated war hero-turned-war critic lifted a fist in the air. As the evening wore on, Kerry failed to tell any stories or jokes. Almost every answer ended with some sign of anger. Was the guy a *militant* pacifist? What exactly should people watching at home make of the Democrats' nominee?

Perhaps realizing the error of being overly harsh, in the third debate Kerry returned to smiling more. All in all, the guy really was a flip-flopper, emotionally speaking. Over the course of the three debates, Kerry went from happy to angry, back to happiness (in fact, joy). And Kerry compounded his problems by grinning wildly about how he'd "married up." Why, the guy looked downright smug about having a wife who's an heiress-by-marriage to the Heinz company fortune. How the average voter, and especially the Democrats' traditional blue-collar base, was supposed to identify with Kerry was a real mystery.

The optics were already in Bush's favor. Kerry stood ramrod straight, had a massive brow (maybe bigger than Michael Dukakis's), plus hooded eyes, and studied hand

QUESTION: Why did you block imported drugs from Canada?

KERRY LOSES THE LIKEABILITY GAME

In the first debate, Kerry came off well thanks to Bush's imitation of a spoiled brat. Smiles helped. But then too often, Kerry settled into coming across as an angry know-it-all, telling Bush he was a dumb-ass (smart enough to win the election).

gestures. Whether acting on advice from Rove or being informed by his own instincts, a consternated Bush relaxed more and more over time. An increase in the amount of the Bush family's usual crooked smiles was matched by a corresponding decrease in the amount of contemptuous smirks on display.

During the second debate, Bush joked, saying that one answer from Kerry "almost made me want to scowl." By the third debate, Bush was downright goofy at times. For example, one smile came on learning he had an investment he didn't know about: "I own a timber company? You need some wood?" That kind of flippancy was hardly a sign of presidential sagacity. On the other hand, if the only alternate to appearing smug was to go this route, maybe the bet was that voters wouldn't object to seeing Bush as the second coming of Alfred E. Neuman from *Mad* magazine.

2008: JOHN MCCAIN VS. BARACK OBAMA

Background

By now, the hypothetical question about a fiscal disaster that had worried '43 Bush during a debate in 2000 had come to pass. Bush hadn't had a good answer then, and John McCain didn't seem to have a good answer when it mattered. At a White House meeting where both candidates were invited to participate in a discussion about what to do, the press reported that the Republican nominee had remained almost eerily silent amid a series of probing inquiries from Barack Obama.

Around that time, McCain even momentarily suspended his campaign in response to the unfolding calamity that became known as the Great Recession. With the economy front and center on everybody's mind, a series of one-sided debates would be beyond strange! What would and could McCain say when the topic of the hour was fiscal policy instead of military strength?

Emotion Displayed	Debate 1 Highlights (more than rival)	Debate 2 Highlights (more than rival)	Debate 3 Highlights (more than rival)
Skepticism	★ - Obama	★★★ - Obama	★★ - Obama
Satisfaction (HELPS)	★ - McCain		
Fear	★★★ - McCain	★★★ – McCain	★★★ - McCain
Pleasure			
Joy (HURTS)	★★★ - Obama	★ - Obama	★★★ - McCain
Anger		★★ - Obama	★ - McCain
Sadness		★★★ – Obama	★ - Obama

2008 DEBATES: EMOTIONAL PROFILE

It's almost as if there's a template here: first Dole, then another wounded veteran faces a smoother, more verbally and emotionally fluent Democratic candidate. Things ultimately didn't work out any better for McCain against Obama then they had for Dole against Clinton. Invoking "Joe the Plumber" in the third debate brought joy to McCain's face, but otherwise fear was his dominant response to the experience of being on stage and up against Obama's mostly cool, confident contempt.

A Man Always Ready for Another Fight

The summer before the 2008 primary season kicked into gear, I had traveled to neighboring Iowa to watch all the candidates from either party up close over a pair of weekends. I happened to catch McCain just days after the I-35W bridge spanning the Mississippi River had collapsed in my home state of Minnesota. Such inattention to our nation's infrastructure "makes me mad" McCain told everyone assembled in a church basement. I was sitting just feet from the guy and wanted to laugh: not because of the disaster (I had driven under a span of the bridge only a minute or two before it collapsed), but because McCain was *always* mad. If it wasn't one pet peeve, it would be another.

Over the course of these three debates, McCain would be surpassed only by John Kerry in terms of the frequency with which he showed anger. The only reason why not more than a trace of McCain's anger shows up in the 2008 Debates: Emotional Profile chart is that both men were often pretty angry. No series of U.S. presidential debates ever held, in fact, was as cantankerous. Therefore, McCain's level of anger rising significantly about Obama's was going to be a heavy lift. That said, sometimes McCain managed that feat during these debates. For instance, McCain's anger arose as he discussed

the need for spending cuts (at a time of recession) on behalf of exercising greater fiscal responsibility. The subjects of Iran and negative campaigning got plenty of grief, too.

To my surprise, after analyzing these debates, it proved to be fear and surprise—not anger—where McCain was most clearly different from Obama. Part of the reason is, again, that Obama showed a lot of more subdued anger, too, in conveying a sense of purpose. In fact, Obama *out-angered* McCain during the second debate (when he also showed more sadness, and lost the debate). But it's likewise true that Obama demonstrated remarkably little discomfort during every debate.

MCCAIN ON EDGE, AND BENEATH THE SMILES NEITHER MAN WAS HAPPY FOR LONG

McCain was all-revved up, even jacked up, with fear as he sought to declare the danger electing Obama would pose. Yes, eyes-wide-with-fear was part of McCain's non-verbal message, as well as quite possibly also a sign of his unease on stage. While Obama often smiled graciously in response to McCain's jabs, make no mistake about it: in emotional terms, the debates of 2008 were harshly fought back and forth, with Obama winning the first debate, McCain the second, and the third tipping Obama's way as he went from joy to skepticism the longer these debates wore on.

QUESTION: What is the threat from Iran to the U.S.?

During the 1996 debates, Bob Dole had often seemed lost in a time warp as he kept referencing World War Two and even the Great Depression. In 2008, McCain likewise came across as out-of-touch and ill at ease. For one thing, he couldn't get enough of heralding Ronald Reagan's administration of two decades ago. For another, only latching onto Joe the Plumber, the archetypal citizen opposed to soak-the-rich class warfare, made McCain happy (indeed, joyously happy in the third debate). Otherwise, McCain was a man obsessed with worrisome military threats abroad.

Regarding McCain's performances, a few details stand out. One was his complete lack of eye contact with Obama during the first debate, as if to suggest his opponent was so "naïve" as to not even be worthy of a glance. Whether accusing Obama of being too soft on Moscow or suggesting that to elect the first-term Senator as President was "dangerous", McCain was on the attack. Some tart jokes aside, the bulge that anger can create below pressed lips made McCain seem, at times, like a snake coiling to strike its victim.

By the third debate, all the poll numbers were against McCain. The race was slipping away. In response, McCain glared and rolled his eyes repeatedly while Obama was talking, looking even more agitated than before. With the country in two wars and heading deeper toward the edge of possibly a complete financial meltdown, McCain's best defense was to remind voters he wasn't George W. Bush. A mouth that pulled wide in fear more than once when the economy was mentioned did nothing to make McCain seem like the candidate most likely to steer the ship-of-state with a steady hand.

Calm, Cool and Contemptuous

The emotional formula for being a successful presidential debater has nothing to do with either contempt or disgust, the two scorning emotions. Again, they neither help nor hurt a candidate's chances. That said, in 2008 those two emotions had *everything* to do with Obama's reaction to being on stage against McCain. Contempt ran high for Obama across all three debates, joined in the third and final debate by a heavy dose of disgust.

Certain Supreme Court rulings, along with some of McCain's taunts, were among the triggers of Obama's disdain. For Obama, "Joe the Plumber" as a rationale for assuming the presidency didn't make the grade, either. "When I'm President," Obama calmly, matter-of-factly declared more than once, as if the election results were already a done deal.

An air of calm, cool superiority bordering on arrogance might seem like the wrong move, emotionally speaking, for a candidate to take. Then again, maybe 2008 was an election year like no other year since Franklin D. Roosevelt took office amid the Great Depression. What are the odds rattled voters saw in Obama's emotional demeanor somebody up to handling a crisis? No doubt Obama had plenty of ammunition to work with. McCain had called the U.S. economy fundamentally "strong" and had promised that the American soldiers in Iraq would be greeted as liberators. "You were wrong," Obama told McCain more than once during these debates, looking poised. Two fingers lightly pressed together became Obama's go-to hand gesture, as if it embodied his promise to bring America back together again, and onto its collective feet.

2012: BARACK OBAMA VS. MITT ROMNEY

Background

Just before the Iowa caucuses in 2008, I told my media agent in New York City that I was convinced Mike Huckabee would beat supposed front-runner Mitt Romney in that state. Why? Well, my gut-instinct was Romney couldn't take Iowa because he looked like the banker who turned down your farm loan. As this election cycle began to play out, Romney reinforced his privileged, stilted persona. There was a story in circulation, for instance, about how, during a 1983 family vacation, Romney drove twelve hours with his dog on top of the car in a windshield-equipped carrier. *Who owns a windshield-equipped carrier?* The candidate claimed that the dog, Seamus, loved the crate. During the Republican primaries, Newt Gingrich aired an anti-Romney attack ad featuring the story. To top it off, protesters were waving "Dogs Against Romney" signs outside the Westminster Dog Show.

Then, less than three weeks before the first debate, video was released of Romney telling millionaire donors at a May fundraiser that essentially half of all Americans were free-loaders: "There are forty-seven percent of the people who will vote for the President no matter what," Romney said, referring to Barack Obama. These people's sin? In Romney's words, it was their being "dependent upon government" while paying "no income tax."

What a gift to Obama, who was still living down having told donors at a San Francisco gathering in 2008 that small-town voters can "get bitter, they cling to guns or religion or antipathy toward people who aren't like them . . . to explain their frustrations." Truth be told, Obama could be as imperious as Romney, despite being able to honestly say what Romney claimed at the videotaped fundraiser: "I have inherited nothing." Which guy would prevail on stage was now the question of the hour.

2012 DEBATES: EMOTIONAL PROFILE

The first debate was almost all Romney, with Obama mostly caught feeling ineffective disgust. It wouldn't be until the third debate that Obama really found his mojo. Dreading a debate focused on his weakest subject matter (foreign affairs), Romney hit the stage literally sick to his stomach.

Emotion Displayed		Debate 1 Highlights (more than rival)	Debate 2 Highlights (more than rival)	Debate 3 Highlights (more than rival)
Skepticism	HELPS			
Satisfaction		★★★ – Romney		★★★ - Obama
Fear		★ – Romney		★ - Romney
Pleasure		★ – Romney	★ - Romney	
Joy	HURTS		★ - Obama	
Anger				
Sadness			★ - Obama	

When Romney and Obama Were at Their Best

For Romney, what worked best was certainly the opening debate. When the topic became his desire to cut government spending to hold down the federal deficit, the Republican nominee swung into action. "I like PBS, I love Big Bird. I actually like you, too," Romney added, referring to the debate's moderator, PBS *News Hour* anchor Jim Lehrer. Although the evening's most memorable line emerged somewhat awkwardly, at least Romney avoided coming across like another Muppet character from *Sesame Street*: Oscar the Grouch. The "Big Bird" reference was offered with a skeptical smile, and overall Romney exhibited lots of cheerful satisfaction.

OBAMA OUT OF SORTS, ROMNEY PROFESSES LOVE FOR BIG BIRD

Romney told us he hated funding PBS but loved *Sesame Street's* Big Bird, and smiled. He told us he was all wet behind the ears with awe for the Constitution, and smiled again. Now it was Obama's turn to come across as peevishly as Bush '43 had during his first debate four years earlier.

Romney was twice as happy during the opening debate as he would be in either of his two other debates with Obama. Avoiding smirks helped Romney as well, as often his smiles ran the risk of making him look smug. Romney's rhapsodizing with eyes-wide-open about being "in awe" of the Declaration of Independence was potentially a little too precious, but the candidate was enough of a dork to make his pollyannish quality believable.

In Obama's case, it took until the third debate for him to warm up. How he must have relished an evening of discussing foreign policy, knowing Romney wouldn't be on familiar turf. Finally, Obama was full of smiles. The amount of happiness evident on Obama's face tripled in volume compared to the first debate, making more tolerable moments of withering scorn thinly disguised as irony.

No moment was more prominent than when Obama seized on Romney's complaints about the reduced size of the military, specifically fewer U.S. Navy ships than at any time since 1917. That remark led to Obama's retort: "Well,

Governor, we also have fewer horses and bayonets." In schooling Romney on the news that a smaller navy was possible due to "these things called aircraft carriers," Obama indulged in more than a few skeptical smiles. All in all, during the third debate I got the impression that Obama was having the time of his life imposing revenge for all of the Republican obstructionism he'd faced since taking office.

Obama and Romney at Their Worst

During the first and second debates, Obama smiled even less than he did during the debates held in 2008 amid the onset of the Great Recession. Large doses of disgust were mostly the culprit, as if he'd grown prematurely weary of Romney's lines of attack. Several times over, Obama's chin pressed upwards, forming an upside-down smile that conveyed resentful exasperation. George W. Bush had given off an impression of imperial isolation in the first debate in 2004, as if nobody had dared cross him since assuming the presidency (except perhaps Dick Cheney). Now, Obama was following suit. At one point he even balled one of his hands into a fist.

The Obama of the third debate was softer and gentler only to the extent that he smiled more. Almost gleefully vengeful, he piled on a hapless Romney with finger pointing and cold stares, his eyes narrowed in anger. The palm of Obama's hand, being held upside down at one point with fingers extended, resembled a claw. Obama cut in on Romney's answers repeatedly, which was just as well because the Romney of the third debate was often either cringing in fear or showing contempt in reaction to being kicked while he was so obviously down-and-out.

OBAMA POURS IT ON

The third debate was a slaughterfest. Romney showed up sick (at the prospect of showing how little he knew about foreign policy). Obama struck again and again as Romney washed out to sea.

2016: HILLARY CLINTON VS. DONALD TRUMP

Background

What can you say? Normally, the presidential debates are among the high-lights of the general election campaign, the moment when the media frenzy hits a series of peaks. But in 2016, Donald Trump's tweets and campaign rally stump remarks were repeatedly jarring. The no-holds-barred style that had begun with the Republican candidate coming down the elevator in Trump Tower to declare that so many of the Hispanic immigrants crossing our southern border illegally were "rapists" got toned down only slightly during the debates. Case in point: Trump invited three women who had accused Bill Clinton of sexually inappropriate behavior to the second debate, hoping to seat them alongside the former President.

Round One

While Hillary Clinton was emotionally twice as negative during this debate as during the other two, she was only half as negative as Trump. There were smiles, notably a big, joyous smile when the moderator, NBC news anchor, Lester Holt reminded Trump that he had at first supported the Iraq War before speaking out against it. The same was true when Trump insisted that "I have a much better temperament than her." Another memorable moment was when Clinton let her shoulder blades bob-and-weave in coquettish fashion during another of Trump's attacks, as if light on her (emotional) feet in confronting an ogre.

Since Trump avoids joy and happiness, in general, like the plague, none of these moments met with an equivalent emotional response from the Repub-lican candidate. So Clinton ended up dominating in terms of exhibiting joy. The bad news for her was that the emotional formula for debates suggests that joy actually harms a candidate's effectiveness. In this case, while two-thirds of surveyed voters said they thought Clinton had won the debate, the poll numbers changed little.[9]

What might have also helped Trump see his way through what was largely a mediocre, if not terrible debate performance was his reliance on skepticism. That is where he held an advantage over Clinton, even if she wasn't exactly immune to offering smiles laced with sarcastic comments herself. In this debate there was, for instance, Trump's answer in reply to Clinton's suspicion that he rarely if ever pays income tax ("That makes me smart"). How did she respond? Trump's answer elicited a mix of an eye roll, a smirk, a skeptical smile, and a thin-lipped display of anger, all in one tight sequence.

Given that Clinton also, at times, emitted irritated sighs like Al Gore had in 2000, there can be little doubt that Clinton was far from perfect in the first debate. Many, maybe even most of her smiles appeared to be forced. She gulped during her first answer, and blinked nervously in suggesting that racism was the real motivation behind Trump's calls for "law and order." Clinton also first demonstrated in this debate a habit of lowering her eyes or closing them entirely, at times, as if she couldn't abide sharing the stage with Trump.

CLINTON OUTSHINES THE GRUMP, BUT TO NO AVAIL

At times, Clinton was more buoyant than Trump (not hard to do). At other times, she could hardly abide what she was hearing from her opponent and closed her eyes in dismay. Feeling off his game, perhaps at the thought that Lester Holt's probing questions meant it was a supposedly two-on-one debate, Trump was grouchy, displaying his characteristic upside-down smile. Now and again, however, he simply seemed at a loss as to what to say.

Emotions		Clinton > Trump	Trump > Clinton
HELPS	Skepticism		
	Satisfaction		
	Fear	★	
	Pleasure	★★	
HURTS	Joy	★★	
	Anger		★
	Sadness		★

DEBATE 1: EMOTIONAL PROFILE

Trump played the Grinch Who Stole Christmas, complete with endless "humbug" expressions of disgust. In a nutshell, Clinton danced between not-always authentic smiles and more than a smattering of utterly sincere smirks.

Those relatively minor hiccups were nothing, however, compared to Trump's travails on stage that night. Maybe the Republican candidate really did feel like it was a two-on-one debate, with NBC's Lester Holt taking an active role against him, as would be Trump's claim afterwards. Whatever the cause, Trump, a man who rarely smiled, found his way to smiling even less on this occasion. In fact, if it hadn't been for flashing his trademark skeptical smiles, he would have hardly smiled at all. If Barack Obama sold hope in 2008, Trump was selling fear of impending doom in 2016.

Trump didn't quite match Clinton's volume of smirks during the first debate, but he always had disgust to fall back to as an automatic response. Like a Christmas gift getting re-gifted, Trump took Clinton's expressions of disdain when the topic was his remarks about women and returned the favor in calling her remarks about his boorish behavior "Not nice" ("I don't deserve it").

Most of all, though, Trump whiffed. There were many issues he might have raised but didn't during the first debate: Clinton's handling of the attack on the American compound in Benghazi, illegal immigration, Clinton's missing emails, and the Clinton Foundation. Instead, he flailed around by saying that Clinton didn't "have the stamina" for the job, when her decades of dedicated and unwavering service to the country proved otherwise.

Round Two

Clinton appeared slightly friendlier during the second debate (a town-hall forum format), but the unease signaled by signs of fear, and surprise in particular, hadn't subsided any despite seemingly having "won" the first debate. All during her campaign, Clinton had kept the crowds behind red velvet rope lines, even distancing herself from much of her staff. To be on stage for an evening, surrounded by voters, wasn't something she enjoyed nearly as much as her husband had. She liked policy, he liked people. Again, that emotional reality emerged as the evening's debate progressed.

Sure, satisfaction flowed—but so did surprise reactions. Twice in particular, Clinton's eyes went extra wide, alert to danger. Once was when she took "responsibility" for her emails (while asserting that there wasn't any "evidence" her server had ever been hacked). The second time was when the issue of whether to use ground forces in Syria came too close to echoing the debate over war with Iraq and her vote to authorize it, leading to more wariness.

DEBATE 2: EMOTIONAL PROFILE

Clinton's previous, occasional ebullience now came down a notch: there were more muted, satisfaction smiles instead this time around. As for Trump, he basically delivered a re-run of his previous stage performance: disgust, disgust, disgust.

Emotions		Clinton > Trump	Trump > Clinton
	Skepticism		
HELPS	Satisfaction	★★★	
	Fear	★	
	Pleasure		
	Joy		
HURTS	Anger		★
	Sadness		★

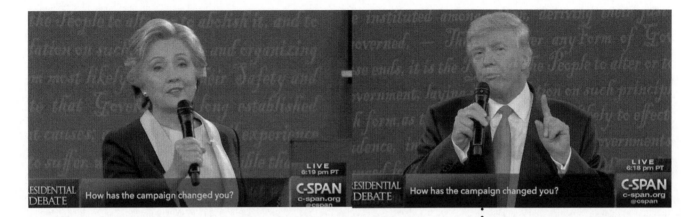

Trump mellowed a bit too, in the presence of voters. Ever so occasionally he smiled, but mostly displays of disgust continued to characterize him to a degree far greater than what was true of Clinton. On hearing a verbal attack, Trump would feel revulsion no matter the merits of the attack. Regarding his attitudes toward women, for instance, Trump shot back that "Nobody" has "more respect for women than me." In the broader sense, however, Trump didn't show up again. *Muted* is a very relative, tongue-in-cheek term when discussing Trump and his emoting habits. Not until the third debate would Trump be at his most sarcastic.

Round Three

Whatever smiles Trump did flash were pretty much always of the skeptical variety, at a volume greater than either of the two previous debates. Challenged to renounce Russia, he dismissively smiled while replying that Vladimir Putin had "outsmarted " both his election opponent and Barack Obama. From foreign trade to border security, Trump damned Clinton with the faint praise of insincere smiles whenever he wasn't showing one of his familiar expressions of disgust, from a raised upper lip to a raised chin.

The anger Trump had displayed during the first debate was due to frustration with questions and topics that put him on the defensive. Now, whatever anger he felt was more a matter of lashing out, and his disgust was revulsion for what he didn't find tolerable. "She's been found to be a liar in so many ways," Trump said of Clinton, his eyes narrowed and his mouth contorted by disgust. "Thanks for doing a great job," he said at another point in the debate, combining a look of rebuke with a skeptical smile. If he stumbled at all, it was in how to handle the *Access Hollywood* tape about his groping. For a moment, Trump's mouth pulled wide in fear, and then he was Trump again.

CLINTON HESITANTLY SMILES, THE DONALD DOUBTS EVERYTHING EXCEPT HIMSELF

Expressions of being seemingly caught by surprise are typical of Clinton. Here her eyebrows have risen in fielding a question. For Trump, the second debate was another case of being relatively subdued, at least by his standards. Knitted eyebrows revealed Trump being about as reflective as he ever gets.

TRUMP CONTINUES TO PLAY DOUBTING THOMAS

Trump's feral-like emotional expertise involves two attributes: doubting what exists, and doubting any solutions anyone other than himself has either tried or thought of. That makes him the perfect cynic. In the third debate, his skeptical smiles were ubiquitous, looking in this case like a boy happy about pulling off a prank. Also here, his "Cherrios" O-ring disgust expression— upper lip raised, lower lip dropped— made more stage appearances and attracted, at times, a largely similar response from Clinton.

Probably falsely believing she was going to win, Clinton mostly played it safe, enduring Trump's attacks for the most part like a boxer leaning back into the ropes, absorbing punches. Big joyful smiles made a return into her emotional repertoire. Yes, attempts to push back on abortion rights drew her ire more than most issues during this third and final debate. On the other hand, when Trump was busy talking down democracy, Clinton objected less, perhaps, than she might have done had she suspected her opponent could, and would, emerge victorious on election night.

DEBATE 3: EMOTIONAL PROFILE

Clinton got the memo, and returned to her smiling, first-debate ways. Only now she was matched by Trump pushing skeptical smiles her way. Otherwise, both candidates were their usual selves: that meant wide-eyed surprise in Clinton's case, more grumpy, upside-down smiles in Trump's case.

	Emotions	Clinton > Trump	Trump > Clinton
	Skepticism		★★
HELPS	Satisfaction	★	
	Fear	★	
	Pleasure		
HURTS	Joy	★★	
	Anger		
	Sadness		★

ODDS & ENDS

Sooner than later, the 2020 presidential debates will be upon us and maybe the candidates, whoever they prove to be, can learn from these results. To take any possible insights one step further, let's explore a few patterns in closing. One of them is by party. Are there any differences, overall, in how the Democratic, Republican, and the two Independent candidates have emoted on average? And have they, by party, exhibited emotions that mostly help or hurt their chances with voters?

The results show that the Democrats have a lock on smiling. They show more joy (which doesn't help them) and more skeptical smiles (which help them a lot). As Democrats show more sadness, too, they're *not* being at a disadvantage depends on their using sadness effectively to exhibit empathy for others rather than ego-centric regrets.

Republicans it would seem are not, Despite being the party

	Emotion Displayed	The Formula (recap)	Democrats > Republicans	Republicans > Democrats	Independents (+/- the two-party average)
HELPS	Skepticism	★★★★	★		-
	Satisfaction	★★★★			
	Fear	★★★		★	
	Pleasure	★★			
HURTS	Joy	★★★	★		+
	Anger	★★		★	-
	Sadness	★★	★		-
NO IMPACT	Contempt	★			
	Disgust	★	★		
	Surprise	★			+

of Ronald Reagan, it would seem that Republicans are not nearly as comfortable about being on stage typically. Fear favors them, however, all the same. Where they have to be careful is a tendency to feel too much anger, which hurts their chances of winning The White House. With only two Independent candidates on whom to base any insights, about the most that can be said with any assurance is that they don't align emotionally with either party; in other words, they truly are independent.

All in all, every campaign cycle is unique in its way and so is every candidate. So let's move to the question: which candidates have "owned" a particular emotion during their time on stage, and have any of them been so emotionally promiscuous as to own more than one emotion?

As might be expected, Bill Clinton, always happy to have an audience, "owns" the more intense levels of happiness: joy and pleasure. But he's also third for sadness, given his "I feel your pain" empathy expertise as demonstrated especially in debates using a town-hall format. Richard Nixon, on the other hand, worked the lower register of happiness—plus skeptical smiles. That's where he excelled. Right there with Nixon was John F. Kennedy, with the difference being that whereas Nixon worked hard to

WHICH PARTY DOMINATES WHICH EMOTION(S) ON AVERAGE

The Democratic candidates are, on average, aided by being more given to skepticism than their Republican counterparts, whose apparent advantage is exhibiting more fear. On the negative side of the ledger, Democrats run into trouble showing too much joy and sadness. For Republicans, the issue is their propensity for anger.

Emotion Displayed		Highest Amount	2nd Highest	3rd Highest
HELPS	Skepticism	Kennedy	Nixon	Trump
	Satisfaction	H. Clinton	B. Clinton	Dukakis
	Fear	Reagan	Anderson	Bush '41
	Pleasure	B. Clinton	Carter	Reagan
HURTS	Joy	Mondale	Perot	B. Clinton
	Anger	Carter	Kerry	Bush '41
	Sadness	Dole	Bush '41	B. Clinton
NO IMPACT	Contempt	Anderson	Obama	Bush '43
	Disgust	Trump	Dukakis	Obama
	Surprise	Dukakis	Anderson	H. Clinton

WHICH CANDIDATES OWNED WHICH EMOTION(S)

There are four debaters—Bill Clinton, Richard Nixon, John F. Kennedy, and John Anderson—who appear the most often here. The difference is that for all of them, except Anderson, two of the three emotional categories in which they were dominant were positive in orientation. Every other candidate appears here at least once, except Romney.

overcome the first debate and showed plenty of pleasure in subsequent debates, Kennedy never quite shook off being nervous. John Anderson is the fourth of those candidates who shows up all over this chart. With him, however, the results are inevitably a disaster: surprise, fear, and contempt are the emotions he was prone to revealing during his disastrous 1980 *mano a mano* debate with Reagan.

Outside of those four candidates showing up repeatedly in my chart, what else is notable? That depends on your expectations, of course. A methodical Michael Dukakis showing surprise as he tackled questions he couldn't know were coming doesn't surprise me, at least. A doleful Bob Dole is in the same category. A germophobic Donald Trump scoring the highest for disgust is likewise no surprise. But John Kerry's trying to press George W. Bush and, therefore, leading the way with anger is, I admit, something of a surprise.

Finally, I'll address two other questions. First, considering all the emotions that tend to either help or hurt a candidate on stage, who came the closest as a debater in getting it right? The answer is Kennedy, given that fear actually appears to be a plus rather than a negative for debaters.

Second, in these fiercely, even rudely partisan times, have the debates gotten uglier not just in tone but in the feelings expressed? The answer is a qualified yes. Based on the emotions shown by the candidates across all debates in that election cycle, three of the five most *negative*, mean-spirited debate series have happened in the 21st century. In contrast, three of the five more *positive* debate series were in the history books by the end of 1984. Now, you might think the ugliest, most rancorous series of debates happened in 2016, but you would be wrong. They come in second place. In first place are (as mentioned earlier) the harsh debates held in 2008, when the Great Recession was unfolding. Therefore, heaven help us should the next election happen during another economic downturn.

PART 3

World Leaders and the Return of Strongmen

ORIENTATION

The Ups and Downs of Democracy

Is it possible to spot a dictator in the making? As a former KGB agent, Russia's president Vladimir Putin might have been easy to peg as somebody with no real commitment to democracy. But how about making the call early on about Recep Tayyip Erdogan of Turkey? I remember the Turkish businesswomen who invited me to Istanbul twice in the mid-2000s being worried about him. Well, their worries proved prescient, as Erdogan has increasingly become an out-and-out despot. That same guessing game of who will or will not prove to be an authoritarian leader is played out, country by country, with disastrous results for the (voting) citizens who guess wrong.

Once upon a time we might have thought of the ultimate triumph of democracy as inevitable. The first chart here tracks the progress of democracy, beginning with the American Revolution and the French Revolution, the harbingers of modern democracy.[1] Four major processes since then have produced intense periods of democratization:

- the collapse of monarchies following the end of World War One in 1918;

- the defeat of dictatorial regimes that flourished due to start of the Great Depression in 1929, and lasted until the end of World War Two in 1945;

- the twilight of European colonialism in Africa and Asia (beginning in 1957);

- and the fall of the Soviet Union and the Iron Curtain from 1989 to 1991.

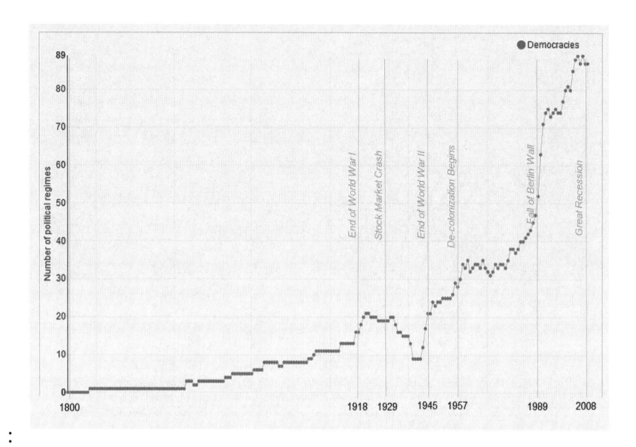

THE GROWTH OF DEMOCRACY

Although the above Polity IV Project chart does not cover the past decade, during that time so-called 'illiberal' hollow democracies have been multiplying, reducing the number of fully functional democracies in the world. The economic pain caused by the Great Recession of 2008 has, no doubt, been a contributing factor to this faltering halt in the growth of genuine democracies. The latest Freedom House information indicates that between 2005-2018 the percentage of countries classified as free dropped by 2%, while the percentage of not-free countries increased by 3%.

The end of several military dictatorships in Latin America since the late 1970s can be included as a fifth, though more limited, phenomenon. All in all, the chart shows only two downswings in the number of democratic countries. The first came during the run-up to World War Two, as populist strongmen and dictators rose to power after the onset of the Great Depression and the concomitant global economic crisis. The other instance is much more recent: the aftermath of the Great Recession of 2008.

For a decade the world has been in something of a democratic recession, and the situation seems to be growing worse. From Donald Trump to an "anything goes" spirit overseas, authoritarian pronouncements and practices are flourishing around the globe.[2] This reality makes my quest to find a formula for identifying a dictator in the making timely and urgent. To that end, I've facially coded 79 notable foreign leaders who have held power sometime between the late 18th century and today, most of them since 1972.

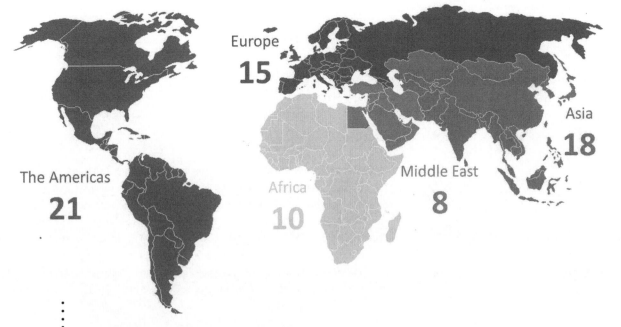

LEADERS PER CONTINENT, 1972–PRESENT

This map shows the geographical distribution of the 66 modern-day leaders, domestic and foreign, whose emotional results have been compared to the annual 1972–2018 Freedom House survey findings.

1972 is an important cut-off point because that is the year the non-profit organization Freedom House began publishing data on the levels of political and civil freedoms present in most countries in the world. Using around 25 indicators, the organization classifies countries as Free, Partly Free, or Not Free.

To the pool of foreign leaders in the post-1972 period, I have added the U.S. presidents from Richard Nixon onward. So in all 66 world leaders constitute the heart of my data set, including an emphasis on leaders in power during the 21st century. That pool of 66 leaders gives me a basis for correlating the results from facial coding to the annual survey findings by Freedom House. The result is a formula for predicting the likelihood that a leader will either favor democracy or authoritarianism.

I took into account all ten emotional states facial coding can identify to discern the tendencies of leaders of countries classified as Free, Partly Free, or Not Free. In the end, only four emotions proved to have predictive power. For simplicity's sake, those four emotions were then re-worked to form a pair of measures with a robust .39 correlation in predicting whether a leader will be pro- or anti-democratic. (As noted earlier in this book, with correlations related to human behavior and with no direct access to the people involved, a correlation of .50 is considered to be downright excellent. Therefore, .39 is a pretty strong correlation.)Those two measures are as follows:

- *Exuberance* (intense happiness), which combines the two most intense levels of happiness, namely, joy and pleasure. These are expansive emotions that fit well with a leader being open-hearted and favorable towards democracy. There is a .31 correlation between the emotions of joy and pleasure and a leader proving to be pro-democratic.

- *Harshness* (anger and disgust), which combines the instinct to "hit" (anger) and to be "fed-up" or repulsed (disgust). There is a .34 correlation between the emotions of anger and disgust and a leader proving to be anti-democratic.

The other six emotions are non-factors. By that I mean they do not rise to an adequate level of predictive power in terms of correlating to leaders who promote or reject democracy. Those other six emotions are listed in the Emotions and Freedom chart in descending rank order, with fear having practically no predictive power at all. Atop the non-factor list is acceptance, which has only a modest correlation to leaders who are anti-democratic in nature. With a formula in hand that balances exuberance against harshness, it's then possible to look at how the formula performs within the three categories that Freedom House operates by.

Emotion Helps Democracy (Exuberance)	Emotion Is Non-Factor	Emotion Hurts Democracy (Harshness)
Joy	Acceptance	Anger
Pleasure	Surprise	Disgust
	Sadness	
	Contempt	
	Satisfaction	
	Fear	

EMOTIONS AND FREEDOM

At one end of the spectrum are the two emotions that correlate well to the facial expressions of democratically inclined leaders. At the other end lie anger and disgust. In between are six other emotions that aren't significantly correlated to either pro- or anti-democratically inclined leaders.

DEGREES OF FREEDOM

Overview of Results

The average for leaders of countries deemed by Freedom House to be Free, i.e., fully democratic, proves to be the most exuberant and least harsh. Results from twenty leaders constitute the Free average. Almost half of them hail from Europe. A second average that appears here is the outcome when the results for those twenty Free country leaders are combined with the results for nine U.S. presidents, from Richard Nixon to Donald Trump. Then the average is a little less emotionally exuberant, primarily due to Trump's inclusion. Close to that second, Free + USA average is a third average, based on the results for the 18 leaders of Partly Free countries. Half of these diluted democracies are located in Asia.

Left to discuss are the results for the 19 leaders of countries deemed Not Free, i.e., authoritarian states. Two-thirds of them are either in Africa or the Middle East. With the average for the leaders of the Not Free countries, a marked shift occurs. Not only does the exuberance level decline some, the level of harshness becomes much more pronounced.

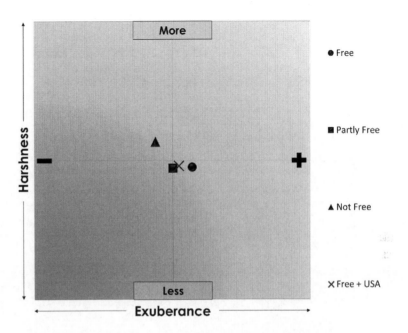

AVERAGES BY TYPE OF COUNTRY

Take away the results for Trump, and the Free + USA average would be basically the same as the Free average. Add Trump in, however, and a shift toward the Partly Free average emerges, thereby highlighting the influence one leader can have on developments worldwide.

Free Countries and Their Leaders

Three-quarters of these leaders land in the right two quadrants of my workhorse Exuberance and Harshness chart, meaning these leaders exhibit more exuberance than is typical of the overall pool of leaders. No leader exemplifies this outcome better than South Africa's first president after apartheid, Nelson Mandela. He is at once the most exuberant and the second least harsh leader included here, behind South Korea's Moon Jae-in.

The harshest of these leaders is the Netherlands' far-right, anti-immigrant politician Geert Wilders. Never yet accepted into any of the country's various

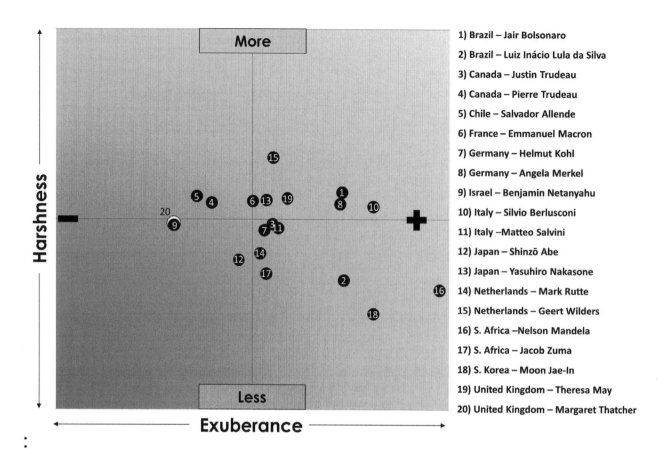

More

Less

Harshness

Exuberance

1) Brazil – Jair Bolsonaro
2) Brazil – Luiz Inácio Lula da Silva
3) Canada – Justin Trudeau
4) Canada – Pierre Trudeau
5) Chile – Salvador Allende
6) France – Emmanuel Macron
7) Germany – Helmut Kohl
8) Germany – Angela Merkel
9) Israel – Benjamin Netanyahu
10) Italy – Silvio Berlusconi
11) Italy –Matteo Salvini
12) Japan – Shinzō Abe
13) Japan – Yasuhiro Nakasone
14) Netherlands – Mark Rutte
15) Netherlands – Geert Wilders
16) S. Africa –Nelson Mandela
17) S. Africa – Jacob Zuma
18) S. Korea – Moon Jae-In
19) United Kingdom – Theresa May
20) United Kingdom – Margaret Thatcher

LEADERS OF FREE COUNTRIES

These 20 individual results provide the basis for the Free country leaders' average, which lands in the lower right quadrant of this chart. In all, 14 out of 20 of these leaders are more, rather than less, exuberant than is typical of the leaders in this study. In all, 11 out of 20 of these leaders are not as harsh than is typical of leaders in this study.

coalition governments, Wilders continues to operate as the major dissident voice on the fringe of Dutch public affairs. Other outlier performers include Great Britain's former prime minister, Margaret Thatcher, and Israel's current prime minister, Benjamin Netanyahu, a leader whose illiberal tendencies have become more pronounced in recent years.[1] While their degree of harshness is middling, it is their lack of exuberance that puts Thatcher and Netanyahu more in league with leaders of Not Free countries.

In general, Free countries and leaders who are happier and more exuberant go together. As already mentioned, Mandela fits the bill perfectly. A single incident from early in his career exemplifies his qualities as a benevolent leader. Thirty years before Mandela was released from prison, the world had seen him deliver a speech in court while on trial for sabotage. "I have fought against white domination," Mandela said that day, "and I have fought against black

Nelson Mandela   Benjamin Netanyahu

domination. I have cherished the idea of a democratic and free society in which all persons live together in harmony." On trial with Mandela was Walter Sisulu, who likewise expected to be hanged if found guilty as charged. Years later Sisulu would remember being encouraged by Mandela's "flexibility, by his ability to change, by his attitude to people. Amazing."[2]

Netanyahu is quite different from Mandela. With Israel's leader, joyful smiles are rare. He is a man more likely to keep his eyes wide, alert to both opportunity and danger, while also being more contemptuous than is usual for Free country leaders. Observers have used words like "arrogant" and "aggressive" to describe him. A prime example of Netanyahu's headstrong tendencies is his recent alliance with an anti-Arab party whose agenda includes resettling all Israeli Arabs in neighboring countries.[4]

Next, let's explore the results for the Free + USA average by considering all the U.S. presidents from 1972 to today, from Richard Nixon to Donald Trump. (Since this part of *Two Cheers for Democracy* broadens its focus, at times, to cover the past century, U.S. presidents all the way back in time to Franklin D. Roosevelt are included in this next chart as a frame of reference.) What the results for the recent U.S. presidents reveal is that blustery Trump and "worrywart" George H. W. Bush emerge as relatively similar in that they're the two least exuberant of our country's post-1972 leaders.

Moreover, if these results are compared to the Free country leader results, it becomes clear that Netanyahu and Trump aren't just good friends in political terms; they are also similar emotionally speaking. Though Trump is harsher, the two men are quite alike in regards to their low amount of exuberance—an outcome at odds with the far greater amount of exuberance typical of Free country leaders.

LEADERS OF FREE COUNTRIES WHO ARE EMOTIONAL OUTLIERS

Mandela served 27 years in prison prior to becoming the first black president of South Africa from 1994-1999. Netanyahu was the prime minister of Israeli from 1996-1999, prior to resuming office in 2009. He's the first Israeli prime minister to have been born in Israel after the country was established.

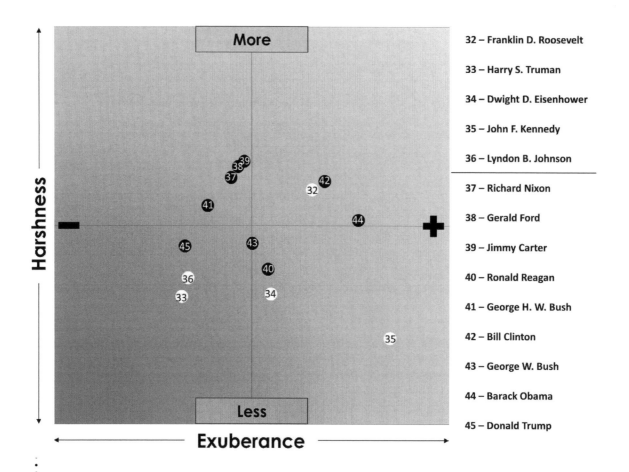

More

Less

Harshness

Exuberance

32 – Franklin D. Roosevelt

33 – Harry S. Truman

34 – Dwight D. Eisenhower

35 – John F. Kennedy

36 – Lyndon B. Johnson

37 – Richard Nixon

38 – Gerald Ford

39 – Jimmy Carter

40 – Ronald Reagan

41 – George H. W. Bush

42 – Bill Clinton

43 – George W. Bush

44 – Barack Obama

45 – Donald Trump

U.S. PRESIDENTS 1972-PRESENT (PLUS ALL THE WAY BACK TO FDR)

As a group, the nine most recent American leaders favor harshness over exuberance. Reagan is closest to the Free country average. Obama and Clinton are the most exuberant, Trump the least so. Note that five presidents prior to the Freedom House 1972 timeframe have been included as additional reference points.

Partly Free Countries and Their Leaders

The 18 leaders from countries Freedom House classifies as Partly Free, with only a few exceptions, exhibit less exuberance than Free country leaders. Whereas 70% of the Free country leaders are fairly exuberant, the percentage of fairly exuberant Partly Free country leaders drops to 39%. The outliers in this case are two extremely exuberant leaders—Indonesia's Joko Widodo and Liberia's former leader Ellen Johnson Sirleaf—and a pair of leaders notable for their relative harshness: Chile's former president Augusto Pinochet and Venezuela's former president Hugo Chávez.

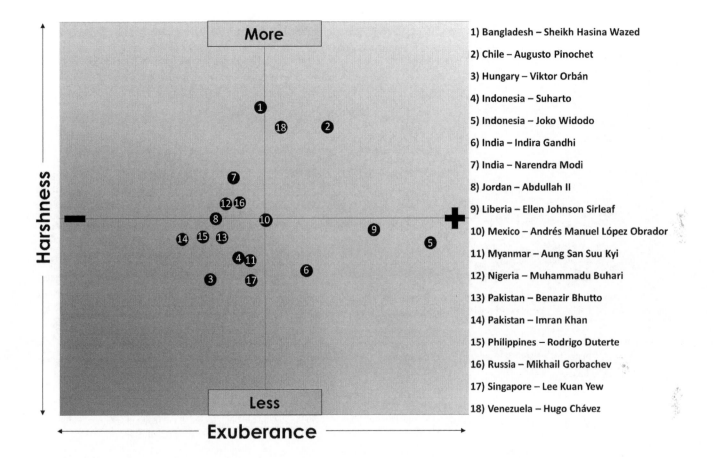

More

1) Bangladesh – Sheikh Hasina Wazed

2) Chile – Augusto Pinochet

3) Hungary – Viktor Orbán

4) Indonesia – Suharto

5) Indonesia – Joko Widodo

6) India – Indira Gandhi

7) India – Narendra Modi

8) Jordan – Abdullah II

9) Liberia – Ellen Johnson Sirleaf

10) Mexico – Andrés Manuel López Obrador

11) Myanmar – Aung San Suu Kyi

12) Nigeria – Muhammadu Buhari

13) Pakistan – Benazir Bhutto

14) Pakistan – Imran Khan

15) Philippines – Rodrigo Duterte

16) Russia – Mikhail Gorbachev

17) Singapore – Lee Kuan Yew

18) Venezuela – Hugo Chávez

Harshness

Less

Exuberance

It is probably safe to assume most people have not heard of Sirleaf, even though she was awarded the Nobel Peace Prize in 2011. Among her other accomplishments, Sirleaf was Africa's first elected female president and one of only five African leaders (along with Nelson Mandela) to have won the $5 million Ibrahim Prize for Achievement in African Leadership,[5] a recognition of her efforts to strengthen democracy and promote human rights. She managed to introduce fiscal vigilance in Liberia, though certainly not an end to corruption. "I beg you no magician," Sirleaf quipped on the radio during her re-election campaign.[6]

LEADERS OF PARTLY FREE COUNTRIES

Six wildly divergent individual results definitely change the Partially Free average. If not for leaders ranging from Indonesia's Widodo to Venezuela's Chavez and Bangladesh's Hasina, where most Partly Free leaders cluster would be obvious: not so harsh, but definitely not exuberant either.

Ellen Johnson Sirleaf **Hugo Chavez**

Chávez's personality, on the other hand, was characterized by extreme harshness. Machismo and all that it involves (bombast, bravado, and a tough-guy cult of personality) never seems to quite go out of style in Latin America, and Chávez was a prime example. This habit was evident in his rhetorical style. "The descendants of those who crucified Christ," Chávez often defiantly asserted, "have taken ownership of the riches of the world."[7]

PARTLY FREE LEADERS WHO ARE EMOTIONAL OUTLIERS

Sirleaf was the president of Liberia from 2006 to 2018 and became the first elected female head of state in Africa. Chavez was the president of Venezuela from 1999 until his death in 2013. Chavez called his blend of imported Marxism and native Latin American machismo "Chavismo."

Not Free Countries and Their Leaders

The 19 leaders from countries Freedom House classifies as Not Free constitute the least exuberant, harshest crowd. In most of these countries civil rights never seem to fully emerge. Consider Uganda, where president Yoweri Museveni recently sent troops onto the floor of Parliament to accost lawmakers who objected to letting him rule for life.[8] Given that nobody died in that extraordinary incident, Museveni's rule qualifies as mild compared to those of two leaders who did get facially coded for the purposes of this study. North Korea's Kim Jong-un and Saudi Arabia's Mohammad bin Salman are at once both harsh and exuberant. They stand at the opposite end of the spectrum emotionally from Iran's former leader, Ruhollah Khomeini, who rarely smiled, and was more prone to sadness and fear than to anger or disgust.

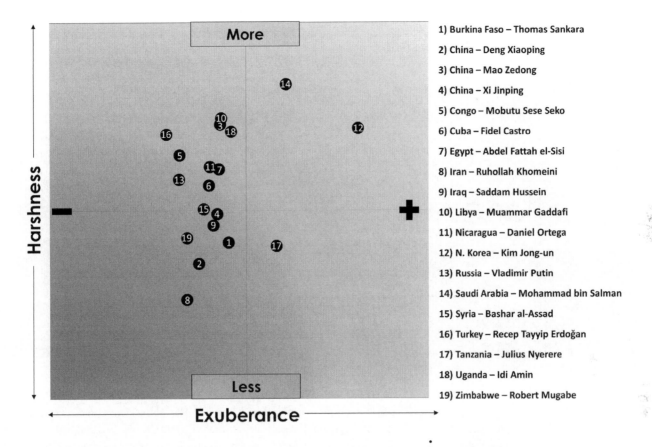

1) Burkina Faso – Thomas Sankara

2) China – Deng Xiaoping

3) China – Mao Zedong

4) China – Xi Jinping

5) Congo – Mobutu Sese Seko

6) Cuba – Fidel Castro

7) Egypt – Abdel Fattah el-Sisi

8) Iran – Ruhollah Khomeini

9) Iraq – Saddam Hussein

10) Libya – Muammar Gaddafi

11) Nicaragua – Daniel Ortega

12) N. Korea – Kim Jong-un

13) Russia – Vladimir Putin

14) Saudi Arabia – Mohammad bin Salman

15) Syria – Bashar al-Assad

16) Turkey – Recep Tayyip Erdoğan

17) Tanzania – Julius Nyerere

18) Uganda – Idi Amin

19) Zimbabwe – Robert Mugabe

Kim fits the mold of Not Free country leaders by being emotionally harsh. Indeed, 58% of these leaders exhibit that quality. On the other hand, only 16% are at all exuberant. There, Kim is a clear-cut exception. Somehow he manages to stay upbeat while threatening death and destruction to America or having his half-brother and uncle killed (the former by poisoning in an airport, and the latter by using troops armed with anti-aircraft guns in lieu of the usual firing squad).[9]

LEADERS OF NOT FREE COUNTRIES

When anger and disgust almost entirely displace intense, exuberant happiness, odds are that you're looking at the leader of a Not Free country. Are the two blatant exceptions to that rule, Saudi Arabia's bin Salman and North Korea's Kim, in effect a pair of psycho-killers? I leave that judgment to you.

Kim Jong-un

Mohammad Bin Salman

NOT FREE LEADERS WHO ARE EMOTIONAL OUTLIERS

Kim became the supreme leader of North Korea in 2011 and is the first North Korean leader born after the country's founding. Saudi Arabia's bin Salman became the country's deputy prime minister in 2017; he's widely considered to be heir presumptive to the throne.

As to bin Salman's signature facial expression, it combines a big, beaming smile with a nose wrinkled in disgust, or alternatively an upper lip raised in a show of disgust and anger. What offends him? Clearly, getting criticized isn't acceptable; just ask journalist Jamal Khashoggi, if only anyone could. After Khashoggi disappeared inside the Saudi Arabian embassy in Istanbul, Turkey, revelations about a bone saw being used to dismember him were about as close as anybody ever came to finding his body. Known by his initials, MbS may now be as well known as Muhammad Bone Sawman.

LEADERSHIP BY ERA

Earlier Eras: Setting the Stage

Not covered by the Freedom House results are another 22 leaders whom I want to include here. The comparison between earlier and post-1972, contemporary leaders, however, can only be partial. That's because leaders in the past were much less likely to exhibit broad smiles than is now the case. So only the harshness measure offers fair comparable data.

As previously discussed, there were no more than ten democracies in the world as late as 1900 and merely 25 as late as 1960, when former European colonies were beginning to gain independence. Naturally, many important world leaders from this earlier period ruled over monarchical or aristocratic regimes. This study covers six individuals who held power prior to 1920: Great Britain's George III and Queen Victoria, France's Napoleon Bonaparte, Germany's Otto von Bismarck, Russia's Catherine the Great, and Venezuela's Simón Bolívar. Of these, only Napoleon and Bismarck led countries in which men could vote (whereas female suffrage was still off in the future in every case).

HARSHNESS LEVEL BY ERA

How quickly the world forgets, and falls back into old, bad habits. The era of 1920-1945 isn't one people should want to re-live, and yet slowly, degree by degree, the average for harsh leaders keep creeping ever closer to the old, awful era of monsters like Hitler and Stalin.

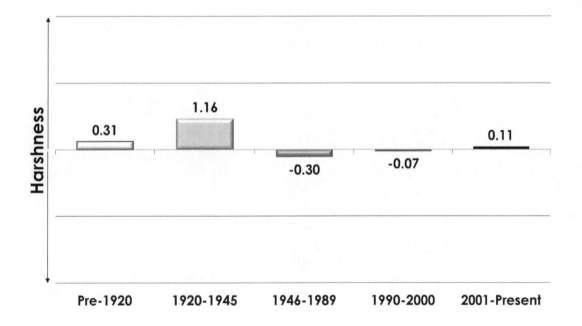

Between Victorian era stuffiness and leaders not needing the approval of their subjects, pre-1920 is the second harshest era. It is, however, no match for what came next. The era from 1920 to 1945 is clearly the one with the highest levels of emotional harshness, as befits the years that spanned The Great Depression and the depravities of World War Two. Meet the era of monsters. The data for this time span draws on the study of seven leaders, including Germany's Adolf Hitler, Italy's Benito Mussolini, Russia's Joseph Stalin, and Brazil's military strongman Getulio Vargas. Not even the inclusion of Great Britain's Winston Churchill, Turkey's Mustafa Kemal Ataturk, and America's Franklin D. Roosevelt can soften the era's standing as the height of harshness in the world to date.

Once the monsters were gone, the degree of harshness subsided. The era from the start of the Cold War in 1946 to the breaching of the Soviet Union's Iron Curtain across Eastern Europe between 1989 and 1991 was much gentler by comparison. The following period, from the end of the Cold War to the attack on the Twin Towers in New York City on September 11, 2001, was almost as gentle. As a group, leaders from both eras came in well below the average for harshness in respect to the individuals examined for this study.

It is only since 9/11, and especially since the Great Recession of 2008, that the average for harshness among political leaders has begun to rise again. Although far less severe than the era of the monsters, the current timeframe comes close to matching the pre-1920's era of monarchs and aristocrats. The similarity is suitably ironic, as these days we have imperial-type leaders assuming their posts seemingly for life. China's Xi Jinping, the country's new emperor, fits that mold. So does Russia's Vladimir Putin as a latter-day czar, Egypt's Abdel Fattah el-Sisi as a pharaoh, Turkey's Recep Tayyip Erdogan as a caliph,[1] and so forth.

Three leaders, each an embodiment of his time period, played such pivotal roles that they deserve special consideration. They consist of Germany's Bismarck, Turkey's Ataturk, and the Soviet Union's final leader, Mikhail Gorbachev.

Otto von Bismarck

Mustafa Kemal Ataturk

Mikhail Gorbachev

PIVOTAL FIGURES ACROSS THE ERAS

Bismarck was a Prussian statesman who became the first Chancellor of the German Empire serving in that role from 1871 to 1890. Ataturk was a Turkish field marshal and secularist reformer. After founding the country, Ataturk became the first president of the Republic of Turkey from 1923 to 1938. Gorbachev was the eighth and last leader of the Soviet Union, serving as the country's communist party secretary from 1985 to 1991.

Nobody better represents the pre-World War One era than the man who gave the United Kingdom its first formidable opponent in decades, Germany's Bismarck, known as the "Iron Chancellor." He united Germany in 1871, rejecting England's values of liberty and individualism in favor of "duty, order, and justice" based on obedience to an all-powerful state. "The great questions of the time," he declared to the world, "will not be resolved by speeches and majority decisions . . . but by iron and blood." Such was his sway that when the European powers met to divide up Africa in 1880, the conference was held in Berlin.

By the end of World War One, no other major combatant had lost a larger percentage of its population than the Ottoman Empire, whose death gave birth to Turkey. Eager to salvage the part the British and the French had not yet divvied up, Ataturk took Turkey and transformed it into a secular democracy and a model for other non-Western powers to follow in the years ahead. Like Bismarck, Ataturk was a military man highly prone to anger. Unlike Bismarck, however, he was often beset by sadness. "I have a reputation for drinking a lot. Indeed, I drink quite much,"[2] he once admitted, and was dead from cirrhosis of the liver at age 57.

Third is Gorbachev. The Russian people remember him for how their living standard fell to Bangladesh's level in the aftermath of the Soviet Union's implosion in 1991.[3] Vladimir Putin has called the loss of Eastern Europe and other former Soviet Republics "the greatest geopolitical catastrophe of the 20th century."[4] To Gorbachev, the course of events was inevitable because whatever economic progress the Soviet Union had once achieved was gone. Accordingly, he told the Politburo: "We have no choice. We are . . . at the end of our tether."

What's Happening Now

Back in the early 1990s, the historian Francis Fukuyama famously declared: "What we may be witnessing is not just the end of the Cold War . . . but the end of history. That is, the end of mankind's ideological evolution and the universalization of Western liberal democracy as the final form of human government." Over time, however, Fukuyama's optimistic judgment has been eclipsed by these more somber words: "We are seeing a new type of threat that I don't really think we've seen in my lifetime."[5] More and more people live in countries where elections have become less meaningful as democracy gets hollowed out.[6]

One of the world leaders most notably engaged in weakening democracy is Hungary's Viktor Orban. On a visit to Budapest in 2018, Donald Trump's former advisor Steve Bannon hailed Orban as "Trump before Trump."

Orban, Bannon, and Trump share many ideological positions, including skepticism of the European Union and a commitment to building a barrier along their two countries' respective southern borders. In Hungary's case, the stated aim is to ensure "the survival of the Judeo-Christian west" from Syrian and other Middle East refugees making their way across Europe.[7] As if to reinforce Bannon's endorsement of Orban, Trump called the Hungarian prime minister to congratulate him after his latest re-election triumph. Such favoritism brings up the question: who else has Trump chosen to hail as his type of "strong" foreign leader or, in turn, disparage, and why?

As this chart shows, Trump has no natural emotional affinity for the three Free country leaders shown here. Instead, it's collectively the strongmen role models that Trump has embraced who have emotional results that look a lot like his own. They are generally harsh leaders, and not exuberant or open-hearted when it comes to embracing others. Temperamentally similar Trump allies deemed worthy of praise have included:[8]

- The Philippine leader Rodrigo Duterte, whose crackdown on drugs has left over 7,000 coun-

trymen dead as a result of what have been called "extra-judicial" killings, often handled by government sponsored vigilantes. Trump has praised Duterte for the "unbelievable job" he is doing handling the country's "drug problem."

- The Russian leader Vladimir Putin, whose critics and opponents, including journalists, have repeatedly been harassed, poisoned or imprisoned. In Trump's words: "If he says great things about me,

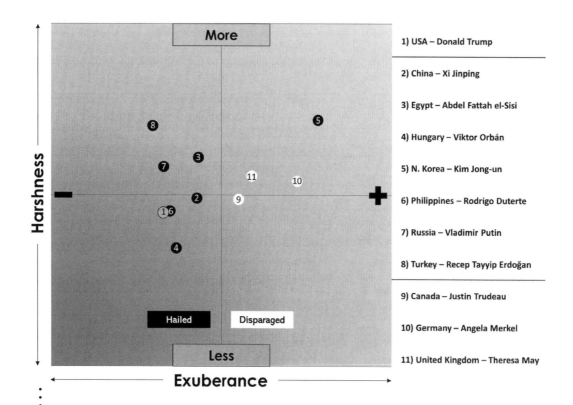

1) USA – Donald Trump

2) China – Xi Jinping

3) Egypt – Abdel Fattah el-Sisi

4) Hungary – Viktor Orbán

5) N. Korea – Kim Jong-un

6) Philippines – Rodrigo Duterte

7) Russia – Vladimir Putin

8) Turkey – Recep Tayyip Erdoğan

9) Canada – Justin Trudeau

10) Germany – Angela Merkel

11) United Kingdom – Theresa May

WHO TRUMP HAS HAILED AND DISPARAGED

Take away the results for North Korea's oddball leader, Kim, and it's a perfect match: Trump is emotionally surrounded by leaders given to acting like bullies.

I'm going to say great things about him" and "he is really very much of a leader."

- The Chinese leader Xi Jinping, whose country leads the world in executions and is engaged in the detention of as many as two million Uighur Muslims in northwest China. "He is a good man," Trump has said. Later, on learning Xi had now been named president for life, Trump replied: "I think it's great. Maybe we'll have to give that a shot some day."

- The North Korean leader Kim Jong-un, whose country the U.N. Commission of Inquiry in 2014 concluded is without equal today in being abusive of its citizens. "He's a pretty smart cookie," Trump has said of Kim and that "we fell in love" on meeting in Singapore.

- The Egyptian leader Abdel-Fattah el-Sissi, whose bloody coup resulted in some 800 protesters being killed in a single day. Trump's verdict: "He's done a fantastic job."

- The Turkish leader Recep Tayyip Erdogan, whose revenge has resulted in over 50,000 people detained since a thwarted coup. A rigged re-election? No problem. Erdogan also earned Trump's praise because the two men "have a great friendship."

Meanwhile, who gets singled out for criticism? First and foremost, anybody associated with the European Union. When asked to name America's biggest foe, who did Trump choose? Not Russia, China, North Korea or Iran—but rather the E.U. As a germaphobe scoring high on disgust, is any of the following language surprising? Trump has described Brussels, the host city of the E.U., as a "hell hole" and Germany, under the leadership of Angela Merkel, as a "total mess." Meanwhile, Europe's leaders have been dismissed in general as "weak leaders."

This same dichotomy, between "strong" leaders Trump admires and "weak" leaders that Trump denigrates, is clearly seen in his wildly different attitudes toward Hungary's Viktor Orban and Canada's Justin Trudeau. Never mind that every recent American president except Trump made either a trip to Ottawa or receiving the Canadian prime minister in Washington, D.C. one of their very first presidential duties. In Trudeau, Trump has found a convenient punching bag, a barrier to reconstructing the North American Free Trade Agreement (NAFTA) as a "win" for America, and accordingly called Trudeau "dishonest and weak" in a tweet during the NAFTA negotiations.

Viktor Orban

Justin Trudeau

A TRUMP BROMANCE AND FOE

Orban of Hungary served as the country's prime minister from 1998 to 2002, before resuming the post in 2010. Trudeau has been Canada's prime minister since 2015 and is the first person in that role to be related to a previous office holder, namely his father, Pierre Trudeau, who served from 1968 to 1984.

In July 2014, Orban gave a speech to an ethnic Hungarian audience in Romania.[9] In what was said that day lie the seeds of the challenge democracy is facing worldwide. It is notable that Orban was speaking to a crowd of people he has granted voting rights in Hungarian elections even though they are not citizens. By choosing ethnicity over borders established after World War One, Orban is signaling that ethnicity and tribalism matter more than the rule of law.

Orban urged his audience that day, and oftentimes since then, not to look back to 1989 and the flowering of democracy after the collapse of communism as a point of reference. No, far better was to denounce liberal, Western, democratic, capitalist values that "embody corruption, sex, and violence" in favor of an Eastern model.

The key to success, Orban said that day, are regimes that are "not Western, not liberal, not liberal democracies, and perhaps not even democracies." The stars to follow are countries like Singapore, China, India, Russia, and Turkey. It is a list remarkably similar to that of countries Trump has praised. These are countries whose leaders Trump and Orban have more emotional affinity with than they do with the leaders of Free countries posited on pluralism and tolerance for minority groups.

THE STATUS QUO

STATUS QUO

International Organizations

Despite numerous conflicts, the world has been relatively calm since the end of World War Two. Increasingly, though, the organizations and alliances put in place decades ago are now under strain or at risk of becoming less relevant. Not only is the "establishment" being attacked by populist leaders, the world's economic center of gravity is shifting to Asia. It's in that context that somebody like Viktor Orban proclaims "the era of liberal democracy is over," while looking East, to China in particular. It's in that context that Orban also says: "There is a race underway to find the method of community organization, the state, which is most capable of making a nation and a community internationally competitive."[1]

In "looking East," what gets bypassed? The countries that form much of the Free world are Western democracies that have pooled their military and monetary muscle to create international organizations to promote stability and security. They form the backbone of the current global status quo. The mantle of leadership in the Western world, at least since 1973, has been held by the so-called G-7: Canada, France, Germany, Italy, Japan, the United Kingdom, and the United States. This group of countries has largely shared a vision of the world order and has sought to maintain order together. For a while, it seemed that Russia would remain part of a broader G-8. But after Russia annexed the Crimea region of Ukraine, the G-8 went back to being the G-7.

More up to date and complete is the G-20, formed in 1999. The G-20 is about money pure and simple. Its roster covers 85% of the world's economic output. In addition to the G-7, the other member nations are Argentina, Australia, Brazil, China, India, Indonesia, Mexico, Russia, Saudi Arabia, South Africa, South Korea, Turkey, as well as a representative from the European Union. Like the E.U. and the G-7, the G-20 still lands in emotional territory associated with the leaders of Free countries.

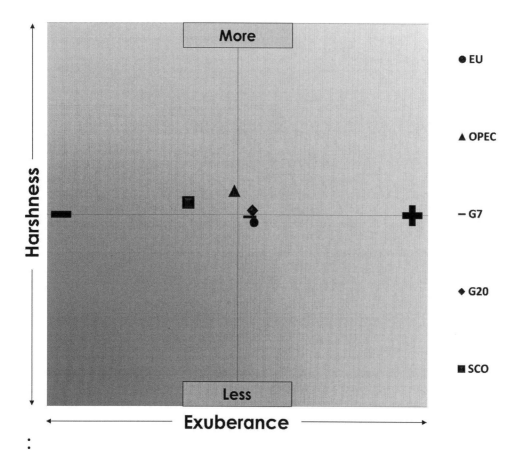

More

Less

Harshness

Exuberance

● EU

▲ OPEC

— G7

◆ G20

■ SCO

SOME KEY WORLD ORGANIZATIONS

If it's true you're defined by who your friends are, the membership rosters of the G-7, G-20, and European Union (E.U.) remain pretty simpatico. The challenge comes from organizations with fewer if any Free leaders, i.e., OPEC's mostly Middle Eastern membership, and the SCO countries led by China.

Two other international organizations are close in emotional territory to the Not Free countries. One is the Organization of Petroleum Exporting Countries (OPEC), founded in Bagdad, Iraq in 1960. OPEC's five founding members, Iran, Iraq, Kuwait, Saudi Arabia, and Venezuela, have over the years been joined by Qatar, Indonesia, Libya, the United Arab Emirates, Algeria, Nigeria, Ecuador, Gabon, Angola, Equatorial Guinea, and Congo. The second is the Shanghai Cooperation Organization (SCO), a Eurasian alliance founded in 2001 comprising China, Russia, four former Soviet Republics (Kazakhstan, Kyrgyzstan, Tajikistan, Uzbekistan), Pakistan, and India.

The further east an organization's leadership contingent is on the globe, the more it veers emotionally and politically away from a democratic orientation. If, or shall we be honest and say *when,* American global dominance ends, will these two spheres, East and West, exist peacefully in tandem or will they find themselves falling into overt competition, philosophically, economically, even militarily? A lot depends on that eventual answer.

Military Might

Multinational organizations are unwieldy and generally slow to act. The United Nations' Security Council, with Russia, China, the U.S., France, and the U.K. able to exercise veto power, is a case in point. Persuasion requires patience. It's easier for a leader to put an army into the field. Here, military strength involves weapons, manpower, and logistical abilities, but not these countries' nuclear stockpiles (if any). Lists vary somewhat regarding the exact rank order. But in averaging three recent lists to determine the top ten major military forces in the world, a likely list in descending order of strength looks like this:[2]

- Led by Donald Trump, the U.S. military has 2,363,000 troops and a huge budget of $587 billion. America has a well-trained army, which also includes almost a million reservists.

- Led by Vladimir Putin, Russia has 3,571,000 troops and a budget of $44 billion. The country's military features the largest tank force in the world.

- Led by Xi Jinping, China has 3,712,000 troops and a budget of $161 billion. Include its reservists and China has the world's largest land force. With growing budgets and success in stealing sensitive military technology from America, China is surely a competitor to be reckoned with.

- Led by Narendra Modi, India has 4,207,000 troops and a budget of $51 billion. The country has the largest army in the world, but many of its weapons are merely "vintage" stock.

- Led by Emmanuel Macron, France has 387,000 troops and a $35 billion military budget. France has continuously chosen to intervene militarily in Africa.

- Led by Theresa May, the United Kingdom has 232,000 troops and a $46 billion budget. The U.K. and U.S. forces frequently coordinate their efforts.

- Led by Moon Jae-in, South Korea has over 640,000 troops and 2.9 million reservists to counter the immediate threat posed by North Korea and also to meet the increasing armament of China.

- Led by Shinzo Abe, Japan has 311,000 troops and a $43.8 billion budget. The country's constitution prohibits Japan from having an offensively oriented army, but given the risk of future disputes with China that limitation may change over time.

- Led by Recep Tayyip Erdogan, Turkey has 743,415 troops and an $8.2 billion budget. The country faces a Kurdish separatist organization, the PKK, and borders an unstable region. Although a member of the North American Treaty Organization (NATO), Turkey is buying arms from Russia.

- Led by Angela Merkel, Germany has 210,000 troops and a $39 billion budget. Economically strong, Germany deliberately punches below its weight in military terms for historical reasons. In other words, its Nazi past still haunts the country.

What is notable about this chart? Most leaders here occupy emotional territory that puts them in league with the average results for the Not Free countries. Free country leaders like America's Trump and Japan's Abe join that trend, as does India's Modi among the leaders of countries classified as Partly Free. Indeed, if it were not for South Korea's Moon and three European leaders, the depicted results would diverge entirely from the Free country average.

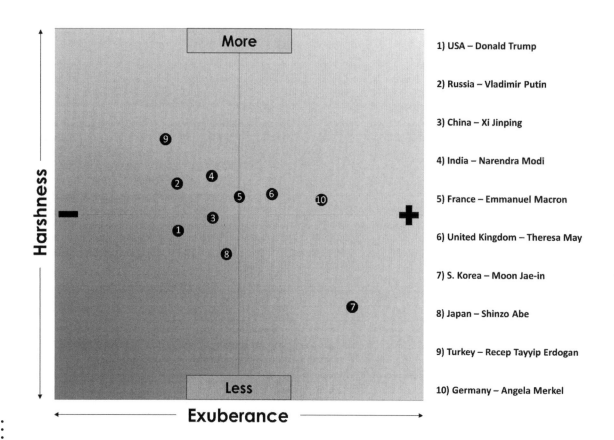

More

Harshness

Less

Exuberance

1) USA – Donald Trump

2) Russia – Vladimir Putin

3) China – Xi Jinping

4) India – Narendra Modi

5) France – Emmanuel Macron

6) United Kingdom – Theresa May

7) S. Korea – Moon Jae-in

8) Japan – Shinzo Abe

9) Turkey – Recep Tayyip Erdogan

10) Germany – Angela Merkel

THE WORLD'S STRONGEST ARMIES

Only three leaders of countries with the strongest armies are more exuberant than the Free country leaders' average, and two of them are the only women here: Germany's Merkel and the U.K.'s May. Who looks to be most belligerent? Turkey's Erdogan and Russia's Putin qualify most of all.

In 2018, *Time* magazine short-listed Moon for its Person of the Year award due to his successful efforts to get North Korea's Kim Jong-un and Trump to talk face-to-face after the U.S. president threatened Kim's regime with "fire and fury like the world has never seen." The son of parents who fled North Korea during the Korean War, Moon admits his agenda is first "economic cooperation, then economic integration and finally full reunification" between the two Koreas.[3] Whether that agenda is a fantasy or not, it's what motivates Moon's presidency.

The polar opposite of Moon, emotionally speaking, is Turkey's Erdogan. No leader among those shown in the military chart is harsher or less exuberant. Critics believe that Turkey now resembles an elective dictatorship, and Erdogan has lent support to that concern by having remarked: "Democracy is like a tram. You ride it until you arrive at your destination, then you step off."[4]

Recep Tayyip Erdoğan

Moon Jae-in

Two Koreas

When the Arab Spring movement reached Turkey, Erdogan crushed it, ending any hopes that he might prove to be a more tolerant, modern-day caliph (in keeping with the country's former Ottoman model). Turkey's founder Mustafa Kemal Ataturk did not have a mild temperament either. But Erdogan is, by comparison, even more given to the scorning emotions of disgust and contempt.

Ataturk felt he was engaged in a game of "catch-up" with the West. Erdogan despises the West. In Erdogan's mind, he remains the poor boy from Kasim-pasa, a working-class district of Istanbul dismissed by the nearby cosmopolitan district of Pera, where secular Western values and affluent lifestyles remain dominant. Erdogan is, in short, a man with a chip on his shoulders.

Cyber Warfare and "Soft Power"

Cyber warfare could destabilize the status quo quickly and decisively. This approach is cost-efficient, with immense potential impact that is very difficult to deter. China, Russia, Iran, North Korea, and, to a lesser degree, India have all sponsored cyber attacks against their political rivals over the past decade.[5] Although the U.S. is by far the greatest victim of cyber attacks, at a cost of over a billion dollars, the country is also one of cyber warfare's occasional practitioners. Could it do more? Yes, for as former president Barack Obama once observed, the U.S. "has the world's foremost cyber arsenal."

UNDER-THE-RADAR LEADERS OF MAJOR ARMIES

Erdogan transitioned from being the prime minister of Turkey from 2003 to 2014 to then becoming its president. His previous stint at mayor of Istanbul ended in 1998 with four months in prison for reciting religious poetry at a public rally. Born during the last year of the Korean War, Moon became the president of South Korea in 2017, and now has to deal with both Trump and Kim in trying to secure an official end to the Korean War.

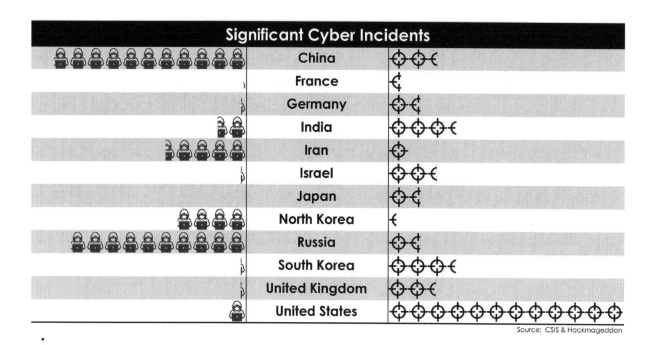

Significant Cyber Incidents

🔒🔒🔒🔒🔒🔒🔒🔒🔒🔒🔒	China	⊕ ⊕ ⊂
ꞌ	France	⊂
ꞌ	Germany	⊕ ⊂
🔒🔒	India	⊕ ⊕ ⊕ ⊂
🔒🔒🔒🔒🔒	Iran	⊕
ꞌ	Israel	⊕ ⊕ ⊂
	Japan	⊕ ⊂
🔒🔒🔒🔒	North Korea	⊂
🔒🔒🔒🔒🔒🔒🔒🔒🔒	Russia	⊕ ⊂
ꞌ	South Korea	⊕ ⊕ ⊕ ⊂
ꞌ	United Kingdom	⊕ ⊕ ⊂
🔒	United States	⊕ ⊕ ⊕ ⊕ ⊕ ⊕ ⊕ ⊕ ⊕ ⊕ ⊕ ⊕ ⊕ ⊕

Source: CSIS & Hackmageddon

SIGNIFICANT CYBER INCIDENTS

The left side of the chart indicates where state-sponsored cyber espionage and cyber warfare attacks originate from. The four main countries—China, Russia, Iran, and North Korea—are all Not Free countries with emotionally harsh leaders. On the right side of the chart are the countries most subject to cyber attacks (excluding cyber crime), with America being clearly the biggest target of those attacks.

The results of analyzing the leaders of the major cyber warfare nations match those of leaders of militarily powerful nations. If it were not for the strange, harsh exuberance of North Korea's Kim, all of the results would land in emotional territory antithetical to the average for Free country leaders.

Directly contrary to the practice of cyber warfare is the more benign, passive concept of "soft power." Its originator was Joseph Nye of Harvard University, who defines soft power as a country's ability to attract and co-opt other countries, rather than coerce them through hard power. Shaping the preferences of other nations by being a model worth emulating is the essence of soft power. In practical terms, when used effectively soft power takes advantage of social trends to influence public opinion by various means, including lobbying through organizations, diplomacy, communications, foreign assistance, and economic reconstruction and development.

Before Trump came to office, the U.S. was often listed first in *The Soft Power 30*, an annual index that ranks countries by this measure.[6] China still struggles as a user of soft power, despite a push to become a "socialist cultural superpower." In 2014, Xi Jinping declared: "We should increase China's soft power, give a good Chinese narrative, and better communicate China's messages to the world."[7]

In 2018, the top ten countries in the soft power rankings were the U.K., France, Germany, the U.S., Japan, Canada, and the Netherlands, along with three countries whose leaders were not analyzed for this study: Switzerland, Sweden, and Australia. Despite losing the leadership of Lee Kuan Yew and being an underdog in pure demographic terms, Singapore is still such a positive, aspiring model for developing countries that it ranks #21, ahead of Hungary, China, Russia, and Brazil.

Here is how the leaders of the two groups emotionally compare, contrasting countries in the top ten in terms of soft power versus countries ranked from 21 to 30. If it were not for two leaders—Trump and Brazil's Jair Bolsonaro—the symmetry would be nearly perfect. Those with less soft power are less exuberant; those with more soft power more upbeat. In other words, more democratically inclined emotional results befit soft power. The opposite is true as well: leaders less upbeat, less embracing, are at the helm of countries less influential in terms of emanating soft power.

BOTH THE WORLD'S TOP AND MIDDLING SOFT POWERS

Despite two outliers, America's Trump and Brazil's Bolsonaro, the picture is pretty clear. The most admired, top-level soft powers have more exuberant leaders than the countries trying to become soft-power powerhouses themselves.

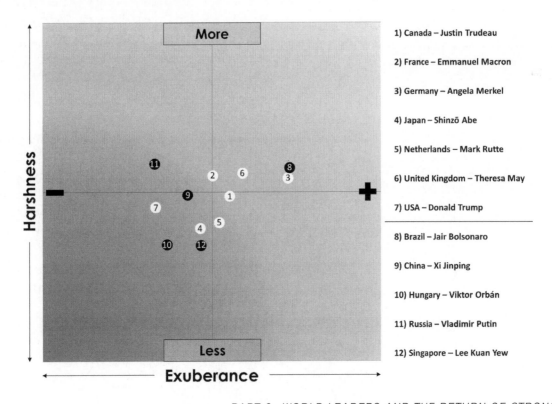

1) Canada – Justin Trudeau

2) France – Emmanuel Macron

3) Germany – Angela Merkel

4) Japan – Shinzō Abe

5) Netherlands – Mark Rutte

6) United Kingdom – Theresa May

7) USA – Donald Trump

8) Brazil – Jair Bolsonaro

9) China – Xi Jinping

10) Hungary – Viktor Orbán

11) Russia – Vladimir Putin

12) Singapore – Lee Kuan Yew

COUNTRY SPOTLIGHTS

The Giants of the Earth

It is a crowded world, and getting more crowded. When I was born in 1959, the world's population was a little over three billion people. Today it approaches 7.5 billion. And if I live the 76 years of a typical white male citizen of America, then in 2035 the world's population will have reached 8.5 billion. Here are the world's biggest countries by population:

- China with 1.4 billion people accounts for 18% of the world's population.

- India will soon surpass China. At present, India has 1.3 billion people and 17.5% of the world's population.

- The U.S. is third, but way back at 4% of the world's population with 327 million people.

- Barack Obama lived in Indonesia as a boy. Lots of people do. It is the home of 3.5% of the world's population, with 265 million people.

- Pakistan is fifth in size with a little under 3% of the world's population and 212 million people. It is a nuclear power and politically unstable.

- Brazil is sixth in world population, almost equal to Pakistan, with some 209 million people.

- Nigeria is Africa's most populous nation. Its 193 million people represent 2.5% of the world's population.

- Bangladesh is in eighth place with 165 million people, meaning that if the entirety of Great Britain's former colony of India had held together, combining India, Pakistan and Bangladesh, then "India" would be far and away the world's largest country, with 1.712 million people.

- Russia has almost 2% of the world's population with 146 million people. Its demographics are declining, however, so time does not favor Vladimir Putin's regime.

- Tenth is Japan, almost as demographically challenged as Russia. Japan has 1.5% of the world's population with 126 million people and an aversion to permitting immigrants.

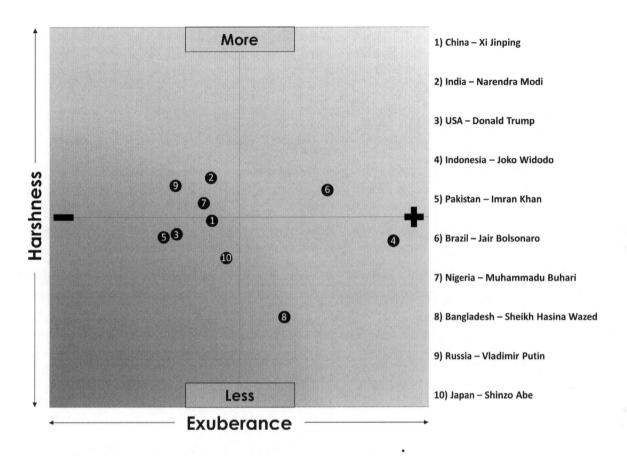

More

Harshness

— **+**

Less

Exuberance

1) China – Xi Jinping

2) India – Narendra Modi

3) USA – Donald Trump

4) Indonesia – Joko Widodo

5) Pakistan – Imran Khan

6) Brazil – Jair Bolsonaro

7) Nigeria – Muhammadu Buhari

8) Bangladesh – Sheikh Hasina Wazed

9) Russia – Vladimir Putin

10) Japan – Shinzo Abe

As these results show, the majority of the leaders of today's biggest countries by population do not emote in ways that typically fit the democratically oriented, Free country mode. Among the exceptions is Bangladesh's Sheikh Hasina Wazed, which suggests that in looking for appropriate allies a democracy like the U.S. might want to look to countries led by women. Where else might the U.S. find allies with whom it has an affinity based on sharing fairly similar democratic practices? The exuberance of Indonesia's leader, Joko Widodo, might help prompt greater consideration of that key country, along with another country too often overlooked by Americans: Nigeria, led by Muhammadu Buhari.

THE LEADERS OF THE BIGGEST COUNTRIES

While India's Modi and the leader of its neighboring rival, Pakistan's Khan, are far from exuberant, India's other big neighbor breaks the mold. Bangladesh's Hasina is an exuberant, emotionally gentle leader, without equal among her peers here when it comes to being less harsh.

Joko Widodo   Muhammadu Buhari

THE LEADERS OF COUNTRIES THE U.S. MIGHT FOCUS ON MORE

Buhari became the president of Nigeria in 2015. Following a military coup d'etat, he previously served as head of state from 1983 to 1985. Widodo was elected president of Indonesia in 2014, becoming the first person of a non-military or elite background to assume that role in the country.

In Widodo's case, he heads the world's third largest democracy. Since 1999 and the end of Suharto's three-decade long presidency, Indonesia has succeeded in showing that Islam and democracy can go hand-in-hand. Many people may associate Islam with the Middle East and North Africa, but almost two-thirds of all Muslims live in Asia. Islam will in the decades to come surpass Christianity as the world's largest religion.[1] By most accounts, Widodo is doing a good job balancing populist, nationalist, and religious tensions in multi-ethnic Indonesia as he endeavors to be an honest, inclusive leader.[2]

Nigeria's Buhari probably suffers by comparison to Widodo. A Muslim himself, Buhari has struggled to contain the Islamic extremists operating in northern Nigeria. Moreover, corruption remains an endemic problem in the country. Nevertheless, as is true regarding Indonesia, the community of Free nations has a vested interest in Buhari's success.

After all, Nigeria exemplifies some important demographic trends of its own. Sub-Saharan Africa has, as a region, the highest fertility rate in the world.[3] Africa is booming in size, and Nigeria is its most significant bellwether nation. People there need and deserve a viable, attractive future. Otherwise they will join the record number of people living outside their birth countries (today's 244 million migrants would qualify as the fifth largest country in the world). Eight of the ten fastest growing international migrant populations are from sub-Saharan countries.[4] How well a figure like Buhari governs, therefore, impacts not only his country and Africa in general, but also the world at large—especially Europe, where so many African immigrants hope to relocate.

Nine Key Countries, Yesterday and Today

The United Nations' Security Council includes five permanent members that were victorious allies during World War Two. China occupies the seat originally designated for the Republic of China and Russia the seat formerly held by the Soviet Union. They are joined by the U.S. and two of its European allies: the U.K. and France. All five of these permanent members have nuclear weapons, among the world's biggest militaries, and are five of the world's six largest arms exporters (Germany is the other).

Given that these Big Five wield veto power, enabling them to prevent the adoption of any substantive Security Council resolution, gaining admission to this club has long been a sought-after privilege. The so-called G4 nations are the ones most often cited as possible permanent member additions to the Security Council: Brazil, Germany, India, and Japan.

The focus here will be on these nine nations—the Big Five and the G4—specifically, the emotional trajectory of each country's leadership. The analysis will rely on three touch points per country: first, a seminal figure from the era before the U.N.'s charter of 1945 was enacted; second, a leader from the period in which the Iron Curtain finally fell and a large number of countries became democracies; and third, that country's current leader. Taken together, those three touch points are meant to provide some sense of each country's emotional orientation over time.

AVERAGES FOR THE BIG FIVE AND THE G4

With the notable exception of Germany, all of the European powers central to World War One and Two reveal less than exuberant results. Only Germany seems to have made a dramatic break from its past. China and Japan are less exuberant, too, the antithesis of samba-loving Brazil.

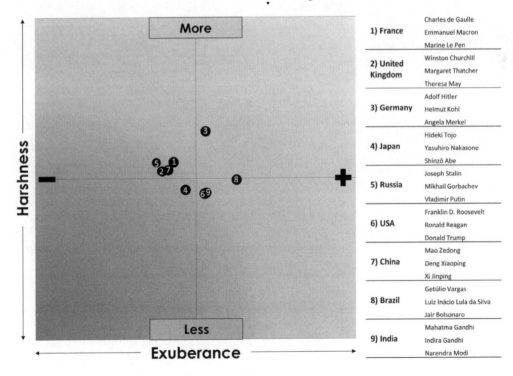

1) France	Charles de Gaulle
	Emmanuel Macron
	Marine Le Pen
2) United Kingdom	Winston Churchill
	Margaret Thatcher
	Theresa May
3) Germany	Adolf Hitler
	Helmut Kohl
	Angela Merkel
4) Japan	Hideki Tojo
	Yasuhiro Nakasone
	Shinzō Abe
5) Russia	Joseph Stalin
	Mikhail Gorbachev
	Vladimir Putin
6) USA	Franklin D. Roosevelt
	Ronald Reagan
	Donald Trump
7) China	Mao Zedong
	Deng Xiaoping
	Xi Jinping
8) Brazil	Getúlio Vargas
	Luiz Inácio Lula da Silva
	Jair Bolsonaro
9) India	Mahatma Gandhi
	Indira Gandhi
	Narendra Modi

Notable results emerge. Due to Adolf Hitler's previous role in its history, Germany scores the highest for harshness. Meanwhile, Russia's trio of leaders qualifies as the least exuberant and Brazil's the most exuberant. As to which country's leaders are the least harsh, the U.S., Japan, and India are pretty much dead even. Those results serve as background for considering each country represented on the chart with a historically appropriate counterpart, except for China, which is a force onto itself.

The Original, Modern Duopoly: The United Kingdom and France

The U.S. had to fight one of these two countries to gain its independence, making the other our first international ally. One was the first to industrialize, while the other in many ways is still primarily an agriculture-oriented country. One was a naval power, the other once threw its army across the European continent, and beyond, in search of hegemony. One had a colonial empire on which the sun "never set," including its "crown jewel" of India, and the other had an empire,

FRENCH AND BRITISH LEADERS

Two results stand out here. The U.K.'s Theresa May is clearly the most disposed to exuberance, a Free country leader tendency. In contrast, France's Charles de Gaulle exhibits harshness, an emotional habit of more autocratic leaders.

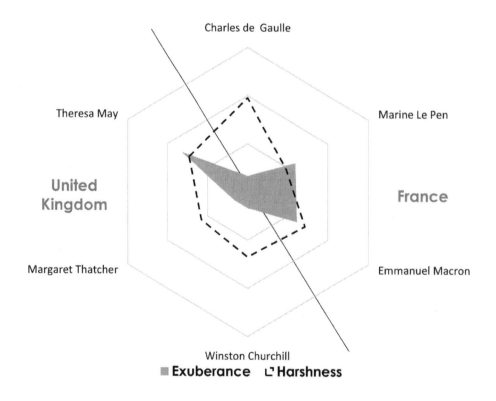

■ **Exuberance** ∟ **Harshness**

too, though it was never especially profitable.[5] One has had many female leaders (going back to Queen Elizabeth and Queen Victoria), while the other joined countries like Italy and Switzerland in being among the last in Western Europe to grant women the right to vote.

They were the first rulers of the modern world. During the 19th century, Western empires that constituted only 7% of the world's land surface controlled as much as 37% of its territory.[6] None were more powerful than the U.K. and France. Notably, except for the era from 1803 to 1815, when Napoleon Bonaparte barnstormed across Europe (and as far as Egypt), the U.K. has always had the advantage.

The source of that advantage might surprise many people. In taking over the slave trade from the Netherlands by 1700 and running it at as a high-profit margin business until 1867, England gained in every leg of the so-called triangular trade route: African slaves imported to the Americas; raw resources (like tobacco, sugar and cotton) to feed the people and textile mills of England; and clothing, rum, and manufactured goods that could be sold worldwide, including back to Africa.[7]

The leader who presided over the British Empire's last hour of glory, Winston Churchill, had more in common emotionally with autocrats than with Free country leaders. This is hardly surprising, as Churchill was not just fighting against the Nazis. In 1931, he declared: "Our fight is hard. It will also be long . . . But win or lose, we must do our duty. If the British people are to lose their Indian Empire, they shall do so with their eyes open."

Why fight so hard for India? Follow the money. While France struggled to turn a profit after seizing colonies in western Africa and Indo-China, in India the U.K. made out well. One measure of that success is India's comparative misfortune. In 1700, India had a per capita gross domestic product (GDP) level of $550. Over the next 250 years, mostly under British rule, India's GDP only rose to $619. In other words, on the brink of gaining its independence in 1947, India had been standing still for over two centuries thanks to the British.[8] Just as the U.K.'s control of as much as four-fifths of the slave trade was a disaster for Africa (whose population did not increase from 1600 to 1900), so did the U.K.'s colonization of India lead to stagnation—and worse.

Winston Churchill

Theresa May

GREAT BRITAIN: PAST AND PRESENT LEADERS

Churchill served as the United Kingdom's prime minister from 1940 to 1945 and again from 1951 to 1955. A winner of the Nobel Prize for Literature, he was an economic liberal and self-professed imperialist. May became the country's prime minister in 2016 and has suffered from a headache called Brexit ever since.

Charles de Gaulle

Emmanuel Macron

FRANCE: PAST AND PRESENT LEADERS

De Gaulle led the French resistance in World War Two, was asked to rewrite the country's constitution in 1958 and subsequently became France's president until resigning in 1969. Macron became the president of France in 2017 after having previously been an investment banker at Rothschild & Cie Banque.

Theresa May and Emmanuel Macron, the current leaders of the U.K. and France, are certainly friendlier, more exuberant, than their respective predecessors: Margaret Thatcher and Charles de Gaulle. But they both have significant challenges to confront.

Macron, the youngest president in the history of the French Fifth Republic, portrays himself as a self-made political entrepreneur turning France into a "startup nation."[9] Critics, however, call this ex-banker the "president of the rich" and dub him "Jupiter" after the Roman god-of-gods for his aloof, arrogant manner. May, on her part, has it no better. Not long after declaring that Britain needs "to send an empathetic message about what we do want," she saw her original Brexit Plan voted down by the largest margin of defeat in British parliamentary history.[10] Holding on rather than holding forth would certainly seem to be both countries' near-term fate, in the shadow of their former, dynastic grandeur.

The Upstarts: Germany and Japan

These two countries were the primary instigators of World War Two, but in comparison are otherwise both a mixture of similarities and profound differences. A case in point is that, yes, both Germany and Japan industrialized during the late 19th century. But in Germany, development was *internally* motivated by Otto von Bismarck's drive to unite and strengthen the country, whereas in Japan change was instigated by the arrival of the U.S. naval

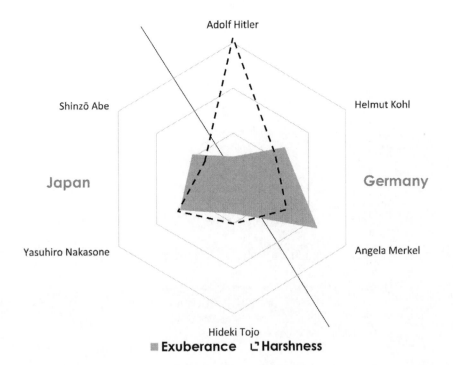

Adolf Hitler

Helmut Kohl

Shinzō Abe

Japan

Germany

Yasuhiro Nakasone

Angela Merkel

Hideki Tojo

■ **Exuberance** ⌐ **Harshness**

commander Matthew Perry and his fleet of black warships in 1853. Told to open its ports or else, Japan responded by engaging in rapid industrialization meant to equal, if not overtake, any and all Western foreigners.

What helped Germany and Japan focus their efforts were the shared national qualities of accepting rules and hard work, attitudes that persist to this day. Surveys have found, for instance, that whereas a commitment to work is considered "important" in the U.S., the U.K., and France by only 8.1% of the people on average, in Germany the figure is 31.3%. In Japan, it's 42.9%. To the question of whether it's acceptable to break the rules, on average 43.9% of Americans, British, and French respond in the affirmative, whereas the figure is 14% in Germany and 15.5% in Japan.[11]

Nevertheless, the two countries are hardly identical—especially in regard to the legacy of World War Two. If there is a specter haunting Germany (and Europe at large), it remains Adolf Hitler, surely the prototype for all of today's right-wing populist leaders. Even in French presidential politics, the issue is often ultimately Hitler. Whether Marine Le Pen's National Front party can ever win her country's presidency, for example, depends to a large degree on whether she can successfully distance herself from her father's anti-Semitic sentiments. Few French have forgotten Jean-Marie Le Pen dismissing the Holocaust as merely a "detail of history,"[12] a comment that led to his expulsion from the party he founded, the one his daughter now leads.

GERMAN AND JAPANESE LEADERS

In this case, there's Hitler and everybody else, given Hitler's towering rage. Merkel could hardly be more different from him, especially when it comes to greater exuberance. Among the Japanese leaders, only Nakasone, the prime minister when Japan was riding high, manages some degree of exuberance.

Adolf Hitler

Angela Merkel

GERMANY: PAST AND PRESENT LEADERS

Hitler was the chancellor of Germany from 1933 to 1945, the instigator of World War Two, and the man most responsible for the Holocaust. Merkel became Germany's chancellor in 2015 and is widely considered to be the de facto leader of the European Union and the world's most powerful woman.

In a similar vein, the degree to which Germany's leaders have sought to distance themselves from Hitler and his legacy can be seen in the emotional results for Helmut Kohl and Angela Merkel. In particular, their greatly subdued degree of harshness is notable. Populist politics tend to involve: overt nationalism, increased military spending, economic protectionism, and bigger budget deficits. Neither Kohl nor Merkel have ever showed a propensity to support such policies. Kohl is most famous for presiding over the reunification of Germany in 1990, under the dual umbrella of the E.U. and NATO. In Merkel's case, she's best known for becoming the de facto leader of the E.U. and, later on, for her decision to welcome a large influx of asylum seekers from Syria and elsewhere in 2014-2015.

In contrast, consider Japan. Both conformity and racial homogeneity are prized there, as Japan continues to look down on its neighbors. Some of that attitude is the result of having been the only non-Western country to industrialize in the 19th century while also avoiding colonization. Another factor is pure racism. There's no law against racial discrimination in Japan. So it's no surprise that while he was presiding over the pinnacle of Japan's return to strength in the 1980s, Yasuhiro Nakasone was caught saying the mental abilities of Americans were lower than in Japan. His reasoning was the presence of racial minorities, specifically "blacks, Puerto Ricans, and Mexicans."[13]

Hideki Tojo

Shinzo Abe

Remarkably adaptable, the Japanese are not exactly famous for their broad smiles. Nakasone is the equivalent of Kohl in terms of exuberance, though a little harsher. Japan's World War Two leader, Tojo Hideki, was in contrast not nearly as harsh as Hitler. Both men were deemed war criminals, even if only Tojo failed to kill himself at war's end and was hanged by the U.S. occupation forces instead.

As for the future, Japan is itching to get out from under the U.S.-Japan security pact originally signed in 1951. Only then can the country adopt a more robust military stance. Article 9 of Japan's Constitution requires the country to "forever renounce war as a sovereign right," a clause that first Nakasone and now Abe would prefer to have amended in order to guard Japan against a resurgent China. In comparison, more intent on maintaining their export-driven economy than anything else, Germany is moving farther away from, rather than closer to, NATO's goal of having members pledge the equivalent of 2% of their GDP to defense spending.

JAPAN: PAST AND PRESENT LEADERS

Tojo was a Japanese army leader and the country's prime minister during much of World War Two. Subsequently arrested by American troops, Tojo was sentenced to death for war crimes and was hanged in 1948. Abe has served as Japan's prime minister since 2012, having previously held the role from 2006 to 2007.

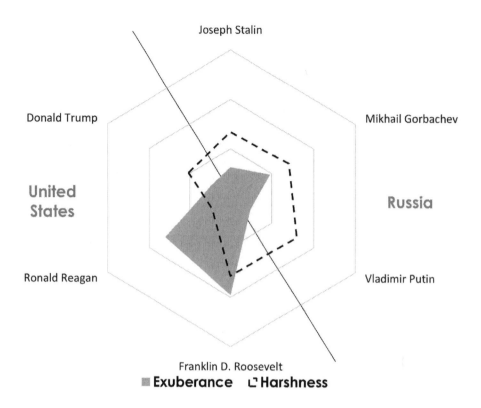

Joseph Stalin

Mikhail Gorbachev

Donald Trump

United
States

Russia

Ronald Reagan

Vladimir Putin

Franklin D. Roosevelt

▇ Exuberance   ⌐ Harshness

**RUSSIAN AND AMERICAN
LEADERS**

Putin and Trump are two peas in a
pod when it comes to not exhibiting
exuberance. Otherwise, Putin
joins his Russian counterparts in
being harsh and dour. Not even
the reform-minded Gorbachev
is exempt from the pattern,
which diverges from this mostly
sunny American leadership
(Trump aside).

The Cold War Adversaries: The United States and Russia

While the U.S. won the Cold War, which resulted in the fall of the Iron
Curtain in 1989 and the dissolution of the old Soviet Union in 1991, it could
be argued that Russia is winning the post Cold War era. "Rich nation, strong
army" is a Japanese saying. In Russia, Vladimir Putin insists on maintaining a
strong army despite not having a rich nation, and has repeatedly dared to use
it. Most recently, that has meant seizing the Crimea and Donbass regions of
Ukraine and deploying forces to help Syria's Bashar al-Assad hold onto power.

There is an argument to be made that when Barack Obama balked at
striking Syria, even after threatening to do so, he was simply exemplifying the
U.S.'s weakening position as upholder of the international security system in
place since World War Two. Putin, for one, is only too happy to reinforce this
notion. Were it not for Donald Trump's lack of exuberance, these two countries' leaders would seemingly have little to nothing in common, emotionally
speaking.

Franklin D. Roosevelt

Donald Trump

Economically the U.S. appears strong and apparently still possesses a fully functioning democracy, despite the partisan sniping. Russia is an entirely different story. Putin's brand of ultranationalist, illiberal "democracy" has become a role model for other leaders like Hungary's Victor Orban and Italy's Matteo Salvini. Even here in America, we have pundits like Matt Drudge calling Putin "the leader of the free world," while praising his strongman style versus so-called Western decadence.[15] The Kremlin refers to Putin's style of leadership as "managed democracy." Others have been more direct. A scholar in Moscow calls Russia's current form of governing "demophilia," i.e., the (induced) death of democracy.[16] Former Russian world chess champion turned political activist Garry Kasparov has an opinion, too. He calls Putin's form of governance a "nonideological kleptocracy."

AMERICA: PAST AND PRESENT LEADERS

FDR brought America to the brink of victory against anti-democratic forces in Japan and Germany, dying less than five months before World War Two ended. Trump became president in 2016, at a time when faith in Congress and the Supreme Court has fallen to historic lows, and one in six Americans believe military rule would be okay.[14]

Joseph Stalin   **Vladimir Putin**

RUSSIA: PAST AND PRESENT LEADERS

Stalin led Russia from 1922 to 1953 as the general secretary of the Soviet Union's communist party and as the country's premier. Due to executions and famines, among other means, the estimate of Stalin's internal victims reaches millions of people. Putin has essentially ruled Russia since 2000, both as its president and prime minister.

As becomes evident from the emotional results, Putin and his idol, Joseph Stalin, are basically aligned. So are the Russian people on the question of Stalin's legacy. Survey results indicate that 38% of Russians consider Stalin to be the "most outstanding person" in world history,[17] despite his being responsible for the deaths of perhaps as many as 20 million Soviet citizens or more.

In the U.S. and Russia chart, the reformer Mikhail Gorbachev represents a weak feint toward a more democratically inclined outcome. A little less harshness and a little more exuberance, and Gorbachev could almost be mistaken for a Free country leader. Not so with Putin. He disrespects and distrusts others. In this study, only China's Xi Jinping and Italy's Silvio Berlusconi show more contempt than Putin does. When not exhibiting anger and disgust, Putin is smirking instead. Gays, Muslims, and atheists are frequent targets of his ire.

The consensus, however, is that it's the prospect of democracy and a related fear of losing power that actually concerns Putin the most. "Politically, the Kremlin wants to insist that any political regime, even if it is catastrophically ineffective, can never be deposed by its own citizens," notes one critic. Even an aide to Putin has acknowledged, "We have no other tradition but to hold out until the end and leave feet first."[18]

Putin has reportedly watched the video of Libya's former leader Muammar Gaddafi meeting his death over and over, horrified that it could portend his own fate. From the Arab Spring to events closer to home like the Rose Revolution in Georgia, the Orange Revolution in Ukraine, the Tulip Revolution in Kyrgyzstan, and protests against President Nicolás Maduro of Venezuela, there's one constant theme in Putin's rhetoric: an aversion to popular uprisings. The world is familiar with the photographs that get released of Putin riding horseback, bare-chested. But Russia's focus on cyber-warfare that aids and abets ideological warfare against democracy and the West is where Putin really has muscle.

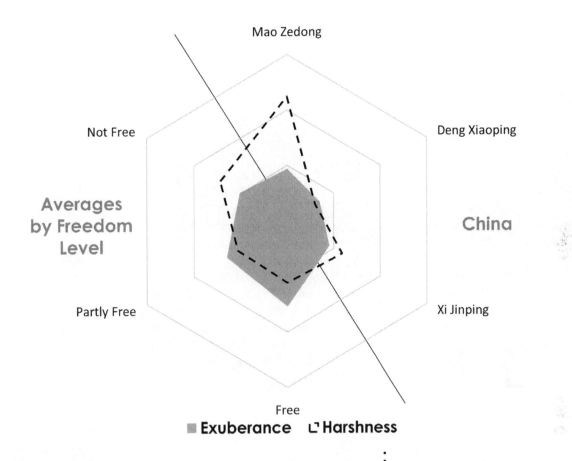

Averages by Freedom Level

China

Mao Zedong · Deng Xiaoping · Xi Jinping

Not Free · Partly Free · Free

■ **Exuberance**   ⌐ **Harshness**

China: A Force onto Itself

"I congratulate you, Xi Jinping, . . . for the openness that you have celebrated and advocated," said the International Monetary Fund chief Christine Lagarde at a conference in China. "The fact that Xi is prepared to give such strong authoritarian guidance within the context of a market economy is great for companies like mine," said Gerry Grimstone, a deputy chairman of Barclays bank. "I simply love Xi Jinping," added the Philippines' leader Rodrigo Duterte at that same event.[19] It's true what Bob Dylan sang: "money doesn't talk, it swears."

CHINESE LEADERS

If the 21st century does prove to be China's century, watch out. None of these three leaders shows exuberance, a tendency of Free and even Partly Free country leaders. While he isn't nearly as harsh as Mao, Xi makes Deng look gentle by comparison.

Mao Zedong   **Deng Xiaoping**   **Xi Jinping**

CHINA: PAST AND PRESENT LEADERS

Mao was the founding father of the People's Republic of China, which he ruled from its creation in 1949 until his death in 1976. Deng was the country's leader from 1978 to 1989, and was responsible for initiating market-economy reforms. Xi has been China's leader since 2012, with an emphasis on national aspirations under the slogan "Chinese Dream."[20]

China's latest leader, Xi, is definitely a force to be reckoned with. Of the previous two major Chinese leaders, Mao Zedong and Deng Xiaoping, Xi is emotionally closer to the former. Yes, the founder of communist China was harsher than Xi is, but neither man could be described as exuberant. The same is true of the less harsh Deng, who hesitated to call for the military to crack down on dissenters in Tiananmen Square (but ultimately sanctioned that move).

Mao inflicted upon his fellow citizens first the trauma of the Great Leap Forward and then the chaos of The Cultural Revolution. Turning private farms into communes led to the mass starvation of as many as 20 million people between 1959 and 1962. During the Cultural Revolution, Red Guard youths were encouraged to purge the "impure" influence of party leaders and intellectuals. Maybe as many as a million people died then, while countless others went to prison, were tortured, or suffered public humiliation.

While Deng believed China should "hide capabilities and bide time," in 2017 Xi declared: "The Chinese nation has gone from standing up, to becoming rich, to becoming strong."[21] If that doesn't sound a little bit like the Soviet Union's Nikita Khrushchev saying "We will bury you" in 1956—and with the means to make it happen in this case—then Western leaders are not paying sufficient attention.

Here are some highlights of Xi's drive to make China great again:[22]

- The "Made in China 2025" initiative to dominate ten vital, next-generation industries.

- The "One Belt, One Road" initiative to create a new Silk Road to Europe, involving vast infrastructure projects to enable a potentially hegemonic transcontinental trading network (that threatens to leave the U.S. on the economic sidelines of the world).

- The 16 + 1 initiative that links eleven Central and Eastern European Union members and another five non-E.U. members, plus China, to foster Chinese bank loans that flout E.U. transparency and accountability requirements.

- The founding of a New Development Bank involving Brazil, Russia, and India, headquartered in Shanghai.

- The militarization of dredged islands in the South China Sea, where runways, ports, hangars, and missiles have been installed, sitting astride some of the world's most commercially vital shipping lanes and air traffic routes.

China is not about "openness" or democracy, no matter what Lagarde would like to believe. Closer to the truth is that China's behavior bristles with Internet censorship, forced intellectual property transfers, state-led economic planning, tariffs, industrial espionage to steal innovations, and so much more. In short, Xi's China combines mercantile ruthlessness with authoritarianism. The prospects for democracy taking root in China someday look dim. In 2013, a Communist Party internal memo pointedly called Western constitutional democracy the kind of Trojan horse that could undermine the country.

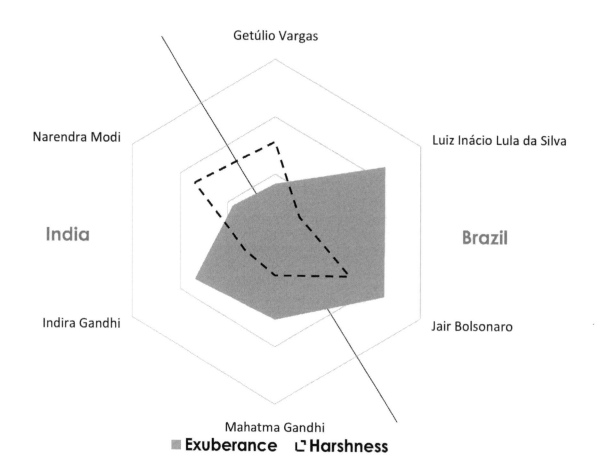

Getúlio Vargas

Luiz Inácio Lula da Silva

Narendra Modi

India

Brazil

Indira Gandhi

Jair Bolsonaro

Mahatma Gandhi

■ **Exuberance** ⌐ **Harshness**

BRAZILIAN AND INDIAN LEADERS

These two countries certainly started from different points, emotionally, in the modern era. Brazil's Vargas was stern, India's Gandhi more benevolent. Since then, the two countries have switched roles. Brazil's leaders have been more exuberant, leaving India to make its way less happily.

India and Brazil: Will They Ever Offset China?

With China ready to potentially dominate the world, the question becomes: what country, if any, can join the U.S. in creating a balance of power? An intriguing candidate is India, which has the demographic heft and looks to be moving headfirst into industrialization on a national scale. Still, it remains to be seen whether India has the drive and discipline necessary to succeed.

Mahatma Gandhi

Narendra Modi

While the country's original guiding force, Mahatma Gandhi, and later his daughter, Indira Gandhi, were in the moderate, essentially democratic vein, the harsher, less exuberant emotional results for Narendra Modi put him squarely in the authoritarian, force-the-initiative camp. In fact, it might well be time to start worrying about the spirit of Modi's ultra-nationalistic, anti-Muslim government. Could it be a harbinger of things to come that a newly issued textbook in India praises Adolf Hitler for giving Germany "dignity and prestige"?[23]

In contrast, no one would suggest that Brazil can really rival China in growth and power on its own, now or perhaps ever. Instead, what Brazil may have to worry about is becoming a version of the joke that used to circulate about Argentina being a country with a great future *behind* it. Brazil has plenty of promise, but likewise faces plenty of challenges.

Nobody outside of Latin America may remember Getúlio Vargas, who ruled in Brazil through much of the 1930s and 40s. For a while, though, he packed a punch. Installed by the military that later deposed him (after which he committed suicide), Vargas was the archetypal dictator of the earlier, populist strongman era. Vargas exhibited as much joy as Italy's Benito Mussolini (almost none) and as much anger, too (well above the average for foreign leaders, but not quite to Hitler's level). Vargas may be most famous for this straightforward description of his ruling style: "For my friends, anything—for my enemies, the law."[24]

INDIA: PAST AND PRESENT LEADERS

Gandhi led the Indian National Congress's efforts against British colonial rule by using nonviolent civil disobedience from 1921 until its independence in 1947, only to be assassinated less than half a year later. Modi has been the prime minister of India since 2014.

Getulio Vargas

Jair Bolsonaro

It's easy to stereotype leadership in Latin America. You start with a caudillo, strongman figure (preferably on horseback), or a populist standing on a balcony Evita Perón style. Next you add rebels battling, sometimes simultaneously, their country's armed forces and paramilitary death squads funded by wealthy landowners. Finally, there are repeated instances of U.S. intervention and some homegrown kleptocracy in action.

BRAZIL: PAST AND PRESENT LEADERS

Vargas ruled Brazil from 1937-1945, before being elected to resume office in 1951. Vargas then served until his suicide in 1954. Bolsonaro is a retired military officer who became Brazil's latest president at the start of 2019.

Therefore, it's encouraging to take note that since 1978, a third wave of democracy has swept the region. First, there was Simón Bolívar, the George Washington of Latin America, liberating the continent. Next, there was the second wave, after World War Two, a wave that disposed of leaders like Vargas. During the latest, third wave, Brazil has seen two elections with entirely different results: the country veering from its first truly working-class president, the union leader Luis Inácio "Lula" da Silva, to the "Trump of the Tropics," Jair Bolsonaro. Yet in their exuberance the two men are quite alike. It's Bolsonaro's greater harshness that marks the difference between them. Besides his various, seemingly offhand, misogynistic, racist, and homophobic remarks, never forget that Bolsonaro is a former army officer who believes: "The mistake of the [Brazilian] dictatorship was to torture without killing."[25]

That's a chilling comment, and all the more so given Latin America's colonial history. The initial era begins, after all, with Christopher Columbus arriving in the New World and writing in his log that the local Arawak "Indians" would "make fine servants . . .. With fifty men we could subjugate them all and make them do whatever we want."[26] During the decades to follow, up to 80% or more of the indigenous population would die at the hands of Conquistadors or by diseases introduced from Europe.

FOLLOW THE MONEY

Sharing the Pie, Then and Now

What's the start of modern world history? It's Columbus sailing West seeking to reach the Far East, too, just as the Portuguese inadvertently initiated the slave trade by going around Africa to reach the Far East themselves. This dual move can be understood only as a game of "follow the money." Every European explorer was trying to get to Asia because that's where the money was back in those days.

There are few studies more eye-opening than the one conducted by legendary economist Angus Maddison, who worked at the Organization for Economic Cooperation and Development (OECD). Using research data from 1500 onward, Maddison sought to map the share of the world's GDP held by the world's most dominant countries over the past 500 years.[1] Before the Western powers colonized them, the global economy was a two-horse race: China and India. As late as 1820, those two countries still accounted for over half of the world's GDP.

GDP HISTORICALLY BY COUNTRY

China's rising economic clout is, in historical terms, just a return to the status quo that prevailed before Western dominance reached its 20th century zenith. The big question is, can India do likewise by reasserting itself, too, economically speaking?

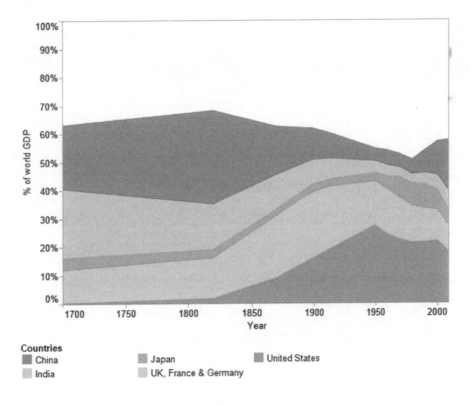

Countries
- China
- India
- Japan
- UK, France & Germany
- United States

Then everything went to hell. The U.K. initiated China's "century of humiliation" by launching the Opium Wars of 1839-1842 and 1856-1860. Eventually, China's share of the world's GDP would fall from 35% to a low of 7%. The outcome was no better for India. That country's share of the world's GDP went from 23% to under 4% soon after the British granted it independence in 1947.[2]

As the U.K.'s fortunes declined, so did America's rise, starting after the Civil War and continuing to this day. Other countries have also had their own heydays, though with relatively smaller pieces of the world's GDP pie. France was strong in 1700, the U.K. and Germany in 1900, Japan during the 1970's and beyond. But India's decline and potential renewal, America's emergence, and the re-emergence of China lately to a level nearer its old economic preeminence, are by far the most striking economic storylines of the twentieth century.

According to the International Monetary Fund (the IMF), the top ten economies in the world today are the U.S., China, Japan, Germany, the U.K., India, France, Italy, Brazil, and Canada. Three of these countries–France, Italy, and Canada–are forecasted to drop out of the top ten global economies by 2050.[3] In their place will be Indonesia, Russia, and Mexico. Meanwhile, of the seven countries likely to maintain a place in the top ten in the future, China, India, and Brazil (5th) are projected to be in the top five, along with the U.S. (3rd) and Indonesia (4th). Japan, Germany, and the U.K. will sink in the rankings to the eighth through tenth spots.

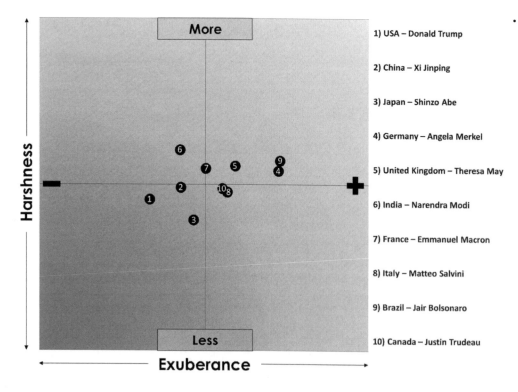

1) USA – Donald Trump

2) China – Xi Jinping

3) Japan – Shinzo Abe

4) Germany – Angela Merkel

5) United Kingdom – Theresa May

6) India – Narendra Modi

7) France – Emmanuel Macron

8) Italy – Matteo Salvini

9) Brazil – Jair Bolsonaro

10) Canada – Justin Trudeau

TOP TEN ECONOMIC POWERS TODAY

At present, these results look comfortable enough: over half of the world's top ten economies have leaders who land in the vicinity of the Free countries' average, after all. But soon the picture will be shifting in a potentially far less democratically-inclined direction.

The addition of Indonesia to these ranks keeps the emotional results of the leaders of the world's top economies from shifting to a less democratic, more authoritarian orientation. That's the good news. Now and well into the future, it seems that the U.S. could be joined by other top-tier economies whose leadership will not drift too far from exuberance or steer too close to harshness. The potential bad news would be the extent to which China's rise might economically sap, and politically undermine, other countries on the top ten list of major economic powers.

What happens when the playing field is more level, when big and small countries alike can compete as equals? Then innovation matters. The quality and nature of a country's leadership can make a tremendous difference in terms of whether a country's fortunes rise or fall. This next chart outlines the countries that are now deemed the most and least innovative.[4] Analysts in this field have concluded that the most innovative are the Netherlands, the U.K., Singapore, the U.S., Germany, Israel, and Japan. The least innovative are Egypt, Nigeria, Nicaragua, Pakistan, and Venezuela.

INNOVATORS: MOST VERSUS LEAST

The pattern is clear: the average for the leaders of the most innovative countries lands basically even with the average for Free countries' leaders. As for the least innovative countries, on average they have at the helm harsh leaders lacking exuberance.

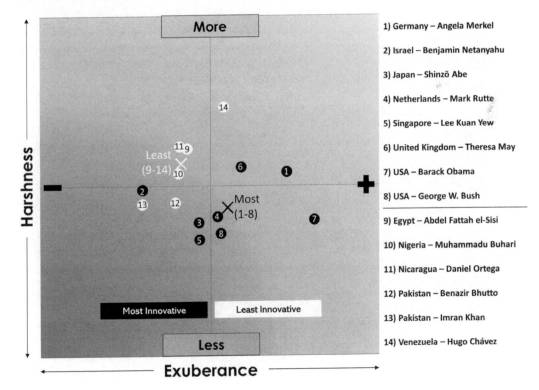

1) Germany – Angela Merkel

2) Israel – Benjamin Netanyahu

3) Japan – Shinzō Abe

4) Netherlands – Mark Rutte

5) Singapore – Lee Kuan Yew

6) United Kingdom – Theresa May

7) USA – Barack Obama

8) USA – George W. Bush

9) Egypt – Abdel Fattah el-Sisi

10) Nigeria – Muhammadu Buhari

11) Nicaragua – Daniel Ortega

12) Pakistan – Benazir Bhutto

13) Pakistan – Imran Khan

14) Venezuela – Hugo Chávez

Countries superior at innovation have, by quite a wide margin, more exuberant, less harsh leaders than countries that struggle to innovate by quite a wide margin. Where the best innovators land as a group matches up well with Free countries, whereas non-innovative countries have leaders strikingly similar, emotionally, to the average for the leaders of Not Free countries. For example, Barack Obama exemplifies exuberance, whereas Venezuela's Hugo Chávez is the epitome of an emotionally harsh leader. The latter led one of the top ten countries in the world, in terms of natural resources, to what has subsequently become the brink of economic and political collapse.

The Realities of Globalization

Notably absent from the list of the top innovators is China, but surely that will change as the country pursues its goal of moving up-market to create products that combine technology and design prowess. Then the outcome for the West is likely to be a double whammy, as China also continues to produce basic consumer goods. Like everything involving China, the scale of the unfolding change will be immense. International trade has become more and more important over the years. The sum of world exports and imports as a share of world GDP was less than 10% during the 1700's, and dominated by England and Portugal. By 1900, and the height of Western colonial rule of the world, the level had reached 30%. Today, after the fall of the Iron Curtain and China's shift to more of a market economy, the level is 60%.[5]

Globalization does not feature a level playing field. There have been winners and losers, as trade has accelerated and countries develop more specialized economies in order to earn a place in the global market.[6] China has been the primary beneficiary, but India has also come out okay.

As a result, the global income distribution for the Asia and Pacific region has improved to a notable degree, as the next two charts reveal. In 1975, that region was below the International Poverty Line level—but no longer. In contrast, Africa has hardly made progress at all. Finally, what's the story in Europe as well as North and South America? As the charts show, those regions continue to lead the world in income. But relative to the Asia and Pacific region, the West's progress is less robust and its lead now potentially open to being eclipsed in the decades to come.

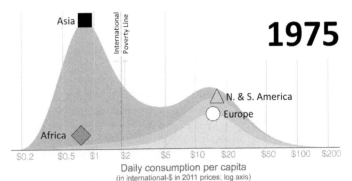

1975

Asia

International Poverty Line

N. & S. America

Europe

Africa

$0.2 $0.5 $1 $2 $5 $10 $20 $50 $100 $200

Daily consumption per capita
(in international-$ in 2011 prices; log axis)

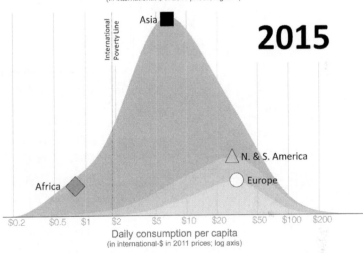

2015

Asia

International Poverty Line

N. & S. America

Europe

Africa

$0.2 $0.5 $1 $2 $5 $10 $20 $50 $100 $200

Daily consumption per capita
(in international-$ in 2011 prices; log axis)

All of this bears on what kind of leadership style might work best for the world's citizens. As Freedom House's latest world map reveals, the Asia and Pacific region consists of a mix of countries fully Free, Partly Free, and Not Free. Of these, China dominates ever since it became the world's "factory floor." That development has led to large job losses in other countries' manufacturing sectors (more than three million in the U.S., for instance, between 2001 and 2007 alone.)[7] Overall, the G-7's share of global GDP fell from over 50% in 1990 to a little above 30% by 2016.[8]

The other group of countries that have not really benefitted from globalization can be found in the developing world. These countries have not seen millions of people lifted out of poverty, as happened in China and, to a lesser extent, in India. These countries are clustered in two regions in particular. The first is Latin America, where places like Cuba, Nicaragua, and Venezuela have gone in reverse. The other is sub-Saharan Africa, which has, at best, been running in place economically as globalization expands its reach.

All in all, globalization is proving to be a mixed blessing for Free countries. In western Europe, America, Canada, and much of South America, globalization present as many economic challenges as opportunities. For many of the Partly Free countries like Mexico, Indonesia, and in eastern Europe, any economic gains are likewise tenuous. Meanwhile, in Africa, a continent characterized by mostly either Not Free or only Partly Free countries, recent initiatives by China and Russia don't bode well for democracy, either, in a region struggling to gain a stronger foothold in the world's economy.

WINNERS AND LOSERS OF GLOBALIZATION

To cope with globalization, to what kind of model should countries turn? G-7 countries are losing out, and with that trend perhaps the authority democracy has enjoyed due, in no small part, to these countries' previously thriving economies. On the other hand, while China's success suggests that authoritarianism might be best, other authoritarian countries like those in Africa are barely getting by.

Whether globalization will ultimately support or undermine democracy remains an open question. With authoritarian China having made such dramatic income gains, the key question then becomes: *might the ends justify the means?* In other words, might it not only be okay–but actually better–for leaders not to be more emotionally open, so that a country can advance more quickly in economic terms?

Economic Progress and Fairness

The argument that authoritarian rule provides superior economic results in comparison to democracy has certainly been made. Hungary's Viktor Orban, for example, has expressed that opinion, despite signs that only support from the E.U. has allowed him to claim progress since he reclaimed power in 2010.[9] Opponents of democracy like to stress three major points:[10]

1. Democracy began in Greece and remains a Western value. So it's solipsistic of Western democratic capitalist countries to assume their values should be universal values.

2. The West is riddled with hypocrisy. It advocates democracy *within* countries but does little to practice democracy *between* countries. For instance, the U.S. holds veto power when it comes to decision-making within the International Monetary Fund (the IMF).

3. Until a country is fully developed, democracy is of secondary concern and perhaps even a "luxury". Europe was autocratic, not democratic, when it grew enough in power to take over much of the world.

Most of all, Orban and fellow-thinkers rely on the ultra-pragmatic argument that democracy often gets in the way of protecting and promoting citizens' standard of living. So, who governs best? To answer that question, let's return to the Free, Partly Free and Not Free classifications introduced earlier, in order to determine whether emotionally positive leaders, democracy, and a better standard of living tend to go together. Put another way, are democracy and a better life mutually reinforcing outcomes or at odds with one another?

To arrive at an answer, this study uses two measures. First, did the average life expectancy increase for a country's citizens while a particular leader was in power? And second, did the country's GDP increase during that same time span?

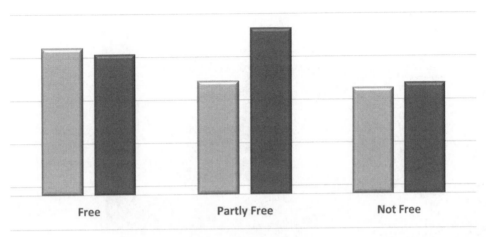

Growth compared to global average during reign

Free   Partly Free   Not Free

◼ GDP   ◼ Life Expectancy

The results show a clear pattern: Free countries outperform Not Free countries across both measures. The gains for life expectancy in Partly Free countries are impressive. But on an economic basis alone, the Partly Free countries fall short of what Free countries accomplish.

In addition, the results for the leaders of Partly Free and Not Free countries would look much worse if corruption were taken into account. This is the case because the two leaders who aided their countries the most in terms of improvements in the standard of living—Indonesia's Suharto and Russia's Vladimir Putin—also appear on lists of leaders who have embezzled the most.[11] In Suharto's case, it's estimated that over his 31 years in power he acquired for himself between $15-35 billion. As for Putin, in 2007 a Kremlin advisor estimated his personal worth at $40 billion, not bad for somebody not born rich and with an annual salary of only a little over $100,000.

Two other leaders of Not Free countries, North Korea's Kim Jong-un and the Congo's Mobutu Sese Seko, also routinely show up on lists of the world's most self-enriching leaders. The saying "power corrupts and absolute power corrupts absolutely" did not come about by chance. By contrast, Singapore's long-time leader, Lee Kuan Yew, by all accounts lived a modest, frugal life. Yes, his salary was a good one. But a measure of Lee's incorruptibility is that now, after his death, none of his heirs have made it onto *Forbes*' list of the 50 wealthiest people in that country.

DEMOCRACY AND STANDARD OF LIVING

Leaders of authoritarian countries may be better able to fudge or hide the outcome for a while. But in the end, the truth is that a lack of freedom for citizens doesn't help a country's leader give them a better life than is found in freer, more democratic societies.

Lee Kuan Yew   **Suharto**

LEE, SUHARTO, AND CORRUPTION: CONTRASTING FIGURES

Lee was Singapore's founding father, leading it from 1959 to 1990, taking the country from the third world to the first world in a single generation under his leadership.[12] Suharto was an Indonesian army general who acquired power in 1967 and served as the country's ruler until resigning from office in 1998.

It's also possible to inquire whether there is a correlation to the likelihood of leaders and their countries being corrupt. The analysis relies on the Corruption Perception Index's annual report on countries' corruptions level.[13] The most recent CPI annual report finds that the most corrupt countries are Venezuela, Libya, Iraq, Syria, and North Korea. In contrast, those countries deemed "spotless," not suffering from corruption, are Singapore, the Netherlands, Canada, and Germany. An emotionally-based comparison of corrupt versus spotlessly led countries derives results similar to those of leaders whose countries suffer the most and least from wealth inequality.

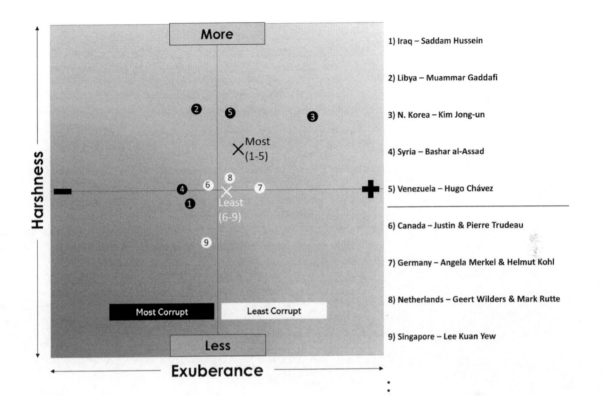

1) Iraq – Saddam Hussein

2) Libya – Muammar Gaddafi

3) N. Korea – Kim Jong-un

4) Syria – Bashar al-Assad

5) Venezuela – Hugo Chávez

_____

6) Canada – Justin & Pierre Trudeau

7) Germany – Angela Merkel & Helmut Kohl

8) Netherlands – Geert Wilders & Mark Rutte

9) Singapore – Lee Kuan Yew

The three harshest results are for leaders of corrupt countries. The same is true for the three least-exuberant results. The pattern appears to be pretty clear: emotionally open leaders tend to be less corrupt. Supporting that conclusion are the two averages added to the chart. They are based on the emotional results of leaders whose countries have a large or small wealth gap.[14] In that case, exuberance does not provide any real distinction, but harshness does. It seems that harsh leaders, corrupt leaders, and leaders of countries not inclined to be fair tend to cluster together.

Surely, with democracy under siege, it's now more important than ever to ensure that voters judge a politician's behavioral tendencies. These results suggest that the odds favor an emotionally harsh leader with few scruples imposing a bad-news style of governance. Corruption festers, increasing rather than assuaging the lack of economic equality and fairness plaguing that leader's country.

CORRUPTION AND INEQUALITY

The surest emotional sign of a leader of a corrupt country is elevated harshness. That result tracks closely to the results for leaders of countries notable for their lack of evenly distributed economic gains. In short, if you want a thief in charge, choose a harsh leader.

TRUST AS THE FINAL KEY FACTOR

Over the course of Part 3, three decisive top ten lists have been introduced: the countries with the strongest militaries, the largest populations, and the greatest economies. The first two charts that follow include every country that appears in at least one of those three lists. Rankings outside the top ten are shown in parentheses, and the overall rank shows each country's score based on its average rank in each of the three lists (the lower the score, the more powerful and important the country). The top ten countries and the seven next most important based on overall rank are designated, too. Among the top ten global players, the U.S. and Brazil represent the Western Hemisphere; China, India, Japan, and Indonesia represent Asia; and Russia, Germany, France, and the U.K. represent Europe.

Country	Military Rank	Population Rank	Economic Rank	Overall Rank (Average)	Freedom Status
U.S.	1	3	1	1st (1.7)	Free
China	3	1	2	2nd (2.0)	Not Free
India	4	2	6	3rd (4.0)	Partly Free
Japan	8	10	3	4th (7.0)	Free
Russia	2	9	(12)	5th (7.7)	Not Free
Brazil	(13)	6	9	6th (9.3)	Free
Germany	10	(17)	4	7th (10.3)	Free
France	5	(21)	7	T-8th (11.0)	Free
U.K.	6	(22)	5	T-8th (11.0)	Free
Indonesia	(15)	4	(16)	10th (11.7)	Partly Free

THE WORLD TODAY: TOP TEN POWERHOUSES

With control of one-seventh of the world's land mass, and its natural resources, Russia can never be counted out. Nevertheless, the potential vulnerability of both China and Russia is that they are the outliers in this list, the two countries entirely Not Free.

Country	Military Rank	Population Rank	Economic Rank	Overall Rank (Average)	Freedom Status
Italy	(11)	(23)	8	14.0	Free
Turkey	9	(19)	(17)	15.0	Not Free
South Korea	7	(27)	(11)	15.7	Free
Pakistan	(17)	5	(41)	21.0	Partly Free
Canada	(20)	(38)	10	22.7	Free
Nigeria	(44)	7	(31)	27.3	Partly Free
Bangladesh	(45)	8	(43)	32.0	Partly Free

Of these top ten countries, half a dozen are Free. India and Indonesia, the two Partly Free countries, provide the next most natural allies for the U.S. Where these ten countries line up emotionally might seem to be all the information required. But as discussed earlier, and in some ways exemplified by Donald Trump's election in 2016, there is a crisis raging within the Western liberal democratic order.

Nothing makes that crisis more obvious than a measure called the Edelman Trust Barometer. It gauges the degree to which citizens trust their respective governments.[1] In the U.S. and China, people have been moving in opposite directions on this question lately, with Americans losing faith in their government at the same time that the Chinese feel surging trust. The latest results put China, Indonesia, and India in a league of their own with scores in the 70%-plus range. Of the other top ten countries, the U.S., Brazil, France, Germany, the U.K., and Japan all have to settle for a high of 49% (the U.S.) to 39% (Japan). Then there's Russia at 29%.

SEVEN OTHER NOTABLE COUNTRIES

This is the other realm in which the battle between democracy and authoritarianism will be waged, and again won or lost. Paying attention to, and aligning with, these countries to foster freedom is also likely to be decisive in determining which direction the world goes.

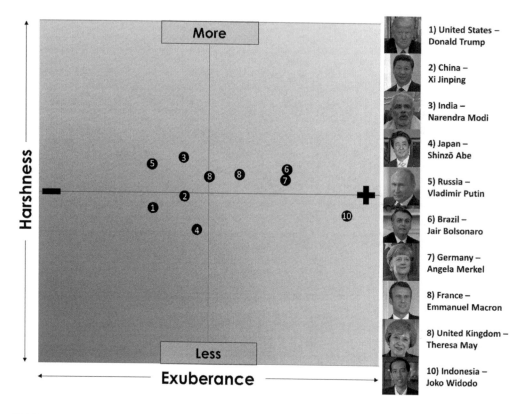

The chart shows a scatter plot with axes "Harshness" (vertical, labeled "More" at top, "Less" at bottom) and "Exuberance" (horizontal). Data points are numbered 1–10 with a legend:

1) United States – Donald Trump
2) China – Xi Jinping
3) India – Narendra Modi
4) Japan – Shinzō Abe
5) Russia – Vladimir Putin
6) Brazil – Jair Bolsonaro
7) Germany – Angela Merkel
8) France – Emmanuel Macron
8) United Kingdom – Theresa May
10) Indonesia – Joko Widodo

THE TOP TEN COUNTRIES, AS THEY BATTLE FOR THE TRUST OF THEIR OWN CITIZENS

The election of Trump has thrown the U.S. into the company, most closely, of Russia's Putin and China's Xi. With more exuberance, the outliers here are the leaders of America's European allies, plus Indonesia's leader.

How could China, with a populace living in a Not Free country and an emotionally unwelcoming leader, garner the top trust score of 79%? Surely much of the answer involves a sense among the people there that China is on the rise. But it's also true that China has no tradition of popular sovereignty. In the political sphere, the government of China has never had to share power with other key players like a church or the business community.[2]

While Indonesia and India, the world's third and fourth most populous democracies, respectively, deal with a surge of Islamic and Hindu influence in their politics,[3] they join China with high trust scores. The issue is that six of the democracies in the top ten overall list exhibit governance trust scores merely half that of China's. Can those countries find their footing again? As China's progress transforms the world, will the leaders of major democratic countries provide peace and prosperity or merely populist rhetoric that often fuels social divisiveness? The eventual answer will determine whether their citizens give none, one, two or ideally three cheers for democracy.

EPILOGUE

2020 Democratic Candidates

How Emotions Drive Leadership Style

Before I conclude by discussing the 2020 Democratic contenders for The White House, let me summarize what we've now learned from this book regarding the impact of emotions on leadership. Across parts 1, 2, and 3 of *Two Cheers for Democracy*, some emotions have emerged as more vital than others.

Joy and anger stand out the most. Regardless of whether the topic is presidential greatness, effectiveness in a debate, or bolstering democracy (as opposed to favoring authoritarian rule), those two emotions have a positive or negative influence in every case. Over the long haul, joy plays a beneficial role. It's only during debates that it seems out of place, and hurts a candidate's chances if shown. Within reason, displays of anger correlate with success in The White House. But anger typically harms a candidate on stage, and is indicative of authoritarian instincts rather than support for democracy.

Other emotions with the most impact consist of pleasure,satisfaction, fear, disgust, and sadness. Of these, pleasure and satisfaction are beneficial, and fear sometimes is. Disgust and sadness, however, have no upside. Disgust harms a president in office, and joins anger as indicative of a leader with authoritarian as opposed to democratic instincts. Sadness, in turn, harms most presidencies in addition to undermining a candidate's odds of getting to The White House in the first place, given its detrimental impact during presidential debates.

Three other emotions—acceptance, surprise, and contempt—are essentially non-players. For the field of political psychology, they are emotions unlikely to be of importance. Of course, no study, including the present study, can ever be absolute. But so long as context is kept in mind, along with recognition that every emotion can have a positive or negative impact on behavior in a given situation, then it's possible to make prudent use of the information provided here.

With their long, even ridiculously long campaign cycles, U.S. presidential races are especially prone to the influence of the one other emotion I haven't mentioned yet: skepticism. As wielded on stage to deflate an opponent's claims, skepticism appears to be a major weapon—and is, therefore, one that we will no doubt see a lot of in the near term. After all, for the Democratic candidates I'm about to discuss, there's a full year ahead (and more) of debates and stump speeches that will precede some candidate

	Greatness	Debates	Democracy
Joy	+	⊘	+
Pleasure	=	+	+
Satisfaction	+	+	=
Acceptance	=	=	=
Surprise	=	=	=
Skepticism		+	
Contempt	⊘	=	=
Disgust	⊘	=	⊘
Anger	+	⊘	⊘
Sadness	⊘	⊘	=
Fear	⊘	+	=

AN OVERVIEW SUMMARY OF EMOTIONAL RESULTS

These are the emotions that matter most, and least, and whether they lead to effective, constructive leadership styles. Pleasure and satisfaction are the most helpful. Joy comes in third for most helpful. Meanwhile, skepticism deserves a shout-out because it's so helpful during debates. In contrast, disgust and sadness—Trump's emotional specialties—are the most harmful.

securing the party's nomination, only to then turn her or his efforts to the general election campaign to follow.

Emotional Affinities

Two Cheers for Democracy has been a journey involving biography, psychology, history, foreign affairs, and the communication skills exhibited on debate stages. As I wrap up this book, the 2020 presidential campaign is already well underway. For the numerous Democratic candidates hoping to be their party's nominee and challenge Donald Trump in the general election, there are obviously lots of factors that will help winnow the field. Among them will be the amount and the nature of the media coverage they receive, their fund-raising prowess, policy positions, and abilities to pull together a strong field operation.

Not to be lost in the mix, however, is fundamentally the candidates' own appeal—which starts with their personalities and the emotions they characteristically shown on the campaign trail. In gender and racial terms, it's an historically diverse group of Democratic candidates seeking the White House. But emotionally, how diverse is this group of candidates and how do they match up with Trump?

To find out, let's run the numbers using all three emotional formulas: presidential greatness, debate success, and a democratic versus authoritarian orientation based on exuberance and harshness. For greatness, all of the U.S. presidents covered in Part 1 become the comparative benchmark in analyzing the Democratic candidates. For the debates, every candidate who took the stage and was covered in Part 2 of this book is now a reference point. For democratic instincts, every

2020 Democratic Candidate	Top Two Distinct Emotions	Most Similar U.S. President(s)
Joe Biden	Pleasure Joy	William Howard Taft, John F. Kennedy
Cory Booker	Surprise Disgust	George Washington
Pete Buttigieg	Satisfaction Disgust	Bill Clinton
Julian Castro	Joy Pleasure	William Howard Taft, John F. Kennedy
Kirsten Gillibrand	Disgust Pleasure	Millard Fillmore (Contempt / Acceptance)
Kamala Harris	Joy Sadness	James Garfield
Amy Klobuchar	Sadness Satisfaction	Abraham Lincoln
Beto O'Rourke	Satisfaction Disgust	Martin Van Buren
Bernie Sanders	Sadness Fear	John Quincy Adams
Elizabeth Warren	Surprise Sadness	Harry S. Truman, Lyndon B. Johnson (Surprise / Acceptance)

FORMER U.S. PRESIDENTS AND CURRENT DEMOCRATIC CONTENDERS: WHO MATCHES UP BEST?

Klobuchar and Booker hits home runs here, while Gillibrand comes the closest to striking out. Instances where a full emotional match-up wasn't available are indicated in parentheses, kind of like the way that realtors work in terms of "comparable" homes in deciding the appropriate asking price for a new listing.

foreign leader covered in Part 3 since 1972 serves, in turn, as a means of populating that additional benchmark.

A top ten list of Democratic candidates is used here, basing that selection on an average of three recent rankings of the candidates' relative strengths.[1] By way of introducing these ten leaders, let's first look at which two emotions they distinctly show most often relative to past presidents. In alphabetical order, the candidates and their comparative results are intriguing.

As you can see, in the sweepstakes of which past U.S. president(s) each of these Democratic candidates emotionally emulates the most, Amy Klobuchar takes the cake. She matches most readily Abraham Lincoln, the president ranked #1 for greatness by presidential historians. Cory Booker is right behind Klobuchar by virtue of matching up well with George Washington, ranked #2 for greatness. Next up might be Elizabeth Warren by this measure, though Harry S. Truman (#6) and Lyndon B. Johnson (#8) are only partial matches based on surprise plus using in this case a tepid form of happiness, namely acceptance, as the feeling that comes the closest to matching the sadness Warren actually shows.

Who comes out the worst here? That might be Kirsten Gillibrand, as Millard Fillmore is a weak comparison twice over. First, Fillmore is the only even close comparison to Gilli-

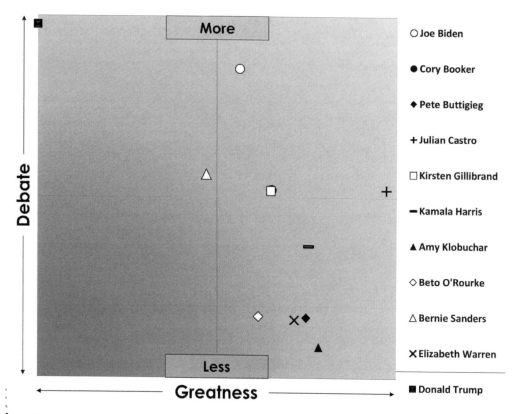

More

Less

Debate

Greatness

○ Joe Biden

● Cory Booker

◆ Pete Buttigieg

+ Julian Castro

□ Kirsten Gillibrand

– Kamala Harris

▲ Amy Klobuchar

◇ Beto O'Rourke

△ Bernie Sanders

✗ Elizabeth Warren

■ Donald Trump

GREATNESS AND DEBATE PROWESS: WHICH DEMOCRATIC CONTENDERS LOOK THE MOST PROMISING?

Castro is aided by his radiant smile. Otherwise, the irony is that two of the likely front-runners, Biden and Sanders, come out looking the most like Trump.

brand's emotional profile. Second, Fillmore is ranked #38 in terms of presidential greatness. Even so, if Gillibrand might somehow come in equal to Fillmore in terms of presidential greatness, that result would still put her ahead of Trump, who to date is ranked #44—as in, dead last—by presidential scholars.

Working the Odds

When the emotional results that best correlate to presidential greatness as well as handling presidential debates are considered, what do we find? Which Democratic 2020 candidates emerge as most likely to do well, and might the strongest of them look more promising than our current president? The answer is that three, maybe four of the contenders do best.

By virtue of basically avoiding sadness (given his radiant happiness), Julia Castro does well regarding greatness. That makes sense because a president feeling lots of sadness is the worst drag anchor on achieving greatness in office. A distant second regarding greatness potential is Klobuchar, followed closely by Kamala Harris and Pete Buttigieg. Bernie Sanders does the worst. Turning to who is likely to be well received

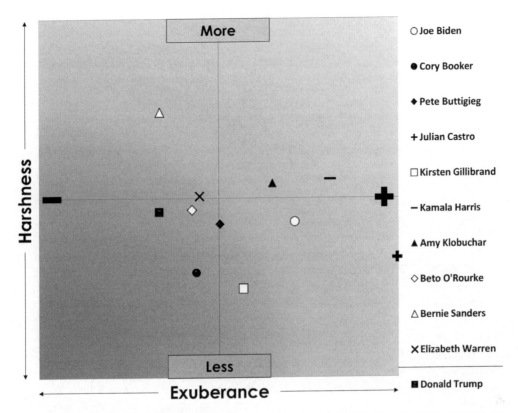

EXUBERANCE AND HARSHNESS: HOW DO THE DEMOCRATIC CONTENDERS STACK UP?

Castro and Harris qualify as super-exuberant, but diverge in terms of Harris being harsher. The single most striking result here, however, is the degree of which Trump and Sanders stand out as de facto soul mates: the former utterly lacking in exuberance, and the latter hands-down the harshest leader of the bunch.

by voters observing a candidate's emotions during a debate, Joe Biden stands far above any other Democratic candidate considered here, with Sanders his distant but nearest rival by this measure. In contrast, Klobuchar isn't likely to be perceived favorably by watching voters. If both factors—greatness potential and likely debate response—are combined, then Castro and Biden come out ahead, but neither provides the complete package. That said, Trump is in far worse shape given his inability to add greatness to a strong debate result.

If the candidates stay true to form, what distinct, signature emotion will voters be likely to see from each of them during debates? Here, the point of reference is only these ten candidates compared to one another, and not to the wider comparison set of previous presidents. Expect Castro to own joy and pleasure, and Beto O'Rourke the milder levels of happiness. Booker is the king of surprise. Turning to the "negative" scorning emotions, Gillibrand is the queen of contempt, and Klobuchar shows a little more disgust than even Harris or Warren. That leaves sadness, fear, and anger. Biden and O'Rourke retreat to sadness, and fear is a problem for Biden and Booker. Should voters be looking for the one consistent, prevalent emotion where a candidates towers above the rest, then hands-down that would be the anger shown by Sanders. No other Democratic candidate shows even two-thirds as much anger as Sanders does. Anger verging on rage is definitely his specialty.

Finally, there is one other formula to consider: the degree of a candidate's exuberance and harshness as a measure of their likelihood to adhere to democratic norms versus exhibiting a more authoritarian bent.

Not surprisingly, Trump veers far from the average results for the leaders of countries Freedom House classifies as Free. His results are more in keeping with the leaders of Not Free countries. In that regard, Trump has one clear kindred spirit among the Democratic contenders: Sanders. While Trump is the second least exuberant, Sanders isn't only the least exuberant leader here, he's also by far the harshest possible entry in the 2020 race. By comparison, Castro, Harris, Biden, and Klobuchar all adhere to—or even pleasantly exceed—the average results for the leaders of Free countries.

Greatness in the White House clearly matters. Domestically, the cost of healthcare and housing weighs people down. The opioid crisis continues unabated. Automation is transforming the workplace and society at large to perhaps a greater extent than any time since the industrialization of America in the late 19th century. A long list of challenges can easily be assembled. Meanwhile, overseas the challenges are no less severe. Never in history has a power like China emerged without a war over what the new status quo will look like. Cyber-warfare poses its own unique problems. Next, add in global warming and suddenly it's not just living standards but living itself that might be at risk sooner than later. To promote prosperity and peace in the midst of all of this change will test whoever occupies the White House. In that context, a candidate's emotional skills during a debate qualify as something more like just the entry ticket to the White House by comparison.

Along with greatness, consider the importance of America maintaining democratic ideals. I for one would argue that those ideals certainly matter, and that in Trump we have had a president who exacerbates, rather than heals, the partisan tensions within the country. More tribalism isn't what America needs right now. Fifty years ago, 5% of Americans said they would be displeased if a child of theirs married somebody from the other party; today 49% of Republicans and 33% of Democrats take that position. Moreover, 49% of Republicans and 55% of Democrats admit the other party leaves them ill-at-ease.[2] Given that one party is largely white and Christian (the Republicans) and the other more racially diverse and secular (the Democrats), mutual tolerance is at extreme risk these days.

When it comes to embracing all Americans, the emotional results are clear. Sanders and Trump alike fit the notion that leaders who are harsh or lacking in exuberance are less likely to cherish what we think of as democratic ideals and behavioral norms. Harsh (angry, disgusted) leaders by their very nature are prone to being confrontational, attacking and delegitimizing opponents. In turn, those lacking the intense happiness that denotes exuberance won't be inclined to embrace new ideas and alternative modes of a society making progress. Exclusivity rather than inclusivity reigns instead.

In a society that leaves the middle of the political and emotional spectrum too often empty, the one thing both sides can agree on often becomes media censorship. That's because new ideas and information threaten a mindset that is already rigidly set. In this book, I've taken exactly the opposite tact. I've asked you, as readers, to look at the concept of leadership in a totally original, open-minded manner, delving into the hearts of presidents and prime ministers through emotional results provided by applying the scientific methodology of facial coding. There are never any guarantees in life, but whenever a president supersedes Trump (whether that happens in 2020 or 2024), odds are that America will urgently need as emotionally intelligent a leader as it can possibly muster.

FACIAL CODING EXPLAINED

The face is where humans best reflect and communicate their emotions. While the correlation of expressions-to-emotions isn't, of course, beyond doubt, in an imperfect world facial coding offers a viable means to readily assess the feelings of others. Supporting explanations and credentials follow.

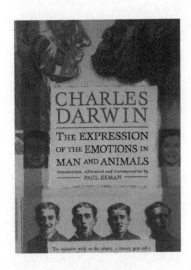

Darwin's Realizations:

The facial coding tool originated with Charles Darwin, who first noted in his travels on The Beagle that facial expressions may have been evolved behaviors meant to express emotion.

1. **Universal:** Even a person born blind has the same expressions. These signals are "hard-wired" into the brain.

2. **Spontaneous:** The face is the only place in the body where muscles either attach to a bone and tissue or tissue only, enabling quicker, real-time reflexes shaped by pulses from the brain. (Other muscles in the body connect to two bones.)

3. **Abundant:** People have more facial muscles than any other species.

Ekman's Refinement:

- Along with colleague Wally Freisen, Dr. Paul Ekman codified the Facial Action Coding System (FACS) from 1965-1978, with refinements added in 2002.

- FACS is based on over 40 facial muscles and 23 movements that correspond to seven core emotions.

- Ekman was named one of *Time* magazine's 100 Most Influential People in 2009, and is ranked as the 16th Most Influential Psychologist of the 21st Century by Scientific Psychology.

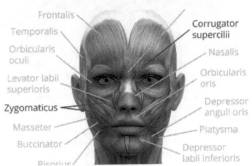

Frontalis

Temporalis

Orbicularis oculi

Levator labii superioris

Zygomaticus

Masseter

Buccinator

Risorius

Corrugator supercilii

Nasalis

Orbicularis oris

Depressor anguli oris

Platysma

Depressor labii inferioris

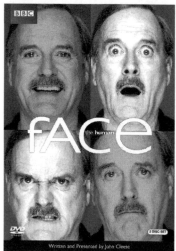

"Darwin was more than just a close and careful observer, he was an explainer. For each and every expression, Darwin asks and answers the question of why a particular movement occurs with a particular emotion."
—Paul Ekman on Charles Darwin

THE 50 MOST INFLUENTIAL PSYCHOLOGISTS IN THE WORLD

 THE BEST SCHOOLS

16. Paul Ekman | Social Psychology, Biological Psychology

Facial Coding in the Mainstream

"The face is an enormously rich source of information about emotions."
—Malcolm Gladwell, *Blink*

"We make snap judgments about personality from people's faces and other tells in fractions of a second, usually showing remarkable consensus in judgment."
—Matthew Hertenstein, *The Tell*

"By the 1980s, psychologists had largely accepted as a 'fundamental axiom of behavioral science' the link between faces and emotions. Emotion therefore explains facial behavior, and facial behavior is an objective index of emotion."
—Russell & Fernandez-Dols, *The Psychology of Facial Expressions*

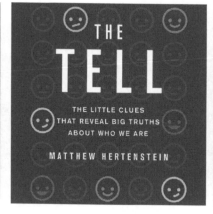

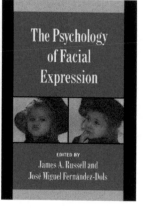

The New York Times

Soon, Your Car May Be Able to Read Your Expressions

By JOHN R. QUAIN   APRIL 6, 2017

Facial Coding Goes Mainstream

From Silicon Valley to China, the automation of facial coding is well under way. Especially as linked to AI (artificial intelligence), the many uses of facial coding are likely to explode in the years ahead – with its application to motor vehicles but one of many ways that facial coding will enter people's lives. It's no wonder *The Economist* has referred to an emerging "facial-industrial complex" that will transform both the business world and society at large.

The Science of Facial Coding

"In a survey of 246 quantitative research experts on emotion, 88% agree that there are universal emotions, and 80% agreed that there are universal facial signals for emotions."
- Dr. Paul Ekman

PERSPECTIVES
on
Psychological
Science

(Vol. 1, 2016)

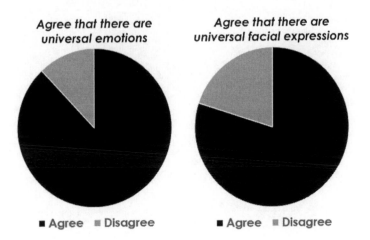

Agree that there are universal emotions

Agree that there are universal facial expressions

■ Agree ■ Disagree   ■ Agree ■ Disagree

There are 23 expressions that correspond to seven emotions:

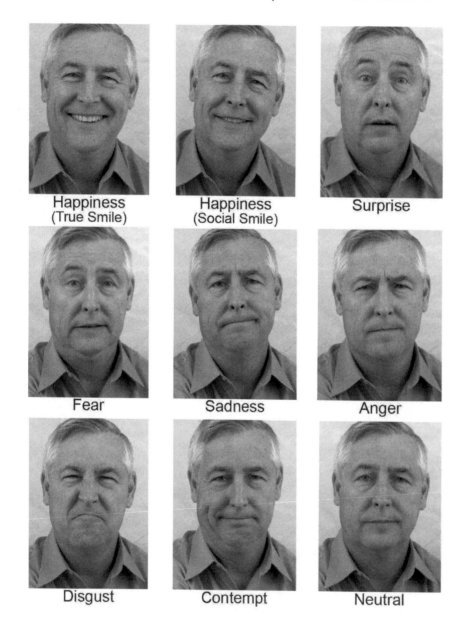

Happiness
(True Smile)

Happiness
(Social Smile)

Surprise

Fear

Sadness

Anger

Disgust

Contempt

Neutral

Two Decades of Facial Coding in Business

Dan Hill's company, Sensory Logic, has received seven U.S. patents related to facial coding including:

- Method and Report Assessing Consumer Reaction to a Stimulus by Matching Eye Position with Facial Coding

- Method of Assessing People's Self-Presentation and Actions to Evaluate Personality Type, Behavioral Tendencies, Credibility, Motivations and Other Insights Through Facial Muscle Activity and Expressions

peg

Facial Action Coding System Final Test

Dan Hill

Your scores on the FACS Final Test show you have

PASSED

this test of skill in scoring facial actions.

From the authors of FACS

Paul Ekman, Wallace V. Friesen, Joseph C. Hager

SOURCES & NOTES

Preface

1. Brandon Rottinghaus and Justin S. Vaughn, "How Does Trump Stack Up Against the Best—and Worst—Presidents?" *The New York Times*, February 19, 2018. A year into his presidency, 170 members of the American Political Science Association completed their latest survey, ranking U.S. presidents on greatness.

2. Justin Wolfers, "An A- for the U.S. Economy, but Failing Grades for Trump's Policies," *The New York Times*, February 4, 2019.

3. Tal Axelrod, "Pence Met with Silence after Mentioning Trump in Munich Speech," *The Hill*, February 16, 2019.

4. David Leonhardt, "The Real State of the Union, in Charts," *The New York Times*, February 5, 2019.

5. Thomas L. Friedman, "When the Cat's Away," *The New York Times*, February 27, 2018.

6. Gamaliel Perruci, "The Study of 'Great' Leaders in Latin America," McDonough Center for Leadership and Business (Marietta College, Ohio).

7. Meltem Ucal, "The Personality and Leadership Style of Recep Tayyip Erdogan: Implications for Turkish Foreign Policy," Research Gate, September 2011.

8. The Facial Action Coding System (FACS) was originated by Paul Ekman and his colleague Wally Freisen. Ekman is regarded as one of the top psychologists working in the world today, and approximately 80% of the academic experts in the specialty of analyzing emotions quantitatively endorse the validity of FACS. The methodology involves 23 different facial muscle movements that correspond to one or more of the seven core emotions of happiness, surprise, anger, fear, sadness, disgust, and contempt. In this study, I utilized photographs available online as well as at times paintings or an occasional sculpture. More information about FACS is available online and in an appendix to this book, as well as from my previous book, *Famous Faces Decoded: A Guidebook for Reading Others*.

9. Robert Plutchik, "Plutchik's Wheel of Emotions," available at https://www.6seconds.org/2017/04/27/plutchiks-model-of-emotions/.

10. The Minitab Blog, "Regression Analysis: How Do I Interrupt R-squared and Assess the Goodness-of-Fit?", May 30, 2013.

11. Michelle Goldberg, "Latvia Above Us, Croatia Below," *The New York Times*, February 4, 2019.

12. Michelle Goldberg, "Madeleine Albright Is Worried. We Should Be, Too," *The New York Times*, April 13, 2018.

13. David Brooks, "The Chaos After Trump," *The New York Times*, March 5, 2018.

Part 1—U.S. Presidents & Their Relative Greatness

Introduction

1. Steven J. Rubenzer and Thomas R. Faschinbauer, *Personality, Character, & Leadership in the White House: Psychologists Assess the Presidents* (Washington, D.C.: Potomac Books, 2004). Nearing publication, I learned about books by Dean Simonton that might also fit the bill.

2. Ezra Pound, *The Cantos of Ezra Pound* (New York: New Directions, 1996). In Canto LI, Pound writes: "Fifth element; mud; said Napoleon." Whether this was truly said by Napoleon or not (maybe during his retreat from Russia), I love the quote!

3. Steven J. Rubenzer, *Op. Cit.*

4. Some but not of all these factors were illuminated nicely in a book by Angus Trumble, *A Brief History of the Smile* (New York: Basic Books, 2004).

Emotions That Enable Greatness

Joy

1. Immelman, Aubrey, "The Political Personality of U.S. President Barack Obama." Paper presented at the 33rd Annual Scientific Meeting of the International Society of Political Psychology, San Francisco, July 7-10, 2010. Available at http://digitalcommons.csbsju.edu/psychology_pubs/25/; and David G. Winter, "Philosopher-King or Polarizing Politician: A Personality Profile of Barack Obama, *Political Psychology*, Vol. 32, No. 6, 2011.

2. Robert Holden, "Barack Obama—Leadership, Happiness and Success," available at https://www.robertholden.com/.

3. David von Drehle, "Honor and Effort: What President Obama Achieved in Eight Years," *Time*, December 22, 2016.

4. Patricia A. Halbert, *I Wish I Knew That: U.S. Presidents: Cool Stuff You Need to Know* (New York: Reader's Digest, 2012).

5. Michael Harvord, "William Howard Taft: Reluctant Leader," ed. Michael Beschloss, *Illustrated History of the Presidents* (New York: Crown, 2000), 328-335.

Satisfaction

1. Steven J. Rubenzer, *Op. Cit.*

2. David Rubel, *Scholastic Encyclopedia of the Presidents and Their Times* (New York: Scholastic, 2013).

3. Steven J. Rubenzer, *Op. Cit.*

4. Wilson Sullivan, "Martin Van Buren: The Red Fox," ed. Michael Beschloss, *Illustrated History of the Presidents* (New York: Crown Publishers, 2000), 114-123.

5. Patricia A. Halbert, *Op. Cit.*; and David Rubel, *Op. Cit.*

6. William A. DeGregorio, *The Complete Book of U.S. Presidents* (Fort Lee, NJ: Barricade Books, 2009).

7. Martin Kelly, "Top 10 Facts about Franklin Pierce," ThoughtCo., available at https://www.thoughtco.com/things-to-know-about-franklin-pierce-104642.

Anger

1. Library of Congress, "Thomas Jefferson," available at https://ww.loc.gov/exhibits/jefferson/jeffworld.html.

2. Lawrence W. Reed, "Grover Cleveland: A Study in Character by Alyn Brodsky," Foundation for Economic Education, available at https://fee.og/articles/grover-cleveland-a-study-in-character-by-alyn-brodsky/.

3. Steven J. Rubenzer, *Op. Cit.*

4. Lewis L. Gould, "Gerald Rudolph Ford: A Time for Healing," ed. Michael Beschloss, *Illustrated History of the Presidents* (New York: Crown, 2000), 454-463.

5. "Calvin Coolidge," History, available at https://www.history.com/us-presidents/calvin-coolidge.

6. The American Moms, "The Centennial President with the Icy Personality," available at http://theamericanmoms.com/centennial-president-icy-personality/.

Emotions That Impair Greatness

Sadness

1. Christine Jarrett, "Clinton's and Trump's Personality Profiles, According to Psychologists," *Research Digest*, available at https://digest.bps.org.uk/2016/11/08/clintons-and-trumps-personality-profiles-according-to-psychologists/.

2. Steven J. Rubenzer, *Op. Cit.*

3. Saul Braun, "Andrew Jackson: Old Hickory," ed. Michael Beschloss, *Illustrated History of the Presidents* (New York: Crown, 2000), 98-113.

4. Steven J. Rubenzer, *Op. Cit.*

5. Ann Bausum, *Our Country's Presidents* (Washington, D.C.: National Geographic Society, 2005).

6. Lewis L. Gould, "Richard Milhouse Nixon: The Road to Watergate," ed. Michael Beschloss, *Illustrated History of the Presidents* (New York: Crown, 2000), 442-453.

7. William A. DeGregorio, *Op. Cit.*

8. Lisa Belkin, "Be a Killer, Be a King: The Education of Donald Trump," Yahoo, July 16, 2016, available at https://www.yahoo.com/news/killer-king-education-donald-trump-000000711.html.

9. Jenna Johnson and Karen Tumulty, "Trump Cites Andrew Jackson as His Hero—And a Reflection of Himself," *The Washington Post*, March 15, 2017.

10. Bob Woodward, *Fear: Trump in the White House* (New York: Simon & Schuster, 2018).

Disgust

1. Wilson Sullivan, "Theodore Roosevelt: the Giant in the Bully Pulpit," ed. Michael Beschloss, *Illustrated History of the Presidents* (New York: Crown, 2000), 314-327.

2. David Rubel, *Op. Cit.*

3. David Jacobs, "Warren Gamaliel Harding: A Babbitt in the White House," ed. Michael Beschloss, *Illustrated History of the Presidents* (New York: Crown, 2000), 350-355.

4. Harding's shortcomings have been amply documented. Sources include: Ann Bausum, *Op. Cit.*; and Kenneth C. Davis, *Don't Know Much about the Presidents* (New York: HarperCollins, 2002).

5. David Jacobs, "Andrew Johnson: Between North and South," ed. Michael Beschloss, *Illustrated History of the Presidents* (New York: Crown, 2000), 208-219.

Contempt

1. Jesse Greenspan, "10 Things You Should Know about Millward Fillmore," *History*, March 7, 2014, available at https://www.history.com/news/10-things-you-should-know-about-millard-fillmore.

2. David Jacobs, "James Monroe: The Era of Good Feelings," ed. Michael Beschloss, *Illustrated History of the United States* (New York: Crown, 2000), 76-87.

3. William A. DeGregorio, *Op. Cit.*

Fear

1. Steven J. Rubenzer, *Op. Cit.*

2. *Ibid.*

3. "James K. Polk: "Facts, Presidency, & Accomplishments" is available at https://www.britannica.com/biography/James-K-Polk. A second, more interesting resource for understanding Polk is by Robert W. Johannsen, "Who Is James K. Polk? The Enigma of Our Eleventh President," a lecture presented on February 14, 1999 at the Hayes Museum.

4. William A. DeGregorio, *Op. Cit.*

Emotions That Qualify as Non-Factors

Surprise

1. Steven J. Rubenzer, *Op. Cit.*

2. *Ibid.*

3. *Ibid.*

4. Michael Harwood, "James Buchanan: An American Nero," ed. Michael Beschloss, *Illustrated History of the Presidents* (New York: Crown, 2000), 178-187.

Acceptance

1. Steven J. Rubenzer, *Op. Cit.*

2. Vince Guerrieri, "Nobody Understands How Great a President McKinley Was," *Politico*, September 14, 2015, available at https://www.politico.com/magazine/story/2015/09/william-mckinley-great-president-denali-213147.

3. Lewis L. Gould, "James Earl Carter: 'Not a Politician,'" ed. Michael Beschloss, *Illustrated History of the Presidents* (New York: Crown, 2000), 464-475.

4. Patricia A. Halbert, *Op. Cit.*

Pleasure

1. Steven J. Rubenzer, *Op. Cit.*

2. Christopher Klein, "10 Things You May Not Know about Herbert Hoover," *History*, October 20, 2014, available at https://www.history.com/news/10-things-you-may-not-know-about-herbert-hoover.

An Extra Twist

1. The ranking for the 10 First Ladies here comes from Jess Bolluyt, "Move Over, Melania Trump: These Are the Most Influential First Ladies in American History, April 27, 2018, available at https://www.cheatsheet.com/culture/most-influential-first-ladies-in-american-history.html/. Other sources that also go into the contributions of these women include: Martin Kelly, "The 10 Most Influential First Ladies," April 12, 2018, available at https://www.thought.co.com/top-most-influential-first-ladies-105458; Kate Anderson Brower, *First Women: The Grace and Power of America's Modern First Ladies* (New York: HarperCollins, 2016); and Amy Pastan, *First Ladies* (New York: DK, 2009).

2. Abigail Geiger, "Number of Women Leaders around the World Has Grown, but They're Still a Small Group," Pew Research Center, March 8, 2017, available at http://www.pewresearch.org/fact-tank/2017/03/08,women-leaders-around-the-world/.

Part 2—U.S. Presidential Debates, Emotionally X-Rayed

3. As background for the debates as well as particulars regarding particular debates, I'm grateful for a pair of books: Jim Lehrer, *Tension City: Inside the Presidential Debates* (New York: Random House, 2011) and Alan Schroeder, *Presidential Debates: Risky Business on the Campaign Trail* (Columbia UP, 2016). I also thank Alan for taking the time to meet and be interviewed by me at Harvard University in 2015.

4. Lydia Saad, "Presidential Debates Rarely Game-Changers (But Have Moved Voter Preferences in Several Elections), Gallup, September 25, 2008, available at http://www.gallup.com/poll/11067/presidential-debates-rarely-gamechangers.aspx).

5. Valerie Strauss, "Many Americans Know Nothing about Their Government. Here's a Bold Way Schools Can Fix That," September 27, 2016, *The Washington Post*; Arthur Levine, "When It Comes to Knowledge of American History, We are a Nation at Risk," *The Hill*, October 17, 2018; David Fouse, "A Republic, If You Can Keep It: The Education Every Student Really Needs," *National Review*, March 21, 2017; and VOA News, "Poll: Americans' Knowledge of Government, History in 'Crisis,' January 19, 2016;

6. Adam Gabbatt, "A Tall Tale? Accuracy of Trump's Medical Report—and New Height—Questioned," *The Guardian*, March 30, 2019.

7. Alan Schroeder, *Op. Cit.*

8. Albert Mahrabian, *Silent Messages* (Belmont, CA: Wadsworth, 1981).

9. Theodore White, *The Making of the President 1960* (New York: Atheneum Books, 1961).

10. James Fallows, "An Acquired Taste," *The Atlantic*, July 2000, available at https://www.theatlantic.com/magazine/archive/2000/07/an-acquired-taste/378263/.

11. Jake Miller, "Polls Say Hillary Clinton Won the Debates—Will It Matter?" CBS News, October 20, 2016.

Part 3—Foreign Leaders and the Return of Strongmen

Introduction

1. Max Roser, "Democracy," available at https://ourworldindata.org/democracy. CC-BY-SA 2.0. Criteria include political rights and civil liberties, free and fair elections, political corruption, and freedom of expression, assembly, education, and religion among other factors. Freedom House, "Freedom in the World 2018: Methodology," available at https://freedomhouse.org/report/methodology-freedom-world-2018.

2. Thomas Friedman, "The Trump Musical: 'Anything Goes,' *The New York Times*, March 5, 2019. To be fair, not everybody agrees that democracy is under siege. For competing viewpoints on that issue consider: "Tom Jacobs, "Democracy Is in Decline in Much of the World," *Pacific Standard*, June 22, 2018, and Melinda Jimenez, "Democracy in a Worldwide Decline? Nope. Here's Our Data," *The Washington Post*, November 15, 2017.

Degrees of Freedom

1. Editorial Board, "Netanyahu Has Descended into New Depths of Demagoguery," *The Washington Post*, April 8, 2019; and Roger Cohen, "Will the Israeli 'King' Be Recrowned?" *The New York Times*, April 8, 2019.

2. PBS *Frontline*, "The Long Walk of Nelson Mandela, aired May 25, 1999, transcript available at https://www.pbs.org/wgbh/pages/frontline/shows/mandela/etc/script.html.

3. Uri Klein, "'King Bibi Explores How Benjamin Netanyahu Became Unbeatable," *Israel News*, December 4, 2018; and

Jeffrey Goldberg, "The Unbearable Smallness of Benjamin Netanyahu," *The Atlantic*, September 29, 2016.

4. Thomas Friedman, *Op. Cit.*

5. Yomi Kazeem, "Africa Has Only Had Four Worthy Leaders in the Last Decade, According to This Prestigious Prize, *Quartz Africa*, June 18, 2016, available at https://qz.com/africa/710869/africa-has-only-had-four-worthy-leaders-in-the-last-decade-according-to-this-prestigious-prize/.

6. Daniel Bergner, "An Uncompromising Woman," *The New York Times*, October 24, 2010, available at https://www.nytimes.com/2010/10/24/magazine/24sirleaf-t.html ; and Tamasin Ford, "Ellen Johnson Sirleaf: The Legacy of Africa's First Elected Female President," BBC News, January 22, 2018, available at https://www.bbc.com/news/world-africa-42748769.

7. "Hugo Chávez," available at https://en.wikiquote.org/wiki/Hugo_Ch%C3%A1vez.

8. Thomas Friedman, *Op. Cit.*

9. Chris Dyer, "King Jong-un Forced His Uncle to Watch Colleagues' Execution by Anti-Aircraft Guns, Then Poured Their Blood Over Him until He Fainted, North Korean Defector Claims," *Daily Mail*, February 25, 2019.

Leadership by Era

1. Thomas Friedman, "When the Cat's Away," *The New York Times*, February 27, 2018.

2. William Durant, quoted in "Mustafa Kemal Ataturk," *Encyclopedia of the Middle East*, available at http://www.midestweb.org/Middle-East-Encyclopedia/kemal-ataturk.htm.

3. David Brooks, "The Most Influential Man on Earth," *The New York Times*, April 3, 2018.

4. Julia Ioffe, "Putin's Game," *The Atlantic*, January/February 2018.

5. Peter S. Goodman, "The Post-World War Two Order Is Under Assault from the Powers That Built It," *The New York Times*, March 26, 2018.

6. Michelle Goldberg, "Madeleine Albright Is Worried. We Should Be, Too," *The New York Times*, April 13, 2018.

7. Gareth Browne, "Orban Is the Original Trumps, Says Bannon in Budapest," *The National*, May 24, 2018.

8. Domenico Montanaro, "6 Strongmen Trump Has Praised— And the Conflicts It Presents," NPR, May 2, 2017; Jasmine C. Lee and Kevin Quealy, "The 567 People, Places and Things Donald Trump Has Insulted on Twitter: A Complete List," *The New York Times*, February 20, 2019; Krishnadev Calamur, "Nine Notorious Dictators, Nine Shout-Outs from Donald Trump," *The Atlantic*, March 4, 2018; Meghan Keneally, "Compiling Donald Trump's Recent Comments on US Allies and Rivals," ABC News, July 16, 2018.

9. Freedom House, "Modern Authoritarianism: Illiberal Democracies," available at https://freedomhouse.org/report/modern-authoritarianism-illiberal-democracies (chapter 5).

The Status Quo

1. Mark Santora, "Soros Foundations to Leave Hungary as Orban Grows More Belligerent," *The New York Times*, May 16, 2018; and Freedom House, "Modern Authoritarianism, Illiberal Democracies," *Op. Cit.*

2. The three sources are Global Firepower's 2019 Military Strength Ranking available at https://www.globalfirepower.com/countries-listing.asp; Young Diplomats Team, "Top 10 Strongest Countries in the World," July 3, 2018, available at http://www.young-diplomats.com/top-10-strongest-countries-world/; and Logan Nye, "The Top 10 Militaries of the World," August 4, 2017, available at https://www.military.com/undertheradar/2017/08/top-10-militaries-world-2017.

3. Charlie Campbell, "Moon Jae-in: TIME Person of the Year 2018 Runner Up," *Time*, available at time.com/person-of-the-year-2018-moon-jae-in-runner-up/.

4. Francois Livet, "Portrait of Recep Tayyip Erdogan—President of the Republic of Turkey," Institute Montaigne, November 8, 2018.

5. The chart is based on data from "Significant Cyber Incidents," published by the Center for Strategic and International Studies and available at https://www.csis.org/programs/cybersecurity-and-governance/technology-policy-program/other-projects-cybersecurity. Other sources here consist of: Anas Baig, "Top 5 Countries Where Cyber Attacks Originate," *Security Today*, March 3, 2017; Bloomberg, "These 3 Countries Post the Biggest Cyber Threats, U.S. Officials Say," *Fortune*, July 26, 2018; and Charles McLellan, "Cyberwar Predictions for 2019: The Stakes Have Been Raised," ZDNet, December 31, 2018.

6. Portland Communications and the USC Center for Public Diplomacy, *The Soft Power 30: A Global Ranking of Soft Power 2018*, available at https://softpower30.com/wp-content/uploads/2018/07/The-Soft-Power-30-Report-2018.pdf.

7. "The Red Carpet, China's Film Industry," *The Economist*, December 21, 2013, available at https://www.economist.com/news/christmas-specials/21591741-red-carpet; and David Shambaugh, "China's Soft-power Push," *Foreign Affairs*, July 16, 2015, available at https://www.foreignaffairs.com/articles/china/2015-06-16/china-s-soft-power-push.

Country Spotlights

1. Drew Desilver and David Masci, "World's Muslim Population More Widespread Than You Might Think," Pew Research, January 31, 2017; and Michael Lipka and Conrad Hackett, "Why Muslims Are the World's Fastest-Growing Religious Group," Pew Research, April 6, 2017.

2. Thomas Pepinsky, Indonesia's Upcoming Elections, Explained," Brookings, March 20, 2019.

3. Anthony Cilluffo and D'Vera Cohn, "7 Demographic Trends Shaping the U.S. and the World in 2018," Pew Research, April 25, 2018.

4. *Ibid*; plus also Pew Charitable Trusts, "3 Demographic Trends Changing Our World," July 19, 2016.

5. Stratfor, "The Geopolitics of France: Maintaining Its Influence in a Changing Europe," September 13, 2010.

6. Martin Jacques, *When China Rules the World*, (New York: Penguin, 2012).

7. Naturally, all sorts of documentation exist regarding the slave trade and its aftermath. Three sources I'm particularly drawing on here consist of: Howard Zinn, *A People's History of the United States* (New York: HarperPerennial, 1999); Susan Schulten, *A History of America in 100 Maps* (Chicago: University of Chicago Press, 2018); Jason Hickel, *The Divide: Global Inequity from Conquest to Free Markets* (New York: W. W. Norton, 2018).

8. *Martin Jacques, Op. Cit; and Jason Hickel, Op. Cit.*

9. Celia Bein and Boris Toucas, "The 'Macron Miracle' Could Transform France into a Global Powerhouse," Brookings, April 22, 2018.

10. Heather Stewart, "May Suffers Heaviest Parliamentary Defeat of a British PM in the Democratic Era," *The Guardian*, January 15, 2019.

11. Martin Jacques, *Op. Cit.*

12. James Masters and Margaux Deygas, "Marine Le Pen Sparks Outrage over Holocaust Comments," CNN, April 10, 2017.

13. Martin Jacques, *Op. Cit.*

14. "Modern Authoritarianism: Illiberal Democracies," *Op. Cit.* (Freedom House).

15. Steven Lee Myers, "The Poison Putin Spreads," *The New York Times*, March 17, 2018.

16. Julia Ioffe, "Putin's Game," *The Atlantic*, January/February 2018.

17. Jochen Bittner, "Who Will Win the New Great Game?" *The New York Times*, April 27, 2018.

18. Neil MacFarquhar, "For the Kremlin, Venezuela Is Not the Next Syria," *The New York Times*, January 30, 2919; Julia Ioffe, *Op. Cit.*; and Bret Stephens, "The Rise of Dictatorship Incorporated," *The New York Times*, March 2, 2018.

19. Alexandra Stevenson, "Xi Jinping Promotes Openness at a China Forum Rife with Restrictions," *The New York Times*, April 11, 2018.

20. "Xi Jinping Calls for a Chinese Dream," *The Daily Telegraph*, March 20, 2013.

21. Kurt M. Campbell and Ely Ratner, "The China Reckoning: How Beijing Defied American Expectations," *Foreign Affairs*, March/April 2018.

22. The sources for this kind of information are almost endless, but include: Panka Misra, "The Rise of China and the Fall of the 'Free Trade' Myth," *The New York Times Magazine*, February 7, 2018; Steven Erlanger, "Europe Once Saw Xi Jinping as a Hedge Against Trump. Not Anymore," *The New York Times*, March 4, 2018; Andrew Witthoeft, "What Is China's Objective with the 2018 16 + 1 Summit?" *The Diplomat*, available at https://thediplomat.com/2018/06/what-is-chinas-objective-with-the-2018-161-summit/; and Jochen Bittner, "Who Will Win the New Great Game?" *The New York Times*, April 27, 2018.

23. Kai Schutz, "Indian Children's Book Lists Hitler as Leader 'Who Will Inspire You,'" *The New York Times*, March 17, 2018.

24. Freedom House, "Latin America Shows That Democratization Is Possible Anywhere," August 3, 2015.

25. The quote comes from a blog by Frederic Louault, "Portrait of Jair Bolsonaro—President of the Federative Republic of Brazil," Institute Montaigne, December 21, 2018. Other sources about Bolsonaro include: Jen Kiby, "4 Things to Know about Jair Bolsonaro, Brazil's Donald Trump," Vox, October 10, 2018, and Tom Phillips, "Trump of the Tropics: The 'Dangerous' Candidate Leading Brazil's Presidential Race," *The Guardian*, April 19, 2018.

26. Howard Zinn, *Op. Cit.*

Follow the Money

1. The story behind Angus Maddison's data is perhaps best recounted in "500 Years of GDP: A Tale of Two Countries," available at http://www.newgeography.com/content/005050-500-years-gdp-a-tale-two-countries. The various charts derived from it have appeared in everything from Derek Thompson, "The Economic History of the Last 2,000 Years in 1 Little Graph," *The Atlantic*, June 19, 2012 to Donald Marron, "2,000 Years of Economic History in One Chart . . . and Another," available at https://dmarron.

com/2012/06/221/2000-years-of-economic-history-in-one-chart-and-another/.

2. Martin Jacques, *Op. Cit.*; and Jason Hickel, *Op. Cit.*

3. Vikas Shukla, "Top 10 Largest Economies by 2050: Emerging Countries to Dominate," PricewaterhouseCoopers report, January 3, 2019.

4. Bruno Lanvin, "The World's Most Innovative Countries, 2018," INSEA Knowledge, July 10, 2018.

5. Adam Shirley, "This Is What 500 Years of Globalization Looks Like," World Economic Forum, May 17, 2016.

6. The global income distribution charts are based on those in an article by Esteban Ortiz-Ospina, "Is Globalization an Engine of Economic Development?" published on August 1, 2017, and available at https://ourworldindata.org/is-globalization-an-engine-of-economic-development. Other sources include: Branko Milanovic, "The Real Winners and Losers of Globalization," *The Globalist*, October 25, 2012; and David Hunkar, "Which Countries Are the Winners and Losers of Globalization?" Top ForeignStocks.com, January 23, 2017.

7. William A. Galston, "The Case for Responsible Nationalism," *The Wall Street Journal*, March 28, 2018.

8. Branko Milanovic, *Op. Cit.*; and David Hunkar, *Op. Cit.*

9. Patrick Kingsley and Benjamin Novak, "Economic Miracle in Hungary, or Just a Mirage?" *The New York Times*, April 3, 2018; and Zoltan Pogastsa and Adam Fabry, "Viktor Orban Is Finally Under Siege," available at https://www.jacobinmag.com/2010/02/hungary-orban-overtime-slave-law-labor-shortage.

10. Martin Jacques, *Op. Cit.*

11. Jeremy Sandbrook, "the 10 Most Corrupt World Leaders of Recent History," Integritas 360, July 20, 2016; and Emily Bella, "top ten Most Corrupt Politicians in the World 2018," BBC News, November 21, 2017.

12. Graham Allison, "Lee Kuan Yew: Lessons for Leaders from Asia's 'Grand Master,'" CNN, April 2, 2015.

13. Aza Wee Sile, "These Are the World's Most Corrupt Nations," CNBC, January 24, 2017, available at https://www.cnbc.com/2017/01/24/these-are-the-worlds-most-corrupt-countries.html.

14. Jason Beaubien, "The Country with the World's Worst Inequality Is . . ." NPR, April 2, 2018. To go right to the Gini Index, see https://www.indexmundi.com/facts/indicators/SI.POV.GINI/rankings.

Trust as the Final Key Factor

1. Niall McCarthy, "The Countries That Trust Their Government Most and Least," *Forbes*, January 22, 2018.

2. Martin Jacques, *Op. Cit.*

3. Thomas Pepinsky, *Op. Cit.*

Epilogue

1. These 10 Democratic contenders for the party's presidential nomination in 2020 were chosen based on the top ten lists from these three sources: "The RS Politics 2020 Democracy Primary Leaderboard," *Rolling Stone*, March 7, 2019; Chris Cillizza and Harry Enten, "2020 Rankings: It's Now or Never for Democrats Who Want To Be President," CNN, March 9, 2019; and, The Ranking Committee, "What 2020 Democrats and Richard Nixon Have in Common," *The Washington Post*, March 22, 2019.

2. The statistics come from Steven Levitsky and Daniel Ziblatt, "How Wobbly Is Our Democracy?" *The New York Times*, January 27, 2018. On that same theme of tribalism, there's Jonathan Rauch, "Have Our Tribes Becomes More Important Than Our Country?" *The Washington Post*, February 16, 2018. Rauch criticizes both sides, citing left-wing "identity-mongering and victim-worshiping" and right-wing "rage-mongering and conspiracy-theorizing."

LEADERSHIP INDEX

IMAGE CREDITS

Introduction

Camden Yards Scoreboard: Oriole Park at Camden Yards in Baltimore, MD. 22 July 2008 by mathplourde. https://commons.wikimedia.org/wiki/File:Camden_Yards%27_scoreboard.jpg. CC BY 2.0; Cropped

Chapter 1

Barack Obama: Official portrait as President-elect. November 2008 by The Obama-Biden Transition Project. https://commons.wikimedia.org/wiki/File:Poster-sized_portrait_of_Barack_Obama.jpg. CC BY 3.0; Cropped

William Howard Taft: USA President elect Woodrow Wilson shares a laugh with outgoing president William Howard Taft outside the White House prior to Wilson's inauguration from The Library of Congress's Prints and Photographs Division (Public Domain). https://commons.wikimedia.org/wiki/File:WilsonTaftLaughing_(cropped).jpg.

Dwight D. Eisenhower: The Commander of American Forces in the European Theatre, Major General Dwight Eisenhower, at his desk from The Imperial War Museum (Public Domain). https://he.wikipedia.org/wiki/%D7%A7%D7%95%D7%91%D7%A5:Major_General_Dwight_Eisenhower,_1942_TR207.jpg.

John F. Kennedy: Television host Jack Paar and John F. Kennedy as a Senator and Presidential candidate when he appeared on The Tonight Show in 1959 by ABC Television (Public Domain). https://commons.wikimedia.org/wiki/File:John_F._Kennedy_Jack_Paar_Tonight_Show_1959.JPG.

Martin Van Buren: The 8th President of the United States circa 1860-1862 from The Library of Congress's Prints and Photographs Division (Public Domain). https://commons.wikimedia.org/wiki/File:Martin_Van_Buren_edit.jpg.

Franklin Pierce: The 14th President of the United States from Bowdoin University (Public Domain). http://community.bowdoin.edu/news/2012/02/president-franklin-pierce-class-of-1824/.

Thomas Jefferson: The Miriam and Ira D. Wallach Division of Art, Prints and Photographs: Print Collection, The New York Public Library. (1798 - 1876). Thomas Jefferson, President of the United States. Retrieved from http://digitalcollections.nypl.org/items/f8dcd8d0-c605-012f-e367-58d385a7bc34.

James Madison: Portrait of James Madison, one of the authors of the Federalist Papers, and the fourth President of the United States by John Vanderlyn (1816) from The White House Historical Association (Public Domain). https://commons.wikimedia.org/wiki/File:James_Madison.jpg.

Grover Cleveland: Hon. Grover Cleveland, head-and-shoulders portrait, facing right August 9, 1892 from The Library of Congress's Prints and Photographs Division (Public Domain). https://commons.wikimedia.org/wiki/File:StephenGroverCleveland.png.

Gerald Ford: President Gerald R. Ford Listening to Kissinger, April 4, 1975 from The National Archives (Public Domain). https://www.flickr.com/photos/pingnews/274991068.

Calvin Coolidge: (Public Domain). http://carrollbryant.blogspot.com/2014/01/calvin-coolidge-presidents.html.

Benjamin Harrison: U.S. President, reproduction of painting from The Library of Congress's Prints and Photographs Division (Public Domain). https://commons.wikimedia.org/wiki/File:Benjamin_Harrison_cph.3g12484.jpg.

Abraham Lincoln: Photo portrait (Public Domain). https://commons.wikimedia.org/wiki/File:Abraham_Lincoln_head_on_shoulders_edit1.jpg.

Andrew Jackson: Photograph 1844 from The Library of Congress's Prints and Photographs Division (Public Domain). https://www.chronicle.com/article/Would-Andrew-Jackson-Have/239966.

Ulysses S. Grant: Portrait photograph of US President Ulysses S. Grant circa 1870 by Mathew Brady from The Library of Congress's Prints and Photographs Division (Public Domain). https://commons.wikimedia.org/wiki/File:Ulysses_S_Grant_by_Brady_c1870-restored.jpg.

John Quincy Adams: National Portrait Gallery painting by George Caleb Bingham circa 1844 (Public Domain). https://commons.wikimedia.org/wiki/File:George_Caleb_Bingham_-_John_Quincy_Adams_-_Google_Art_Project.jpg.

Richard Nixon: Photo of John F. Kennedy and Richard Nixon taken prior to their first debate at WBBM-TV in Chicago on September 26, 1960 by AP (Public Domain). https://commons.wikimedia.org/wiki/File:Kennedy_Nixon_debate_first_Chicago_1960.jpg.

James A. Garfield: Photo of James A. Garfield and Lucretia Rudolph was taken around the time of their engagement, February 16, 2016 by Western Reserve Historical Society. https://en.wikipedia.org/wiki/File:James_A._Garfield_and_Lucretia_Rudolph.jpg.

Donald Trump: Donald Trump after signing the pledge of allegiance September 3, 2015 by Michael Vadon. https://commons.wikimedia.org/wiki/File:Donald_Trump_Signs_The_Pledge_12.jpg. CC BY 4.0; Cropped

Theodore Roosevelt: Portrait photograph of United States President Theodore Roosevelt (1920) by Underwood & Underwood (Public Domain). https://commons.wikimedia.org/wiki/File:Americana_1920_Theodore_Roosevelt_(cropped).jpg.

Warren Harding: Warren G. Harding 29th President of the United States (1921-1923) (Public Domain). https://commons.wikimedia.org/wiki/File:Warren_G._Harding.jpg.

Andrew Johnson: Portrait of Johnson standing from The Library of Congress's Prints and Photographs Division (Public Domain). https://commons.wikimedia.org/wiki/File:President_Andrew_Johnson_standing.jpg.

James Monroe: Portrait of James Monroe, The White House Historical Association circa 1819 from The White House Historical Association (Public Domain). https://commons.wikimedia.org/wiki/File:James_Monroe_White_House_portrait_1819.gif.

Millard Fillmore: 13th president of the United States by Mathew B. Brady circa 1855-1865, from The Library of Congress Brady-Handy photograph collection (Public Domain). https://commons.wikimedia.org/wiki/File:Millard_Fillmore.jpg.

Zachary Taylor: Daguerreotype by Mathew B. Brady from The Library of Congress Brady-Handy photograph collection. https://www.britannica.com/biography/Zachary-Taylor/images-videos/media/584895/14724.

William Henry Harrison: Daguerreotype of an oil painting depicting William Henry Harrison, 9th President of the United States circa 1850 by Albert Sands Southworth and Josiah Johnson Hawes (Public Domain). https://commons.wikimedia.org/wiki/File:William_Henry_Harrison_daguerreotype_edit.jpg.

Ronald Reagan: President Ronald Reagan speaking at a Rally for Senator Durenberger in Minneapolis, Minnesota, February 8, 1982 from The National Archives and Records Administration (Public Domain). https://commons.wikimedia.org/wiki/File:President_Reagan_speaking_in_Minneapolis_1982.jpg.

George H.W. Bush: Former President of the United States George H.W. Bush talks with Airmen Nov. 20 during a visit to the 380th Air Expeditionary Wing in Southwest Asia by Master Sgt. Jason Tudor (Public Domain). https://www.af.mil/News/Article-Display/Article/129009/former-president-visits-airmen/.

James K. Polk: United States president James Knox Polk, three-quarter length portrait, three-quarters to the right, seated, February 14, 1849 by Mathew B. Brady from The Library of Congress Brady-Handy photograph collection (Public Domain). https://commons.wikimedia.org/wiki/File:James_Polk_restored.jpg.

George W. Bush: In the wake of the terrorist attacks of September 11, President George W. Bush delivers remarks discouraging anti-Muslim sentiment, at the Islamic Center of Washington, DC by The Office of White House Management (Public Domain). https://commons.wikimedia.org/wiki/File:911-_President_George_W._Bush_at_Islamic_Center,_09-17-2001._(6124777178).jpg.

Rutherford B. Hayes: Portrait from 1879 by James Landy from The Library of Congress Brady-Handy photograph collection (Public Domain). https://it.wikipedia.org/wiki/File:Rutherford_B_Hayes_-_head_and_shoulders.jpg.

John Tyler: Restored daguerreotype of John Tyler, tenth president of the United States circa 1860 by Edwards & Anthony (Public Domain). https://commons.wikimedia.org/wiki/File:Tyler_Daguerreotype_(restoration).jpg.

George Washington: Portrait March 20, 1797 by Gilbert Stuart from the Clark Art Institute (Public Domain). https://commons.wikimedia.org/wiki/File:Gilbert_Stuart_Williamstown_Portrait_of_George_Washington.jpg.

Harry Truman: Portrait of President Harry S. Truman circa 1947 by The Harry S. Truman Library & Museum (Public Domain). https://commons.wikimedia.org/wiki/File:Truman_58-766-09_(3x4_C).jpg.

Lyndon B. Johnson: Photo portrait of President Lyndon B. Johnson in the Oval Office, leaning on a chair, March 10, 1964 by Arnold Newman, White House Press Office (Public Domain). https://commons.wikimedia.org/wiki/File:37_Lyndon_Johnson_3x4.jpg.

Woodrow Wilson: Photo by Harris & Ewing from The Library of Congress. https://commons.wikimedia.org/wiki/File:Woodrow_Wilson-H%26E.jpg.

James Buchanan: In his post-presidency years (after 1861)(Public Domain). https://commons.wikimedia.org/wiki/File:James_Buchanan_-_post_presidency.jpg.

Franklin D. Roosevelt: Photo circa 1933 from The National Archives and Records Administration (Franklin D. Roosevelt Library)

(Public Domain). https://commons.wikimedia.org/wiki/File:Franklin_D._Roosevelt_-_NARA_-_196715.jpg.

John Adams: Portrait by Benjamin Blyth, 1766 (Public Domain). https://declaration.fas.harvard.edu/blog/october-abigail-john.

William McKinley: Oil on canvas portrait by August Benziger (1897) from The National Portrait Gallery (Public Domain). https://www.conservapedia.com/File:William_McKinley_by_Benziger.jpg.

Jimmy Carter: Jimmy Carter's Presidential portrait by the Department of Defense (Public Domain). https://commons.wikimedia.org/wiki/File:JimmyCarterPortrait2.jpg.

Chester A. Arthur: From The Library of Congress's Prints and Photographs Division (Public Domain). https://www.whatitmeanstobeamerican.org/engagements/can-a-corrupt-politician-become-a-good-president/.

Bill Clinton: General Session with President Bill Clinton August 29, 2015 by Chris Savas. https://commons.wikimedia.org/wiki/File:Bill_Clinton_(2015).jpg. CC BY 4.0, Cropped.

Herbert Hoover: Herbert Hoover with his pet Belgian Shepherd dog "King Tut" circa 1928 by Herbert E. French from The Library of Congress (Public Domain). https://en.wikipedia.org/wiki/File:Herbert_Hoover_and_King_Tut.jpg.

Eleanor Roosevelt: Eleanor Roosevelt with servicemen during trip to Central and South America from The Franklin D. Roosevelt Library (Public Domain). https://fdrlibrary.tumblr.com/post/92830518864/day-64-eleanor-roosevelt-visits-central-and-south.

Chapter 3

Nelson Mandela: In Johannesburg on May 13, 2008 by South Africa The Good News. https://commons.wikimedia.org/wiki/File:Nelson_Mandela-2008_(edit).jpg. CC BY 2.0; Cropped

Benjamin Netanyahu: White House photo by Pete Souza, May 18, 2009 (Public Domain). https://commons.wikimedia.org/wiki/File:BenjaminNetanyahu.jpg.

Ellen Johnson Sirleaf: President of Liberia, during a state visit to Brazil, April 7, 2010 by Antonio Cruz (Agência Brasil). https://commons.wikimedia.org/wiki/File:Ellen_Johnson-Sirleaf,_April_2010.jpg. CC BY 3.0; Cropped

Hugo Chavez: Interview with Venezuelan President Hugo Chávez after meeting at Granja do Torto January 19, 2006 by Agência Brasil. https://commons.wikimedia.org/wiki/File:Chavez141610.jpg. CC BY 3.0; Cropped

Kim Jong-un: Chairman of North Korea, [Kim Jung-Un]] in the Inter Korean Summit July 28, 2018 courtesy of the Korean Government (Public Domain). https://commons.wikimedia.org/wiki/File:Kim_Jung-Un_-_Inter_Korean_Summit(cropped)_v7.jpg.

Muhammad bin Salman: G20 Summit Argentina, Plenary—Day 2, December 1, 2018. https://commons.wikimedia.org/wiki/File:Plenaria_-_D%C3%ADa_2_(32259145628).jpg. CC BY 2.0; Cropped

Otto von Bismarck: Photo after his resignation on August 31, 1890 by Jacques Pilartz (Public Domain). https://commons.wikimedia.org/wiki/File:Bundesarchiv_Bild_146-2005-0057,_Otto_von_Bismarck.jpg.

Mustafa Kemal Atatürk: Photo from September 23, 1925 (Public Domain). https://commons.wikimedia.org/wiki/File:Atat%C3%BCrk_23_Eyl%C3%BCl_1925%27te_Re%C5%9Fit_Pa%C5%9Fa_Gemisi%27nde.jpg.

Mikhail Gorbachev: Soviet General Secretary Gorbachev in the White House Library December 8, 1987 by The White House Photo Office (Public Domain). https://commons.wikimedia.org/wiki/File:Mikhail_Gorbachev_1987.jpg.

Viktor Orbán: Photo March 22, 2018 by The European People's Pary. https://commons.wikimedia.org/wiki/File:Viktor_Orb%C3%A1n_2018.jpg. CC BY 2.0; Cropped

Jutin Trudeau: President Donald J. Trump is joined by Canadian Prime Minister Justin Trudeau at the USMCA signing ceremony Friday, Nov. 30, 2018, in Buenos Aires, Argentina. (Official White House Photo by Shealah Craighead) (Public Domain). https://commons.wikimedia.org/wiki/File:President_Donald_J._Trump_at_the_G20_Summit_(32245874198).jpg.

Recep Tayyip Erdoğan: At the Annual Meeting 2006 of the World Economic Forum in Davos, Switzerland, January 27, 2006 courtesy of The World Economic Forum. https://commons.wikimedia.org/wiki/File:Prime_Minister_of_Turkey_Recep_Tayyip_Erdogan_cropped.jpg. CC BY 2.0; Cropped

Moon Jae-in: Meeting with President Donald Trump May 22, 2018 courtesy of the Korean Government (Public Domain). https://commons.wikimedia.org/wiki/File:US-Korea_Summit_22_May_v2.jpg.

Kim Jong-un & Moon Jae-in: Attending a banquet on the Peace House in South Korea, April 27,2018 courtesy of The Korea Summit Press Pool (Public Domain). https://globalnews.ca/news/4172994/kim-jong-un-image-jokes-hug-korea-summit/.

Joko Widodo: "The New Mr. President," photo by Ahmad Syauki (username: uyeah). https://www.flickr.com/photos/ukik/14967050094/in/photostream/. CC BY 2.0; Cropped

Winston Churchill: Portrait courtesy of British Government (Public Domain). https://teachingamericanhistory.org/library/document/mass-effects-in-modern-life/

Theresa May: Speaking during an international conference on Somalia at the Lancaster House in London on May 11, 2017 by Air Force Staff Sgt. Jette Carr, Department of Defense (Public Domain). https://www.flickr.com/photos/secdef/34437693922/.

Charles de Gaulle: A WWII photo portrait of General Charles de Gaulle of the Free French Forces circa 1942 from the US Library of Congress (Public Domain). https://commons.wikimedia.org/wiki/File:De_Gaulle-OWI.jpg.

Emmanuel Macron: Photo from July 6, 2017 courtesy of The Office of the President of Mexico. https://www.flickr.com/photos/presidenciamx/35633549951/. CC BY 2.0; Cropped

Adolf Hitler: Adolf Hitler in office seating on his desk. Bavarian national library in 1936 by Heinrich Hoffmann (Public Domain). https://commons.wikimedia.org/wiki/File:Adolf_Hitler_Berghof-1936.jpg.

Angela Merkel: President Dilma Rousseff receives Chancellor of Germany Angela Merkel in official ceremony at the Planalto Palace August 20, 2015 by Elza Fiùza, Agência Brasil. https://commons.wikimedia.org/wiki/File:Merkel_cropped.jpg. CC BY 3.0; Cropped

Hideki Tojo: Portrait of Tojo Hideki before 1946 (Public Domain). https://commons.wikimedia.org/wiki/File:Hideki_Tojo_posing.jpg.

Shinzō Abe: 'The Union Finance Minister, Shri P. Chidambaram called on the Prime Minister of Japan, Mr. Shinzo Abe in Japan April 1, 2013 by India Ministry of Finance (Government of India Open Data License). https://commons.wikimedia.org/wiki/File:%27The_Union_Finance_Minister,_Shri_P._Chidambaram_called_on_the_Prime_Minister_of_Japan,_Mr._Shinzo_Abe_in_Japan_(1).jpg

Franklin D. Roosevelt: Photo circa 1933 from The National Archives and Records Administration (Franklin D. Roosevelt Library) (Public Domain). https://commons.wikimedia.org/wiki/File:Franklin_D._Roosevelt_-_NARA_-_196715.jpg.

Donald Trump: Trump speaking with supporters at Arizona State Fairgrounds by Gage Skidmore. https://en.wikipedia.org/wiki/File:Donald_Trump_(27484750260).jpg. CC BY-SA 2.0

Muhammadu Buhari: The Official Portrait of the President of the Federal Republic of Nigeria, President Muhammadu Buhari taken by Bayo Omoboriowo, May 29, 2015. https://commons.wikimedia.org/wiki/File:Muhammadu_Buhari,_President_of_the_Federal_Republic_of_Nigeria_(cropped).jpg. CC BY 4.0; Cropped

Joseph Stalin: Secretary-general of the Communist party of Soviet Union in 1942 (Public Domain). https://commons.wikimedia.org/wiki/File:JStalin_Secretary_general_CCCP_1942.jpg.

Vladimir Putin: Official portrait of Vladimir Putin (2006) courtesy of The Russian Presidential Press and Information Office. https://commons.wikimedia.org/wiki/File:Vladimir_Putin_-_2006.jpg. CC BY 4.0

Mao Zedong: Photo of Mao Zedong with signature (circa 1960) courtesy of hsxgw.gov.cn (Public Domain). https://commons.wikimedia.org/wiki/File:Mao_Zedong_2.jpg.

Deng Xiaoping: Photo with Jimmy Carter January 29, 1979 courtesy of the Executive Office of the President of the United States (Public Domain). https://commons.wikimedia.org/wiki/File:Deng_Xiaoping.jpg. CC BY 2.0; Cropped

Yi Jinping: Xi Jinping, General Secretary of the Communist Party of China. National Palace, Mexico City on June 4, 2013 by Angélica Rivera de Peña. https://commons.wikimedia.org/wiki/File:Xi_Jinping_Mexico2013.jpg.

Mahatma Ghandi: Studio photograph of Mohandas K. Gandhi, London, 1931 by Elliott & Fry (Public Domain). https://commons.wikimedia.org/wiki/File:Mahatma-Gandhi,_studio,_1931.jpg.

Narendra Modi: Image of Narendra Modi at the World Economic Forum in India on November 16, 2008 by Norbert Schiller, World Economic Forum. https://commons.wikimedia.org/wiki/File:Modi-WEF.jpg. CC BY-SA 2.0

Getulio Vargas: Official portrait of Getulio Vargas Courtesy of The Gallery of Presidents and the Government of Brazil circa 1930 (Public Domain). https://commons.wikimedia.org/wiki/File:Getulio_Vargas_(1930).jpg.

Jair Bolsonaro: Brazilian President Bolsonaro by Ron Przysucha, United States Department of State (Public Domain). https://commons.wikimedia.org/wiki/File:Presidente_Bolsonaro.png

Lee Kuan Yew: Senior Minister Lee Kuan Yew of Singapore, being escorted by United States Secretary of Defense Donald H. Rumsfeld through an honour cordon and into the Pentagon by United States Department of Defense May 2, 2002 (Public Domain). https://commons.wikimedia.org/wiki/File:Lee_Kuan_Yew.jpg.

Suharto: Suharto, second President of the Republic of Indonesia, at the start of his sixth term in 1993 by State Secretariat of the Republic of Indonesia (Public Domain). https://commons.wikimedia.org/wiki/File:President_Suharto,_1993.jpg.

ABOUT THE AUTHOR

Dan Hill, Ph.D., is the founder and president of Sensory Logic, Inc., which originated the use of facial coding in business beginning in 1998. Dan has received ten U.S. patents in all, and his research-based consulting company has worked for over half of the world's top 100 business-to-consumer oriented companies.

Dan's TV appearances have included: ABC's "Good Morning America," Al Jazeera, Bloomberg TV, CNBC, CNN, ESPN, Fox, MSNBC, NBC's "The Today Show," PBS, and The Tennis Channel. Radio appearances have included the BBC and NPR's "Marketplace." Print and digital coverage of Dan's work has included: *Admap, Advertising Age, Adweek, Allure, Cosmopolitan, China Forbes, Entrepreneur, Fast Company, The Financial Times, Inc., Kiplinger's The Los Angeles Times, The New York Times, Politico, Time, USA Today*, and *The Wall Street Journal*, in addition to his having been a columnist for *Reuters* during the 2016 presidential race. His essays were noted with commendation in the 1989, 1991 and 1994 editions of *The Best American Essays*.

Since his education at St. Olaf College, Oxford University, Brown University, and Rutgers University, Dan has given speeches and workshops in over 25 countries, Along with his wife, Karen Bernthal, he lives in St. Paul, Minnesota and Palm Desert, California. To sign up for Dan's *Faces of the Week* blog series or to learn about his other offerings, please visit www.sensorylogic.com.

OTHER BOOKS BY DAN HILL

Emotionomics (2007, 2008, 2010 editions)

There are two currencies in business: money and emotions. The book that first brought behavior economics into business on an actionable basis reveals how breakthroughs in brain science have revelatory implications for how companies should be conducting business in the 21st century. Gone is the old consumer and worker model in which appeals to utilitarian benefits alone will carry the day. Instead, step ahead of competitors by stepping closer to customers and employees, the two groups of people on whom profitability depends. *Emotionomics* covers the role of emotions in both the marketplace and workplace, from branding, to offer design, packaging, usability, advertising, sales, and the customer shopping experience, as well as leadership and employee management. Chosen by *Advertising Age* as one of the top ten must-read books of 2009, *Emotionomics* includes a foreword by Sam Simon, co-creator of *The Simpsons*, and is endorsed by business luminaries like Seth Godin, Philip Kotler, Martin Lindstrom, Jeffrey Gitomer, Paco Underhill, and Faith Popcorn.

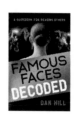

Famous Faces Decoded (2018, 2019 editions)

Unless you've never been lied to in life, you know that words aren't enough in assessing people and situations. Vital to emotional intelligence is fluently reading the language of facial expressions. *Famous Faces Decoded* shows you that emotions are hidden in plain sight on all of our faces. You'll learn how emotions shape and reflect our personalities, driving behavior. There is no better, in-the-moment way to reliably grasp what's going on with those you love or work with. This book is full of lively stories about stars you know, or think you know, from the realms of Hollywood, music, sports, and the media, to leading politicians and business people. The examples highlight celebrities from four eras: The Silent Generation, Baby Boomers, Gen X-ers, and Millennials. From whom to hire, to sales, negotiations, and interacting with your boss, colleagues or customers, as well as in dating, marriage or handling your kids, *Famous Faces Decoded* will help anyone keen on securing more steadfast rapport with others. Endorsed by Daniel Pink, Jeanne Moos, Mary Carillo, Jon Gordon, B. Joseph Pine II, and EQ co-founder John D. Mayer.

First Blush (2019)

What we choose to focus on, and how we feel about what we're seeing, defines us. In today's hyper-visual world that stretches from TV shows and advertising to online videos (and more), how good are we at truly understanding what does and doesn't grab our attention and make us care? This groundbreaking book tackles that question by using two unique scientific tools to provide objective, quantifiable see/feel answers. *First Blush* is twice as large in scope as any study ever conducted before that links eye-tracking and world-class art works. This book simultaneously draws on facial coding to capture and identify people's quick, real-time emotional responses to 88 notable art works, spanning the eras from masters like da Vinci and Rembrandt to contemporary painters, photographers, and sculptors like Basquiat, Liebovitz, and Koons. "Art is either plagiarism or revolution," wrote Paul Gauguin. Welcome to revolution. You won't find another richly-illustrated, full-color art book like *First Blush* anywhere else.

Made in the USA
Middletown, DE
02 August 2021